SIREN LAND

SIREN LAND

by

NORMAN DOUGLAS

SECKER & WARBURG
London
IN ASSOCIATION WITH THE ARTS COUNCIL OF GREAT BRITAIN

First published (J. M. Dent) 1911
Second edition 1923
Third edition (New Adelphi Library) 1927
Reprinted 1929
Fourth edition (Penguin Books) 1948
Combined edition with *Fountains in the Sand* (Secker & Warburg) 1957
This edition first published in England 1982 by
Martin Secker & Warburg Limited
in association with the Arts Council of Great Britain
54 Poland Street, London W1V 3DF

Introduction copyright © 1982 by Mark Holloway

ISBN 0-436-13204-4

Printed and bound in Great Britain by
Biddles Ltd, Guildford and King's Lynn

CONTENTS

INTRODUCTION

MARK HOLLOWAY

Siren Land was the first book written entirely by Norman Douglas. It was first published in 1911, when he was forty-three years old. Partly Scottish and partly German, overtly aristocratic and covertly rather raffish, he was a bold, wayward, persuasive, charming and perverse man. He was also filled with an insatiable curiosity about anything that interested him, and since a great many things did, his mind was stocked with a lavish and wide-embracing assortment of knowledge. Knowledge he loved for its own sake, and being bookish as well as a physically active pragmatist in daily life, he pressed out, as he said, both his experiences and his researches to the last drop. To the last drop also, he loved wine, and good food, friends and lovers – of a lifetime or an hour: his appetites were robust and in excellent fettle to within a year or two of his death. He looked askance at the present, preferred to look backwards rather than forwards, thought humanity had reached its peak in ancient Greece, and that the chief business of life was to enjoy oneself, by which he meant to be able to do what one wants to do.

Most of these characteristics, well-matured, were confidently displayed in this first book, which was a brilliant debut. Fulfilling his own definition (written at a later date) of what the reader of a good travel book is entitled to, he supplies not only all that one would wish to know about the subject – features of landscape with their associative history, geology, zoology, botany, archaeology, etc.– but also that author's "mind worth knowing" that is part of his definition. He presides with an apparently effortless omniscience over the region he has selected. There is nothing he has not read about it, no legend or rumour or myth he has not heard, often from a native of the place. (He heard much by offering sweets to the young, and snuff to the old.) There is nothing observable that he has not seen and carefully examined; and nothing that he has read or heard or seen that he has not thought about. All this might be mere thoroughness, within the compass of any pedant. What makes *Siren Land* exceptional is the quality of the telling. He writes in the manner of one leisured and educated person addressing another of the same kind or of a man making meditative comments for his own pleasure – "I am only dreaming through the summer months to the music of the cicadas" – dreaming perhaps, but sharply aware, and weaving scholarship, impressions, fact, and fantasy into an intricate fabric as enchantingly entertaining and full of human interest as the best of fairy tales or ancient myths. This atmosphere is created without fuss, with economy and elegance, with style and verve, with measure and serenity, eminently considerate of the reader, good mannered, enticing, satisfying.

The opening chapter, "Sirens", which first appeared in *The English Review*, was said by the editor of that famous literary journal Ford Madox Ford (when reminiscing twenty years later) to have been "the most beautiful thing we printed". The research on which "Sirens" is based is prodigious; so also is the reading that lies behind his persuasive defence of Tiberius, or his mischievous analysis of Sister Serafina, or his remarks on the Blue Grotto. In another chapter, "Rain on the Hills", he gives the reader a foretaste of the high spirits, wit, and ironic humour that were to make him famous a few years later when his best-known book, *South Wind*, was published.

South Wind was a novel set in that same southern half of Italy which contains Siren Land (the Sorrentine peninsula). Together with Capri, this forms one arm of the Bay of Naples, and is a region that Douglas knew as well as anyone, and better than most. He had lived in it, walked over every inch of it, loved it, and returned to it frequently. He knew many of its people intimately. He spoke the dialect, knew the finger signs and manual gestures, shared some of the superstitions. This personal and physical familiarity with the country helps to bring the touch and taste of it, its sights and sounds almost as vividly to the reader as if he were there himself.

Apart from *South Wind* and two other novels, Douglas wrote five travel books. Three of these were about Italy. *Old Calabria* (1915), which must be the most comprehensive and idiosyncratic book ever written in English about that region, has been recognised as a classic almost since the day it was published. *Alone* (1921) is the mellowest, most relaxed and meditative of the travel books, and was Douglas's own favourite of all his books. Like much of his work, but perhaps more than most of it, *Alone* gives a good idea of his range of interests, and his abilities as raconteur and conversationalist, by which listeners such as Joseph Conrad, D. H. Lawrence, Rebecca West, Compton Mackenzie, Aldous Huxley and Graham Greene were fascinated – not to mention hundreds of others in all walks of life. *Alone*, mostly about wanderings north of Rome, was followed by *Together* (1923), set in the Vorarlberg, the Austrian province in which Douglas was born and spent his childhood. It is the most autobiographical of the travel books, only exceeded in this particular by his highly original and tantalising *Looking Back* (1933), in which he describes his life and his friends by taking up their calling cards one by one and writing little or much under each name as the mood takes him. It is greatly characteristic and enjoyable, one of the most successful experiments in autobiography written in the first half of the century.

It could be said that there is a progression in Douglas's non-fictional books from the more or less impersonal yet friendly approach of a courteous stranger, towards the more self-revealing and sometimes deliberately indiscreet confidences of a man who knows he has become something of a cult figure (as was the case after about 1925). In this sequence each book offers almost as much, differently, as any other; even so, it is difficult not to have a special affection for *Siren Land*. Here, where the author displays his prodigal gifts for the first time, there is a freshness, a richness of vocabulary and phrasing, an evident delight in the handling of words, a sense of form and style, a serenity and a masterliness, that make the book one of the most memorable of its genre. Irradiated by sunshine and sometimes bathed in the dewy haze of myth, it is as strong as rock, as sparkling as water, as real as daylight. As in almost everything Douglas wrote, there emerges from it a philosophical attitude which celebrates life in all its vividness, and scornfully or with laughter dismisses obstacles to happiness.

SIREN LAND

I

SIRENS AND THEIR ANCESTRY

IT was the Emperor Tiberius who startled his grammarians with the question, what songs the Sirens sang? I suspect he knew more about the matter than they did, for he was a Siren-worshipper all his life, though fate did not allow him to indulge his genius till those last few years which he spent among them on the rock-islet of Capri. The grammarians, if they were prudent, doubtless referred him to Homer, who has preserved a portion of their lay.

Whether Sirens of this true kind are in existence at the present day is rather questionable, for the waste places of earth have been reclaimed, and the sea's untrampled floor is examined and officially reported upon. Not so long ago some such creatures were still found. Jacobus Noierus relates that in 1403 a Siren was captured in the Zuider Zee. She was brought to Haarlem and, being naked, allowed herself to be clothed; she learned to eat like a Dutchman; she could spin thread and take pleasure in other maidenly occupations; she was gentle and lived to a great age. But she never spoke. The honest burghers had no knowledge of the language of the sea-folk to enable them to teach her their own tongue, so she remained mute to the end of her days—a circumstance to be regretted, since, excepting in the Arab tale of "Julnar the Sea-born", little information has been handed down to us regarding the conversational and domestic habits of mediæval Sirens.

In the royal archives of Portugal are preserved the records of a costly litigation between the Crown and the Grand Master of the Order of Saint James, as to who should possess the Sirens cast up by the sea on the Grand Master's shores. The suit ended in the King's favour: BE IT ENACTED—THAT SIRENS AND OTHER MARINE MONSTERS EJECTED BY THE WAVES UPON LAND OWNED BY THE GRAND MASTER SHALL PASS INTO THE POSSESSION OF THE KING. This would show that Sirens were then fairly plentiful. And one of the best authenticated cases is that recorded by the veracious

Captain John Smith—he of Pocahontas fame. "I cannot here omit to mention", says he, "the admirable creature of God which in the year 1610 I saw with these my own eyes. I happened to be standing, at daybreak, on the shore not far from the harbour of St. John, when I observed a marine monster swiftly swimming towards me. Lovely was her shape; eyes, nose, ears, cheeks, mouth, neck, forehead, and the whole face was as that of the fairest maiden; her hair, of azure hue, fell over her shoulders. . . ." Altogether, a strange fish. The rest of the quotation will be found in Gottfried's *Historia Antipodum*.

Consult also Gessner, Rondeletius, Scaliger, and other good folks, from whose relations it appears evident that Sirens were common enough in their days and, doubtless for that reason, of little repute; for whatever is common becomes debased, as the very word "vulgar" proves. This perhaps helps to explain their fishy termination, for the oldest Sirens were of a bird kind. The change took place, I imagine, about the time of Saint Augustine, when so many pagan shapes began to affect new vestments and characters, not always to their advantage. It influenced even those born in Hellenic waters, whom we might have supposed to have remained more respectable and conservative than the others.

Thus Theodorus Gaza, whose name is a guarantee of good faith and intelligence—did he not write the first Greek grammar?—once related in a large and distinguished company (Pontanus was also present) how that, after a great storm in the Peloponnesus, a sea-lady was cast up with other jetsam on the beach. She was still alive and breathing hard; her face and body were "absolutely human" and not uncomely. Immediately a large concourse of people gathered round, but her sighs and heaving breast plainly showed how embarrassed she was by their vulgar curiosity. Presently she began to cry outright. The compassionate scholar ordered the crowd to move away and escorted her, as best he could, to the water's edge. There, throwing herself into the waves with a mighty splash, she vanished from sight. This one, again, partook rather of the nature of a fish than of a bird.

In Greece, too, Sirens of every kind have ceased to sing.

I remember a long-drawn, golden evening among the Cyclades. A spell had fallen over all things; the movement of Nature seemed to be momentarily arrested; there was not a sound below, but, overhead, the sunbeams vibrated with tuneful melodies. Janko, the fisherman, had dropped his oars, and our boat, the only moving object in that preternatural stillness, was drawn by an invisible hand towards the ruddy pool in the west. But athwart our path lay a craggy islet, black and menacing against the background of crimson conflagration. Soon it came in upon us in swarthy confusion of rock and cloven ravine, a few gleams of emerald in its sheltered recesses. Here if anywhere, methought, Sirens might still dwell unmolested. The curly-pated rascal steered with cunning hand towards a Lilliputian inlet; like a true Greek, he appreciated curiosity in every form. But he resolutely refused to set foot on shore. I began my explorations alone, concluding that he had visited the place before.

It was no Siren islet. It was an islet of fleas. I picked them off my clothes in tens, in hundreds, in handfuls. Never was mortal nearer jumping out of his skin. Janko was surprised and shocked.

Now, whether these fleas had inhabited the island from time immemorial, being degenerate descendants of certain heroic creatures that sailed thither in company of Jason and his Argonauts, or had been left there by shipwrecked mariners of modern days; how it came about that they multiplied to the exclusion of every other living thing; what manner of food was theirs—whether, anthropophagous-wise, they preyed upon one another or had learned to content themselves with the silvery dews of morning, like Anacreon's cicada, or else had acquired the faculty of long fasting between rare orgies such as they enjoyed on that afternoon: these and other questions have since occurred to me as not unworthy of consideration. Mr. Hudson, in his *La Plata*, has vexed himself with similar problems. But at that moment I was far too busy to give any thought to such matters.

Ay, they have deserted Greece, the Sirens. It was never more than a half-way house to them. But they stayed there long enough to don new clothes and habits. Nothing indeed ever entered that little country but came out rejuvenated and clarified. A thousand turbid streams, pouring into Hellas from every side, issued thence grandly, in a calm and transparent river, to fertilize the world. So it was with the Sirens. Like many things, they were only an importation, one of the new ideas that, following the trade routes, crept in to feed the artistic imagination of the Greeks. Now that we know a little something of the ancient civilizations of countries like Egypt and Phœnicia that traded with Greece, we can appreciate the wonderful Hellenic genius for borrowing and adapting. Hermes, the intelligent thief, is a typical Greek. For whatever they stole or appropriated—religions, metals, comforts of life, architecture, engineering—they stole with exquisite taste; they discarded the dross and took only what was of value. All traces of the theft quickly vanished; it looked absurd, as Monsieur du Presle has pointed out, to acknowledge indebtedness to others for things which they might as well have invented themselves. For the rest, the stolen material was re-modelled till its original creator could hardly have recognized it. The grotesque, the cruel, became humane. Borrowed gods of frantic aspect put on fair and benignant faces. And every item was forthwith stamped with the hall-mark of Hellas: temperance. All these *objets de vertu* have been handled a good deal since those days; they were sadly knocked about in the uproarious Middle Ages; but this hall-mark is not thumbed away: connoisseurs know it.

I question whether Phorcus himself, the father of the Sirens— or was it Achelous? these old family histories are delicate ground— would have recognized his girls again. How did they look on entering Greece? Ask Messieurs Weicker, Schrader, De Petra, Corcia, Klausen, and their colleagues. They will tell you everything, for they have performed the unknightly task, suggested by Anaxilas, of "plucking the Sirens". In the interests of anatomy it was no doubt desirable, since it enabled them to count the vertebræ and teeth, and perhaps to decide whether the Sirens were really cannibals or not; artists and poets complain of unnecessary mutilation. Dreamers are always complaining. How they looked? They were the personification of sultry dog-days when Sirius (whence their name) burns fiercely in the parching firmament; they were vampires, demons of heat, of putrefaction, of voluptuousness, of lust. But Hellas clothed them anew in virginal hearts and garments and sent them westward—in bad company to be sure, for it seems they travelled with the Teleboeans or Taphians, incorrigible cut-throats and cattle-stealers. It must have been something like "the Baby and the Burglar".

Yes; from the minute specialized researches of scholars it is quite clear that the Sirens were nowise indigenous to Greece; they belonged to wilder, non-Hellenic cycles, "remaining", says Butcher, "as foreign words borrowed into a language, but never wholly nationalized". Like other animistic conceptions common to many seas and lands, they drifted into Hellas and were *deodorized*. Our familiar Sirens are not demons of putrefaction; they are creatures full of charm and go to prove the humanizing influence of the Greeks; not of the Greek crowd, as is sometimes inferred (for a more intemperate set of bigots and ruffians never breathed), but only of its teachers, who resented ugliness as a sin and ever held up to them the ideal of nemesis—measure.

Homer began the work, and nothing is more true than that saying of Herodotus, that "Homer arranged the generations of the gods". The *Odyssey*, which sweeps along its current the legend-wrecks of multitudinous extra-Hellenic races, has wafted down to us a fragment of the foreign and cannibalistic old Siren-lore—

> In verdant meads they sport, and wide around
> Lie human bones, that whiten all the ground;
> The ground polluted floats with human gore,
> And human carnage taints the dreadful shore. . . .

but there is no further elaboration of this ungracious aspect; on the contrary, their song, which follows, is conceived in the true spirit of beauty and quite at variance with this primeval picture of crude bloodthirstiness. A characteristic hellenization, caught in the act. This first step towards purification accomplished, later poets and philosophers dwelt ever more on the human attributes of the Sirens, on their charms of voice and feature, till finally the "whitening bones" and other harsh traits faded from sight.

After Hellas came the Alexandrian period with its philological and historical vagaries, and the prodigious syncretism of gods in the second and third centuries; then mediævalism, which dwarfed Hellenic shapes into caco-demons and with their glories crowned its saints.

The Siren Parthenope escaped by taking refuge during mediæval storms in the narrow confines of an amulet, such Siren-charms as are still seen in the streets of Naples and credited with peculiar efficacity against the evil eye. In this, I seem to see the homœopathic principle at work, for the Sirens themselves were witches at the time—sea-witches, and to this day the bathing population may be observed to cross themselves devoutly before plunging into the water, in order to paralyse these malevolent genii of the deep. Others, such as Venus, sheltered themselves behind musty saints; Santa Venere is in high repute as Healer of certain diseases.

And another point of general interest becomes clear from these scientific disquisitions: that the Sirens of Homer must be sought in the West rather than where Gladstone and others have located them. A variety of speculations are now converging to show that the Odyssean fable is the record of one of many westward processions of gods and men and is, indeed, only another example of that suggestive "westing" law first propounded, I believe, by the Russian naturalist, von Baer. Curiously enough, Baer himself asserted that the adventures of Odysseus, including the Siren episode, took place in the Black Sea; but this may have been due to a kind of patriotism on his part—if we always knew from what motives our profoundest convictions have sprung! An interesting phenomenon, by the way, this of exact thinkers relapsing, in old age, into hazardous theorizings. So Baer, the physiologist, discourses about the legendary Phæacians; Virchow, the pathologist, about prehistoric man; Wallace, the biologist, about the world of spirits. And sometimes the weariness, the acquiescent mood is premature: Lodge, the mathematician, has already begun to preach the æons and ethics. It is the way of individual man and the way of nations; none exemplifies it better than Hellas: from "pillars of unwrought stone" to Aristotle and back again, via Plato, to the *logos*, which is obscurity once more. But not all of us follow this natural curve; some are born old and others never attain maturity, the discords being adjusted in some posthumous or antenatal existence.

The Greek Sirens, at least, are stamped with features of eternal youth. They linger on sea-girt rocks, lyre in hand, or rise from the gleaming water, clash their cymbals, and again vanish. So you may see them pictured on Greek vases. There is a vagueness, remoteness, and restraint about them which permits of multifarious interpretations and constitutes the charm of so many of these Hellenic conceptions. They are not the product of one mind, but a complex, many-faceted growth which reflects the touches of various layers of culture superimposed upon one another—fair but elusive shapes. Here is one aspect. Long ago, the Sirens engaged the Muses in a singing-contest. They were worsted, and the Muses decked themselves with their enemies' feather-plumes. Who is not tempted to detect in this legend the victory of disciplined music over the wild improvisations of natural song? And another: the three sister-Sirens drowned themselves out of love for Odysseus. This is the impress of strong human feelings—a hopeless passion, you perceive: no school-

girl sentimentality. Picture a "demon of putrefaction" casting itself
into the sea for a mortal! Oh, they had changed considerably in
the air of Hellas. The purification—the hallmark. The "*chaste
Parthenope*" found a resting-place and an honoured tomb on the
spot where now stands Naples. For a thousand years she dominated
its social and religious institutions. She dominates them still. Is
Parthenope dead? Who, then, is Santa Lucia? The madonnas of
Naples are all sea-queens whose crowns shine with a borrowed
lustre; the Madonna della Libera, the Stella di Mare—they are all
reincarnations of antique shapes, of the Sirens, of Leucothea,
Euploia, and the Nereids, and their cult to this day is pagan rather
than Christian. You will not find such saints in Tuscany.

A large Siren literature has sprung up within recent times. But I
would still like to see a book which should develop the idea as a
whole, tracing their genealogy from birth through all the changes
of character they have undergone since ancient days—a book which
might be entitled *Les Sirènes à travers les siècles* (why does it sound
better in French?), and which would afford an interesting measure
of the corresponding state of the human intelligence. For we create
our gods in our own likeness.

There is an imp of the imagination called the familiar spirit or
guardian angel, who often runs parallel to these eerie water-ladies.
Like the Sirens that occur everywhere—in Chinese and Saxon
tradition, in Brazil and in the grey-green reaches of Polar seas,*
the attendant demon is of animistic growth, springing up, indepen-
dently, in Burma, among the old Irish, the Eskimos, the Chilians.

Our particular Sirens are probably of Phœnician origin, while
our particular guardian angels come from the Chaldæans. The
crystal spaces of their æther were alive with fluttering divas who
grew in holiness as they receded from earth; Hellenic and Roman
culture took them over from direct contact with the East, but
Christian Europe received them indirectly as a legacy from the
Jews who had imbibed this poetic demonology during their Baby-
lonian sorrows and had enriched their sacred books with these
terrible and lovely creatures of air, which the Gnostics and Sabæans

* Henry Hudson's crew saw one when seeking a passage to the North Pole near
Nova Zemblya. She was like a woman above, "her skin very white and long hair
hanging behind, of colour black". Her tail was speckled and shaped like that of
a porpoise.

elaborated into a glittering hierarchy. So the seven planetary spirits of Persian mythology melted into the seven arch-angels of Cabbalistic dreamings; but our ideas of ordinary ones, of winged forms intermediate between God and man, are purely Chaldæan. Christians were actually forbidden by the Council of Laodicea to call upon the angels, and it was not till the second Council of Nicæa that this "idolatrous practice" was sanctioned; Byzance indeed, rather than Rome, is the mother of angel worship.

Even as the Sirens soon took on fixed æsthetic attributes, so the guardian angel was early installed in his moral functions. Every man had his own; angels and gods likewise; the graves of the dead likewise, and high divinities were sometimes pleased to play the part with deserving mortals like Tobias or Telemachus. Pythagoras, strongly tainted with Orientalism, made his *daimon* perceptible to the senses, whereas the familiar of Socrates was invisible, the "divine voice" of reason. This point of time is approximately the high-water mark of both conceptions—hence onward there is the exuberance of decline. And as in Homer we can designate the precise poetic touch which raised the Sirens from their lowly place, so in Plato we may note the very blunder whereby the familiar became gross once more. For the master can hardly have meant by "a divine something" that which his disciples thought—interpreting literally an allegorical remark of his, they built up that anthropomorphic theory which stultified Socrates and re-materialized the *demon*.

It is characteristic of mankind that only then did he, like the Sirens, become "popular". Xenophon, Menander, Apuleius, and the rest of them waxed eloquent in explanations; Diogenes and Apollonius also began to consult private devils, and of course Plotinus, the ape of Socrates, had one too. And soon the curious spirit of Alexandrian pedantry was at work upon them, dwelling, with erudite dilettantism, upon the origins and meanings of the Sirens, while Philo mixed his astounding *salade russe* of Greek and Jewish demons.

The Romans, busy and honest, had no use for things of beauty, save as plunder of war to decorate their temples and villas. They rejected the Sirens, but the stern Pelasgic cast of their religion led them to identify the *demon* with what philosophers called the idiosyncrasy, the genius. Enlarging upon this sober notion, they gave congenial spirits to corporate bodies and towns, the grandest being that of Rome itself; the patron saints of modern Italian cities and villages are so firmly rooted only because they represent the lineal descendants of these old tutelar deities. And sometimes a good and a bad genius lived conjointly in the body of one man, striving for the mastery: a problem which already confronted these Chaldæans whose religious cursing-tablets (models of what such literature ought to be) are largely taken up with conjurations for the expulsion of malefic demons in favour of beneficial ones. The dilemma was inevitable—one of the two antagonistic forces must preponderate— and so these imaginary intracorporeal mannikins are a microcosmic illustration of the pitfalls of dualistic creeds.

Mediævalism came, and the familiar or paredral spirits went through the same degrading metamorphosis as the Sirens. They grew common; philosophers like Simon Magus, saints like Teresa, poets like Tasso—everybody had one or more of them. That of Cornelius Agrippa lived in the shape of a black dog (Faust): on his death-bed at Lyons the sage thus cursed it—*Hence, beast of damnation, that hast wholly damned me!* (whereupon it vanished), and his great disciple Wier, who also believed in them, is sharply reprimanded for doubting this particular tale. The idea commingled with a host of mandrake legends; idols, of which numbers were sold in England under Henry VIII, were carved out of this plant and gravely consulted.

I think the Crusades and the Western domination of the Arabs, in whose lore the attendant genius plays a conspicuous part, may have helped to spread the superstition throughout Europe, which was then in a fit condition to believe anything. The familiar lived no longer inside man, prompting him to moral actions; he was imprisoned in capsules or rings (Parthenope in her amulet) and could be constrained to appear or dismissed from service (Ariel). Up to this day, *homunculi* in glass phials are bought in German fairs and kept "for luck"—I have seen them hawked about the streets of London—and the following will show that this trade, like others, had its risks: "In the year 1650 a merchant of Augsburg kept some of these quaint spirits sealed up, like flies or ants, in bottles, intending to bring them to the fair of Leipzig; but when, by means of a letter, it was discovered that he was about to offer them for sale, he denied the whole matter—*perhaps they themselves had whispered to him* that he might have to answer awkward questions on their account." Awkward questions!

Despoiled of their pristine ennobling qualities, these beings were still sociable and not without hopes of heaven; the familiar had become realistic, swayed by passions like mankind, sometimes lovable and often tinged with a vein of sadness, while Sirens like Undine and Melusine were strangely human in tears and laughter. We were not yet wholly afraid of these our creatures. But soon enough, by that process of deterioration of which the word "demon" is itself an example, they were absorbed into the essence of the Evil One and became his slaves—past redemption. Witches only, and not philosophers, kept familiars in the shape of cats, and the belief was merged into that of incubi, Satanic Pact; the Church warning its adherents against them: *Ipse simulat se captum, ut te capiat; a te inclusum, ut contra te finaliter concludat.* Thus the rebellious angels confined in copper vessels by the great Lord Solomon have degenerated into a bottled imp, an infant's toy; and from the voice of reason of the Greek sage, from the guardian angel that watches over the slumbers of innocent childhood, from the genius of divine Augustus and eternal Rome, we descend to the "harmless, necessary cat".

I rather question whether the familiar spirit would have maintained its strong fascination if it had not lent itself to practical purposes, and one may speculate how much of the worldly prestige of men like Mahomet, Numa, or Carbajal was due to their fiction of a ghostly counsellor, which justified actions unintelligible to the vulgar. The familiar has lately appeared in a new guise: the control of the medium.

Will he quite die out? No more than the Sirens. The pious Silvio Pellico addressed a prayer to his spiritual custodian; the Catholic Church, however, has never favoured this individualistic tendency, convinced that the rôle of guardian angel is more properly performed by confessors or one of the thousand saints appointed for that purpose. Protestantism, meanwhile, has reverted to the "still, small voice", though in neurotic men, like George Fox, a vision is required to supplement the conscience. All those who fail to attribute their well-being to natural causes will crave for something of the guardian-angel type, even as simple mariners, in moments of danger, may wonder whether there is indeed no truth in those tales of spiteful she-devils lurking in the depths. And if this were a philosophical age, I would endeavour to show that the whole invisible-companion-idea is merely an exemplification of Lotze's views, as to that striving of the human personality to extend and consolidate its sphere of domination which has induced us to carry walking-sticks and to wear tall hats; while the Sirens are—well, no matter. Fortunately, metaphysics are out of fashion just now.

It seems to me that the Sirens, like other old Hellenic ideals, are coming to honour again.

During their westward progress they tarried long about the headland of Athenæum, which is the southern horn of the Bay of Naples now called Punta Campanella, and about its islands. A snowy temple, one of the wonders of the western world, rose in their honour near this wave-beaten promontory—for promontories were sacred in oldest days from their dangers to navigation; colonnades and statues are swept away, but its memory lies embedded in the name of the village of Massa Lubrense (*delubrum*). A wondrous mode of survival, when one comes to think of it: a temple enshrined in the letters of a word whose very meaning is forgotten, handed down from father to son through tumultuous ages of Romans and Goths and Saracens, Normans, French, and Spaniards, and persisting, ever cryptic to the vulgar, after the more perishable records of stone and marble are clean vanished from the earth.

A good idea of the country can be obtained from the well-known Deserto convent above Sorrento or, nearer the point of the promontory, from the summit of Mount San Costanzo which, if I mistake not, ought to be an island like Capri near at hand, but will probably cling to the mainland for another few thousand years. The eye looks down upon the two gulfs of Naples and Salerno, divided by a hilly ridge; the precipitous mass of Sant' Angelo, stretching right across the peninsula in an easterly direction, shuts off the view from the world beyond. This is Siren Land. To the south lie the islets of the Sirens, nowadays known as the Galli; westwards, Capri, appropriately associated with them from its craggy and yet alluring aspect; Sorrento, whose name has been derived from them—I wonder some adventurous scholar has not identified it with the Homeric *Surie*—lies on the northern slope. A favoured land, flowing with milk and honey; particularly the former: Saint-Non mentions as proof of its fertility the fact that you can engage wet-nurses there from the ages of fourteen to fifty-five.

I am not going to describe its natural features; the thing has been done by five hundred travellers already. Imagine to yourself a

tongue of limestone about three miles across and six long, jutting
into the sea; a few islands hanging upon its skirts; villages and
farms whose inhabitants reflect the various cultures that have been
imposed upon them during the last two thousand years of political
changes. A microscopic territory; but overgrown with hoary
traditions of which that of the sea-maidens is only one. We need
merely think of those quaintly carved vessels which in olden days
sailed in between Capri and Point Campanella, bearing westwards certain gods and letters and aspirations—much of what is
best, in fact, in our own modern civilization. And more recent
memories, grim and glorious, cluster thickly about its rocks and
inlets. . . .

It was no doubt during one of those spells of deathlike summer
stagnation, known hereabouts as *scirocco chiaro* or *tempo di bafogna*,
that Odysseus encountered the Sirens—

> While yet I speak the winged galley flies
> And lo! The Siren shores like mists arise.
> Sunk were at once the winds; the air above,
> And waves below, at once forgot to move.
> Some dæmon calmed the air, and smoothed the deep,
> Hushed the loud winds, and charmed the waves to sleep—

for scirocco is the withering blast whose hot and clammy touch
hastens death and putrefaction.

This passage may have suggested to Cerquand the idea that the
Sirens "*sont le calme sous le vent des hautes falaises et des îles*", an interpretation which he subsequently discarded. Loosely speaking, this
would imply that *some* thing had been created out of nothing; even
as, on the same principle, Pan has been called the personification
of the midday hush that can be felt. The Swiss painter Boecklin,
whose Gothic exuberance often ran on lines antithetical to what
we call Hellenic serenity, has yet divined the psychology of the
matter in *Das Schweigen im Walde*—the shudder that attunes the
mind to receive chimerical impressions, the silence that creates;
though I cannot but think that the effect of this particular picture
would have been improved by the omission of Madame Boecklin.
So may those pioneers of navigation have felt when, becalmed in
the noonday heat amid pale-shimmering cliffs, they grew conscious
of the unseen presence. Sirens dwell here! For the genii of earth and
air were ready enough to commune with untutored men of early
ages, to whom everything unknown was marvellous. Such fruitful

shadows cast by inanimate nature upon the human phantasy are not rare; the secondary stage is reached when the artist endeavours to fix in stone these wavering shapes, or the bard in verse; the third is that of the philosopher or grammarian who explains them as the splashing of waves and what not.

What not, indeed? The Sirens, says one, are the charms of the Gulf of Naples. No, says another; they were chaste priestesses. They were neither chaste nor priestesses, but exactly the reverse. They were sunbeams. They were perilous cliffs. They were a race of peaceful shepherds. They were symbols of persuasion. They were cannibals. They were planetary spirits. They were prophets. They were a species of Oriental owl. They were the harmonious faculties of the soul. They were penguins.

Penguins! That is the final pronouncement of commentatorial erudition.

Yet I must add my own mite of conjecture regarding the so-called "eyed Sirens". These, I hold, may well represent a pristine version of the Beasts in the Apocalypse. And Eustathius has already explained how they came by their feather-dresses. They used to be young girls like any other nymphs or naiads, but Venus was so annoyed at their persistent chastity that she changed them into birds. Just like Venus—the Venus of the grammarians.

So may they have felt, those ancient mariners, spell-bound in drowsy scirocco-chains; but I question whether this was the true genesis of the Sirens. The bird-termination. . . . It recurs in the harpies, of Egyptian origin. Those Egyptians, too, had that notable conceit of the dead body being visited by its soul in the shape of a human-headed hawk (*Die Seelenvögel*), and it was also—says Doughty—"an ancient opinion of the idolatrous Arabs, that the departing spirit flitted from man's brain-pan as a wandering fowl, complaining thenceforward in deadly thirst her unavenged wrong". Leucothea, a Phœnician goddess, could likewise assume the bird-form,* and—who knows?—some crazy enthusiast may yet succeed

* Professor Correra gives various reasons for supposing that the cult of Leucothea was more widely diffused in these regions than is generally believed. So, for example, he refers to this divinity the statue of a sea-lady seated upon a marine monster which was found in the ancient Villa Pausilipon and is now in the Naples Museum. I observe that in the Blacas collection there was a gem which exactly reproduces this statue—King has figured it under the title of *Venus Euploia* whose temple is supposed, though not by Beloch, to have stood near the site of this Villa at the western point of the Bay of Naples, facing the Athenæum promontory on

in establishing a cousinship between the Sirens and those enigmatical swan-maidens who winged their way from snowy Himalaya
to grace the bridal couch of northern hero-kings.

For the rest, such days of heavy-lidded atmospheric brooding
are rare in Siren land.

They are clear-eyed and caressing as a rule, these summer
breezes; caressing and cleansing; they set all the shining leaves
a-tremble and scatter town-memories and the fumes of musty
learning. How the bizarre throng of water-witches and familiars
grow uneasy in that brave light, and wan—how they fade away,
like the ghosts they are!

the east. This identical gem is also photographed as "Nereid or Thetis" in the
beautiful work of Furtwaengler, who thinks that the several gems depicting this
subject are antique copies of a stone dating about 400 B.C. Here are three different
versions of one figure: Leucothea, Venus, and Nereid; whence we may conclude
that the sages have not yet quite disentangled the genealogies of these wave-born
divinities. It used to be thought that some of them, like the Sirens, Leucothea and
Aphrodite, had come to these shores with their old Phœnician worshippers. These
traders have doubtless left their mark in certain South Italian local names, such
as Megaris (their depot at Naples), Marata, and Sama—Megaris, Marathon, and
Samos in Greece are also of Phœnician origin—but their gods, as we now know
them, only entered the country later on, under Hellenic auspices.

II

UPLANDS OF SORRENTO

WITH the exception of Capri, which is the only spot within a hundred miles of Naples where a foreigner is reasonably well treated, no accommodation in the septentrional sense of the word can be found in Siren land save at Sorrento and Sant' Agata, the idea being that "foreigners must first come" before anything can be done to welcome the few that flee into these solitudes from the din and confusion of that fair land whose frontier-station bears the ominous name of Chiasso (noise). Massa is rich and populous, but contains not a single hotel or even restaurant; it is a community of peasant-proprietors who live, some of them, in fine country houses built in pre-Bourbon days by Spanish and Neapolitan grandees—indeed, it is one of the surprising things in this district to see mouldering structures with ample courtyards, arched galleries, and noble escutcheons over their gates, now inhabited by mean-looking folk whose manners, at least, are still in harmony with their dwellings. Massa is full of them, but even the humblest village can boast of one or two. The terrors of a century of Bourbonism reduced this country to direst distress. Capri, after the discovery of the Blue Grotto, began to thrive in spite of its sovereigns, but the mainland portions are only just now recovering from the blight. Neapolitans have grown rich again and seek the fine air of the hills as of yore, while the inhabitants themselves bring much money from New York; and from Argentina, where a good half of them are periodically employed in selling potatoes to the Spaniards, who apparently eat nothing else. "Good people" they call them, because they are easily gulled in the matter of weights and measures.

One consequence of this revival is that the price of land is rising once more and new houses are being built. This would be satisfactory, were it not that the style of architecture has changed for the worse. That harmonious medley of small vaulted chambers with

their vine-shaded loggia in front, so becoming to this climate and
charming to look upon, has been displaced by hideous *palazzi* constructed with iron beams, asphalt, and roofing tiles—things formerly
unheard of. No person with a sense of the fitness of things will ever
fall in love with these new dwellings, although they are built, as the
architects will tell you, according to the latest *regola d'arte*. When a
Southerner discourses upon *regola d'arte*, he is generally up to some
mischief.

Even the colossal hand-made house-keys of the olden days, now
replaced by weedy cast-iron abominations, were not without a
certain austere beauty: there was a smack of Saint Peter about
them. And they had their uses, too. Three years ago a wealthy
landowner, returning home at night, was attacked by two ruffians
with knives. Having no ordinary weapon of defence, not even a
walking-stick, he began to wield his house-key with such dexterity
that one of his assailants was brained on the spot, while the other
crawled into the fields, where he was found dead next morning—
at least, he ought to have been.

The ridge of backbone which divides the gulfs of Salerno and
Naples is called *Le Tore*—an obscure and venerable word which is
common all over this region and takes us back to Mount Taurus in
Cilicia and to the Celtic and Sinaitic Tor. Perhaps the poet Statius
was referring to these Tore when he spoke of the "green Tauru-
bulæ" of Sorrento or Capri, but unfortunately nobody can tell us
exactly what he meant, as in the whole of ancient literature the
word occurs only in this one passage. A modern scholar derives the
Tore from the Greek τα ὄρη, the mountains; which, if not correct,
is at least simple. There is a village called Torco on the southern
slope of the ridge just below Sant' Agata, whose name has been
drawn by some from the Latin *torqueo*, because the road "turns"
there, and by others from the Greek *theorica* because, they say, a
religious procession of youths and maidens used to wend thither in
olden days. Though the church of Torco is one of the oldest in the
district, there are no classic remains whatever in the neighbourhood,
and I rather disbelieve this tempting theorica-derivation, although
it is adopted in his *Magic and Astrology* by Maury who copied it, I
suspect, from the old Sorrentine writer, Onofrio Gargiulli. It seems
more natural to connect the word Torco with this backbone or
Tor.

It is not a crest but a rounded plateau, and as the divide

approaches far nearer to the southern shore, the rocks on this incline needs must rush precipitously into the sea, with perilous paths into grottos, and thrifty olives on the middle heights grasping the limestone ledges or climbing warily down the gullies; the northern slope, on which Massa and Sorrento lie, is a gentle declivity planted with vines and oranges and walnuts, and refreshed by streams that run through the heat of the dog-days. The Tore reach their highest elevation immediately behind Sorrento. Here, in the early morning, when sea-mists on either side shroud the two gulfs from view, the wanderer has all the illusion of being on some lonely Alpine meadow—not a sign of human habitation or handiwork; a chill nip in the air; browsing cattle with deep-toned bells round their necks, and real, close-cropped turf under foot. This, I imagine, is the track which the wolves follow when they leave their fastnesses of the Sant' Angelo in winter to scour the richer country.

A path, the *via delle Tore*, runs along the whole summit, passing through Sant' Agata and ending at Termini, which is the last village on the peninsula. An ideal summer walk, for those who do not feel a little dry heat. But if you sit down, it is well to seek out the shadow of some wall or an umbrageous carob, for the reverberation of the light may induce a sun-stroke.

The olives make scanty shade: they are too ferociously pruned hereabouts. The whole of the southern incline is planted with them wherever a little soil can be scraped together, and their oil is excellent —better, says Pliny, than that of Venafrum—probably because the inhabitants know the secret of preparing it. As soon as it is plucked, the fruit must be pressed in those picturesque rustic mills where, by the dim light of a lantern—the work is nearly always done at night— half-naked, Praxitelean shapes of men and boys may be discerned turning the heavy stone wheel which crushes the berry to a clammy pulp. Alas, these trees are now remorselessly uprooted wherever the soil will feed the more profitable grape; Capri has lost half its olives, Ischia all: a consummation to be deplored since the vine, however gladsome in its summer greenery, is bare for six months in the year when its straggling limbs have a peculiarly unkempt and disreputable appearance. Were the landscape alone to be considered, I could wish that some new scourge like phylloxera might be introduced, for there is enough wine in the country already. At this moment it is being sold for three francs a barrel (forty-four litres) on Ischia, whereas the oil-crop has failed altogether; there has been no rain, the grub has invaded the fruit, and the preceding winter was too mild (the olive likes a good shiver once a year). These trees are small in size, mere pigmies beside the writhing monsters of Spain and Greece and Apulia; their upper limbs are stretched in a nervous tension which is the despair of artists, but in those tumid roots there sits—to all appearances—a deep repose. Yet who can tell what passionate alchemy is astir in that subterranean laboratory, sustaining life and fashioning fruit through those scorching summer months, among stones that are often too hot to handle?

At this season the olive's complexion wanes to a yellowish green; with the autumn rains it becomes blue-grey; the plant also varies in tint according to locality. This may help to explain the contradictory colour-epithets which the ancients bestowed upon it. Even now it is still revered as emblem of peace and plenty, a sprig of olive being attached to boats and houses after the Easter blessing. There is this peculiarity in its leaves, that they can make no fluttering movements like those of most plants; they are affixed to the stem like metal plates, and if the wind blows it is the whole limb of the tree which sways. And so a pretty effect may often be seen upon these olive-coloured slopes: the branches bending with one accord to the breeze expose the white under-surface of all the leaves, and the hillside is clothed in silver.

Here, on these remote uplands, I prefer to turn my back on the green undulations of Massa and Sorrento, on Vesuvius and Naples, Ischia and the Phlegræan Fields; all these regions are trite and familiar. I prefer to gaze towards the mysterious South, the mountains of Basilicata and the fabled headland Licosa, where Leucosia, sister-Siren of Parthenope, lies buried. At this height the sea's horizon soars into the firmament smooth as a sheet of sapphire, and the eye never wearies of watching those pearly lines and spirals that crawl upon its surface, the paths of silver-footed Thetis—a restful prospect, with dim suggestions of love and affinity for this encircling element that reach back, for aught we know, to primeval days of Ascidian-life. There is a note of impotence in the sea's wintry storms, for it can but rage against its prison bars or drown a few sailormen, an ignoble business: true grandeur is only in its luminous calm.

Licosa is the furthest point visible but, on rare occasions, other lands with peaks and promontories unknown loom upon the sky-line,

and sometimes, by the same atmospheric witchcraft, the volcanic
cone of Stromboli is projected out of the waves. Early mornings
in spring and autumn are most propitious for these delicate trickeries.
So Hehn saw the island of Ischia from Monte Cavo near Albano,
though it must have been well below the horizon. Dream-pageants,
swift-fading. . . .

This is essentially a land of line, of irreproachable contours, and
your painter had best begin by throwing away his palette and
striving to see it aright: a land of classical parsimony, limestone and
blue sea, whose chastened beauty none save a really great craftsman,
with disciplined hand and heart attuned to eternal melodies, can
hope to disentangle from among the prejudices and traditions of
his own mind. What caricatures are the works of even world-
famous artists who have painted on these shores; what faulty
draughtsmanship, meretricious effects, and lack of decent restraint!
How they fail to see the simplicity underlying those complex
natural formations! For the loveliness of this landscape is not that
of Phryne, and the painter errs who thinks that his inmost thoughts
are met half-way by a smile of encouragement. The smile is there,
but not for him. It is for the constraining mortal who disregards it;
who stands to his work in the relation of God to man.

A gradual change is taking place in the orographical modelling
of the Bay of Naples. Capri and the other limestone portions must
formerly have presented a smoother aspect to the eye, as they were
covered with trees and soil which gave them a rounded look. The
trees being felled, the earth slipped down, exposing the jagged
asperities of the rock. With the volcanic districts it is generally the
reverse, for these craters are of soft material, and the longer they
are exposed, the smoother they become. The lower eminences of
Baiæ and Ischia are now merely a jumble of curving lines, and a
small crater near Fuorigrotta is in the last stage of liquescence;
soon the rain and the plough will have merged it into the earth
whence it arose—the limestone tracts, meanwhile, grow more
peaked every day.

Capri is a microcosm whose perfection of *décor* and hieratic
lineaments can only have been the inspiration of some divinely
frenzied Prometheus. But its beauty, though vital and palpitating,
is now cramped and impaired by the encroachments of humanity.
Rocks are blasted away for driving roads; shrubs are cut down;

high walls and houses everywhere invade its primitive comeliness. The place is too small to endure these affronts without prejudice. It must have been different in the days when the Sirens were its only inhabitants; if, indeed, it was really their island. For I cannot help thinking that commentators of the Homeric cosmography take the "islands" too seriously, and thereby involve themselves in needless trouble. Ancient navigators were inordinately fond of islands, and slow sailing without a compass may well turn an indented coastline or promontory into a group of them. This is plain from *Sindbad the Sailor*, and from Hanno's *Periplus*. People living on continents are more likely to locate marvels in islands—India and America were also "islands"; so was Paradise, according to Lambertus Floridus; to say nothing of Atlantis—and the ingenious Pelliccia has written a book to prove that the whole Sorrentine peninsula was likewise an island in olden days. He argues thus: The Sirens dwelt at Capri; Circe, the enchantress, lived on another island near at hand; Sorrento is near at hand; therefore Sorrento must have been the island of Circe—falsifying geography and geology in order to vindicate a prehistoric sailor's yarn. What strange creatures we are, placing more faith in deductions than in facts—why? God created the facts and they may take care of themselves, but the deductions are our own, to be clung to with parental attachment. Even so Vargas, that monster of misapplied eruditions, insists that the Siren Parthenope was not worshipped at Naples, because—well, it would injure his pet theory about the Semitic races.

A wonderful discovery was made on Capri three years ago: the bones of mammoth, hippopotami, and other improbable beasts embedded together with human weapons of the earliest palæolithic ages. Inasmuch as a pair of mammoths would soon nibble away the last leaf on a rock of this size, we must presume it to have been joined to the mainland in those days. These relics were found below the ashes of the terrific Phlegræan convulsions which may have done the work of detachment later on.

Capri is curious also for its Tyrrhenian fauna and flora; it is part of the wreck of that submerged continent whose ruins still lift their head above the water here and there, and whose configuration is being patiently mapped out by the labours of men like Suess, Blanchard, Parato, and Forsyth Major. The remains of the fallow-deer, a Tyrrhenian creature, have been unearthed here; certain snails and various Tyrrhenian plants still occur on the island, such as the *convolvulus cneorum* with its creamy blossoms, and the wild palm, which used to hang in exquisite clusters, untouched from time immemorial, on the rocky ledges, but is now ruthlessly torn down to decorate gardens, in which ninety per cent of them perish.

How much of this drowned world still saw the light of sun and stars when the Sirens sang, I, for one, would be glad to know. For it can hardly have vanished with a *Hey, presto!* like Graham's Island; doubtless it sank slowly; Odysseus may yet have drawn up his ship on beaches that are now, for aught we can tell, slumbering beneath the waves. We have all heard that story of Plato's, and how the priest of Sais told Solon of the mighty island of Atlantis which lay beyond the Pillars of Hercules and was engulfed by the sea. An old Orphic tradition runs to the same effect. Of the former existence of this true Atlantic continent there are abundant grave indications —may not this legend have become amalgamated in the course of ages with that of the Tyrrhenian catastrophe? Humboldt seems to have thought so.

It is easy to see, from the summit of the Tore, that Capri is merely a prolongation, a dependency, of the mainland. And in point of shape, too, it is almost a repetition—on an enlarged scale, of course —of the mountain of San Costanzo, which terminates the peninsula and is itself something of an island. That the chief beauty of Capri, its insular position and the noble line of cliffs fronting the town on the west, should be due to what they call a "fault", proves that scientific nomenclature is not always appropriate for ordinary purposes.

I often gaze down upon Siren land from those inspiring heights of Faito on Sant' Angelo which afford, from splendour and associations, one of the finest prospects in the world. It is cool up here among the mountain pastures, and there are still ancient beech trees and firs that look strangely out of place—relics of the autochthonous woodlands that have now been stripped of their timber like that once famous Sila forest, which is being eradicated so conscientiously that its chief town already lies in a desert of glaring rocks and to gather a handful of firewood there entails a scramble of half a day. Conceive what this means in a winter of Northern severity, how it makes for misery and depopulation, and how easily it could have been avoided!

It is a relief to think that the wooded tracts above Siren land have fallen into the hands of a man like their present owner. For they are an historical monument worth preserving: they display the flora of the Italian continent as it was in the days when the pious Æneas sailed hitherwards. We are apt to forget that the whole appearance of Italian scenery has been changed owing to imported plants—the very cypress, the orange and maize and a hundred others great and small, which we regard as so characteristic, are aliens to the soil.* And the idea of preserving such tracts, absurd as it may seem to modern Italians, is really not inherently preposterous: certain civilized nations, such as the French, Americans, and English, have already by private gift or public subscription enclosed delectable woodlands to be an eternal delight and precept to their children; and only the other day the German Emperor rescued, in the very heart of Italy, the hoary oaks of Olevano from their impending fate. These, unless I am much mistaken, will be monuments more acceptable and more intelligible to posterity than the forests now growing up in Italy: forests of trousered political nonentities in bronze and marble, whose doctrines, often enough, became a derision before their protagonists were yet fairly in their graves.

The stealthy teachings of the sea, the Sirens' abode, still lie open to all, but those of earth-nature have been sadly misread of late and thwarted; and although we have heard much concerning the hygienic and economic advantages of properly controlled wood-lands, there is room for another benefactor to mankind—for him, namely, who would proclaim their ethical significance, their influence as a refining and civilizing agency in the education of the human race. Who will deny that forests, once they have abandoned their hostile attitude to man's progress upon earth, exercise a benignant power, subtle and profound, upon the mind of a people; that music, architecture, and other generous arts have in forests sought, and found, high inspiration; that some of the sublimest efforts of literary genius could not have been conceived in regions as denuded of timber as Italy, Greece, and Spain now are? Rentzsch ascribes the political decadence of Spain almost wholly to the destruction of forests. Even if this be going too far, I cannot but think

---

* So, for instance, the spiky agave which they call *mal' occhio* because its point is a defence against the evil eye; the mesembryanthemum, known as *unghia di iannara* (witches' claws) from the shape of its leaves; or the grotesque Indian fig— one of God's earliest attempts at tree-making—which Preller, by mistake, depicted in his "Homeric Landscape". The *kaktos* of the Greeks seems to have been a kind of artichoke.

that in sweeping away woodlands many deeply rooted humane aspirations, interwoven in their leafy solitudes, are likewise swept away, and a legion of gracious phantoms, who wandered freely among those solemn aisles ready to converse with all, banished for evermore. Shakespeare's England can still be found by those who look for it, but they who would discover the Italy of her poets must go far afield. Communion with nature, which exalts and purifies the mind, has ceased and in its place has arisen that pest of the South: futile inquisitiveness concerning man in his meanest manifestations.

It was not without an intuition of this truth that the ancients contrived their exquisite fable of Eresichthon, and whoever yet remembers the elves and fairies of his childhood may be envied of a talisman indeed. It would hardly profit us, I think, to withhold from our children the contemplation of woodland marvels, with their tender symbolism of leaf and flower, birth and decay; the wonder-period of our remote ancestors, through which we must all pass in youth, that fleeting hour of nature-worship, may well be abbreviated, but cannot wholly be cut out of the programme of our moral growth without detriment to the race.

The elimination of mystery: what has it not done for modern Italy? Whether the disfigurement of the landscape has not reflected itself upon the race? Whether the listlessness of so many Italian townspeople, and the evil precocity of their children, be not the nymphs' revenge for Eresichthon's crime? The old Greeks felt differently and so do their modern descendants; their humblest mechanic loves the country, and has therefore preserved a far nobler curiosity upon the things of life. The boy of the streets, who sees nothing of the protean witchery of flowers and living waters, is not a veritable boy at any time, since his youth is ended ere it began. We are not yet ripe for growing up in the streets; they stimulate the social instincts of the adult, but stunt the adolescent who craves for solitude and surroundings habitual to earlier periods of human history. We know what is said of the second generation of city-dwellers, even of high social standing; and has any good ever come out of that foul-clustering town-proletariat, beloved of humanitarians? Nothing—never; they are only waiting for a leader, some "inspired idiot", to rend to pieces our poor civilization. Whereas out of the very dregs of the country-folk has often arisen, by the operation of that dark law which regulates the meteoric appearance of "sports", a Lincoln, a Winckelmann, to guide men's footsteps in the path.

On these Siren heights—*Montes Sireniani*, they used to be called—the human element is lacking; there is no sound save the chirping of the cicadas among the olive branches; an azure calm, a calm of life, streams down from on high, permeating every sense with tremulous scintillations of vitality. It is always difficult to analyse sensations—imponderable moods; and in such moments of breathless summer radiance every one will have feelings commensurate to the bent of his mind and habitual associations. Here, in spite of the solitude, it seems to me that no genii of earth or heaven are waiting to hold communion with mankind. I have felt the awe-inspiring midday hush in many wilds and wolds, and often enough the mind, surrounded by the unfamiliar, is prone to conjure up phantoms from inanimate nature. Here it is merely aglow with life; self-centred in the circumambient calm and stimulated to attention by the sun's rays, it is yet at rest. The landscape, therefore, and not only the hour and the man, plays a part when gods are to be created. Perhaps this helps us to understand the enigma of universal Pan. From being an Arcadian forest-god he became, as culture advanced, diffused and impalpable. The forest lost its noonday mystery and its Embodiment was no longer seen of men; he was merged into the brooding meridian stillness of all earth which no clearings, no cornfields, no sparkling cities could impair; his weaker comrades, the fauns and dryads, unable to endure this searching light, took refuge in yet shadier groves, or pined away.

Nor do immortal gods look down from cloudy pavilions, for the sky here is a vast dome, and not a plane. Wherever thunder-clouds touch mountain summits this quaint belief will arise, and Zeus, whatever his origin, found a congenial home in Greece, where the exhalations, formerly more abundant, even now repose upon the hill-tops. In Siren land they do not; they sail overhead in summer-time, a painted argosy that seldom anchors to spill its dewy freight against the mountain-sides, though the *Cloud-gatherer*—when the south wind blows—is busy as at Ægina, collecting out of a sunny sea invisible wreaths of vapour which he spins into a crown about the grey head of Capri. The community of this two-storey-world idea in Scandinavia and Greece is hardly a proof of the boreal descent of some Hellenic gods (we might as well trace it to old Australia, where a Walhalla was fabled among the interlacing boughs of lofty eucalypti); nor yet their violence and unruliness, for in early stages divinity naturally reflects the turbulence of human environment. Wotan, had he survived to this day, would doubtless have become an orderly fellow, even as Zeus did. Altogether, some little nonsense has been written concerning the anthropomorphism of the gods of Greece. As if any deity could afford to dispense with these traits! The Jahveh of the Jews was sufficiently human in his vindictiveness and jealousy; later on, when he became etherealized, the humanity of his son refreshed our interest in him. And what lends the devil his charm? His quasi-human attributes; his bargainings, his ill-treatment at the hands of heaven. Beings wholly divine are inevitably endowed with qualities of good and evil identical with our own: they are mere caricatures of good or bad men. The profoundly divine therefore is, and ever has been, profoundly uninteresting. These Greek gods are extra-human rather than super-human; they are interpenetrations of human motives with new and unaccountable elements. Much might also be said in favour of the view that their absurdities and excesses were deliberately contrived as a foil to the moderation-ideal of the Greeks themselves. Yet, polish away all excrescences and subtilize them to the vanishing point of purity—their pedigrees cannot be wholly expunged; some Lucian will always be there to rake up old scandals; to remind Jupiter Optimus Maximus of certain Cretan meadows and Venus, the *alma mater*, of that affair of the net.

Here, on these odorous Siren heights, far removed from duty's sacred call—for duty has become the Moloch of modern life—it may not be amiss to build a summer hut wherein to undergo a brief period of *katharsis*, of purgation and readjustment. For we do get sadly out of perspective with our environment in the fevered North, out of touch with elemental and permanent things; we are for ever looking up-stream. It is well, now and then, to glance backwards adown that flowing river and to note, before they fade from sight, the strange, half-forgotten landscapes one has traversed. Is it I, one wonders, who thought and felt thus? How one changes! And one's friends—how they change! And even public opinion, that exemplary biped which stands, nose in air and uttering incomprehensible grunts, with one leg in the illusions of the past and the other in those of the future—how it changes!

An old Hebrew, who taught the pleasures of a virtuous life after exhausting those of a voluptuous one, said: Go to the ant; he forgot to remember that the ant sleeps for half the year. Man alone is a perennial drudge. Yet many of us would do well to *mediterraneanize* ourselves for a season, to quicken those ethic roots from which has sprung so much of what is best in our natures. To dream in Siren land, pursuing the moods and memories as they shift in labyrinthine mazes, like shadows on a woodland path in June; to stroll among the hills and fill the mind with new images upon which to browse at leisure, casting off outworn weeds of thought with the painless ease of a serpent and unperplexing, incidentally, some of those "questions of the day" of which the daily papers nevertheless know nothing—this is an antidote for many ills. There is repose in Siren land; there is none of that delirious massing-together in which certain mortals, unable to stand alone, can lean up against one another and so gain, for a moment, a precarious condition of equipoise.

To dream—yes; but, as de Quincey observed, *he whose talk is of oxen will dream of oxen*, and I am not attempting to prescribe for the uncivilized, particularly as they are in loving hands just now: is not the whole trend of our legislation a sustained effort to pamper the unfit at the expense of the fit, to foster the moral delusions of the crowd—of those whose spiritual activities are in abeyance? May they prosper! There will ever remain one badge of distinction to mark them from those of another fibre—their imperviousness to the meaning of certain old Siren voices—

> O stay, oh pride of Greece! Ulysses stay!
> O cease thy course, and listen to our lay!
> Blest is the man our song ordain'd to hear,
> The song instructs the soul, and charms the ear,
> Approach! Thy soul shall into rapture rise!
> Approach! And learn new wisdom from the wise!
> We know whate'er the kings of mighty name
> Achieved at Ilium in the field of fame;
> Whate'er beneath the sun's bright journey lies.
> O stay and learn new wisdom from the wise. . . .

for I perceive in this lay no promise of any of those things which they covet, of gold and diamonds and fair women and long life and earthly honours and the joys of Heaven; but only of enlightenment.

And whoso hears these voices, says Homer, nevermore returns to his home and family, which may be taken to mean that certain persons have rated wisdom higher than domestic bliss; doubtless a poetic exaggeration.

III

THE SIREN ISLETS

OF the five Siren rocks only three lie close together, and these are the so-called Galli. The old name Sirenusæ gradually died out; no earlier reference to them under their present one occurs, I believe, than that contained in the chronicle of the Abbot of Telese (1133), who records their capture by Roger of Sicily. He speaks of them as "Guallo"—evidently, therefore, a patronymic from the family of Guallo or Gallo on the mainland—and, what is more singular, he calls them "a little town placed *infra mare*". Now there is a spot called Guallo on the penin-sula, but wise men will have it that he meant these islands, and I am not for arguing the point.

It is not absolutely clear, from this and other old documents, whether in those days the three rocks had the same configuration as now; presumably, yes; at the same time, they were certainly spoken of as one and single, and the Amalfitan doge, who lived awhile in exile here, might have found it a more tolerable residence if they had all been joined together. But he had been blinded, and they, whose hands are their eyes, may as well grope about on a rock as on a continent.

How fond they were of blindings and mutilations at this period— the straightforward killing of the Romans was too harsh for these Byzantines, who, like all squeamish people, were proportionately cruel.

Perhaps, too, he was confined in a dungeon, although there is no mention of any buildings on the islands when, in 1330, King Robert reared a brave tower there, whose cistern is still resorted to by fishermen and quail-hunters, for the protection of seafaring men against pirates. In fact, the island, or islands, are expressly called "uncultivated" in the deed which confers the guardianship of this keep to his trusty and well-beloved Pasquale Celentano, who established himself there with four soldiers, and seems to have liked it, for it was he who had applied for the post. His family is still extant.

And so they are at this present moment; uncultivated, treeless and, in summer, aflame with heat; struck by the sun's first beams, they glister through the livelong day and remain fiercely glowing, like incandescent rubies, long after the coast-line is drowned in the shades of evening. Yet there are wandering breezes and a harmonious wave-lapping suggestive of coolness. They lie in a rough circle, and anyone but a geologist familiar with the inevitable "quaquaversal dip" would take them to be the relics of a submerged crater, an illusion which is strengthened by the outward slope and half-moon shape of the greater islet, and by the riven pinnacles of stone gnawed by the waves into bizarre shapes and painted, wherever the spray can reach them, to a murky brown. And this is exactly what one old traveller called them—a mistake for which he was sternly rebuked by Breislack. So Dumas talks of the "granitic ramparts" of Capri, and a Swiss, writing only three years ago, praises its "*parois verticales de porphyre et basalte*". A deplorable lack of general intelligence, seeing that the principal charm of all Italian scenery, its graceful outlines and much of its delicate aerial tints, are exclusively due to a peculiar natural formation. Limestone, and no other rock, is able to produce them.

The Galli, again, are nothing but Apennine limestone—wrecks of the neighbouring peninsula which used to slope southward with a gentle incline so as to include them in its body, even as on the other side it still descends gradually seawards: they were torn off in some terrific prehistoric convulsion. In one spot the laminated strata are broken to form a melodious sea-cave—each cave in Siren land sings its own peculiar melody—the haunt of countless sly-twittering* swifts who rear their families in the shelving rock.

Were I writing a guide-book or historical account of this region, I would endeavour to give a systematic description of these legendary islets, supplemented with measurements and hints for travellers. But I am doing nothing of the kind; I am only dreaming through the summer months to the music of the cicadas, and dreams are irresponsible things that flit about aimlessly, dwelling with absurd gravity upon unconsidered trifles and never quoting statistics.

I sail across to the neighbouring rock of La Rotonda and find—nothing, save a peregrine that dashes off the cliff at my approach.

* The epithet applies only to the Alpine species, *C. melba*.

"Ah, if I had brought my gun!" exclaims my companion, with unfeigned anguish. Does he eat peregrines? To be sure he does, and finds them "better than pigeons". Of all the hawk tribe, they are only surpassed by the lesser kestrel, which is *squisitissimo*.

Long ago, the Anjou sovereigns caused the peregrines "in the territory of Capri and Sorrento" to be caught and trained for purposes of falconry.

The third islet, called "Castelletto" from its castellated appearance, is known to sailors as *Punta da Vuccacia* = Boccaccia = a piece of ordnance which, at some period, was placed there to command the straits. A broad rock-cut path, worthy of the Romans, and probably built to allow ships to be drawn on land, ascends part of the way: the rest is rather a dangerous climb. A precipitous crag, inaccessible to invaders; all the summit built over and the limestone chiselled smooth in certain tracts where a sentinel may have paced. I suspect that this fortress dates from 1532, for in that year a native of Sorrento received the grant of all three islets on the condition that one of them should be fortified. It looks as if no inspector had been sent down from head-quarters to see that the work was properly done: a jerry-built affair—King Robert's tower will long outlast it.

Treeless they are, the Siren rocks; but not flowerless. Now that the riot of vegetation has been allowed to grow for the last year or two, one can form some idea of what it would become if left undisturbed for longer periods. Capri, I believe, holds a record for variety of plants on a small space—

> *La Flore est de telle richesse*
> *Que dans ce réduit limité*
> *A huit cents arrive l'espèce,*
> *A trois cents, la variété. . . .*

sings the truthful bard, but nowhere on Capri do flowering plants rush into such reckless overgrowth as here. In the winter months the narcissus dominates; its scent is heavy upon the air and the glossy brown bulbs thrust each other out of the earth; in May the ground is hidden under a radiant tangle of many-hued blossoms that must be seen to be believed. Every flower of Campania seems to have taken refuge on this lonely rock. The rapid evaporation of sea-air no doubt contributes to this luxuriance, and also the rich soil of the outer slope.

I once attempted to draw up a list of the Galli flowers, but abandoned the idea; they shift with every month. Let him, whose mind is at peace, sojourn awhile on these rocks, and there elaborate a catalogue of all of them, great and small, with a shepherd's calendar setting forth their seasons of flowering and decay. Or better still if, detached from sordid cares, he buys the islets outright and replants them with ten thousand shade-giving trees, marrying the rough exhalations of briny sun-scorched rock with the fragrance of rose and cedar. What joy to watch their rapid growth in the deep, warm soil! In these days, when life is so complicated as to lose all homogeneity and unity of purpose, when our fine edges are worn off by never-ending trivialities and meannesses, I often think that planting trees and reclaiming the waste places of earth are among the few occupations that still commend themselves to gentler natures—pleasure and instruction for oneself, health and profit to posterity. . . .

According to Strabo, the Siren islets were "three stony and *desert* little rocks". His words are plain enough, and he uses them twice over.

Were they true, when he wrote?

For whoever, climbing up the usual path from the sea, arrives at the summit of the larger island, will perceive that the rocky surface here has been artificially levelled down for a length of some fifty yards, and, jutting out of the soil, will be seen the substructures of two thick parallel walls of the first century—Strabo's lifetime. Here, then, stood a grandiose edifice, slightly curved so as to follow the natural crescent of the island, with its larger façades fronting east and west. The nameless Siren-worshipper who designed this lordly pleasure-house had studied local conditions of landscape and ventilation; the site could not have been more happily chosen. In the hottest days of midsummer a sea-breeze rustled through those ample halls, and his view was superb, whether, in early morning, he let his eye wander over leagues of violet sea-calm towards Pæstum and the shapely peak of Alburno that fades into mist as the sun gains strength, or glanced westwards into the chaos of rocks and many-hued waters at his feet, with Capri and Ierate in the background, shutting out the world beyond.

The marbles are gone—gone into the mortar of King Robert's tower. Yet, searching among the debris on the hill-side, I found some fragments of white penthelic and *giallo antico* slabs for a pave-ment, and a systematic hunt might yield brick-stamps which would help to decide the age of the building. The ground sounds hollow in certain places, as if there were chambers beneath.

The foundations of this structure are massive enough to have supported a temple, but I question whether they ever did so, because we should probably possess some record of an ancient divinity worshipped here, and also because, at the water's edge on the inner side of the islet, are the remains of a bathing-house or harbour, or both combined, without which such a large establish-ment as that above could hardly have been considered complete. Its flooring, of irregular shape, is surrounded by formidable walls of reticulated Posilipo tufa leaning against the hill-side: in the centre stands a modern lime-kiln. Rocks have tumbled upon it and into the sea beyond, but I can detect no traces of its continuation below the waves. At the promontory of Marciano near Massa, on the contrary—a highly interesting point—there is another (con-temporary) Roman villa with its little *dépendence* at sea-level, and here the masonry descends into the deep. These are the sites which ought to be examined by those who wish to settle the debated question of the former water-level.

Altogether, it would be well if some trained archæologist were to investigate this and other remains upon the southern shore of the peninsula, of whose existence no one seems to be aware.* No great outlay would be required to lay bare what is left of this building on the Galli-rock, and nothing more enjoyable or interesting could be imagined than this kind of work. Crusades are gone out of fashion for the moment and the only warfare at present worthy of the name is the bloodless crusade against fools ("The Warfare of the Future?")—can any nobler participation in it be imagined than that of unearthing those monuments of bygone ages in whose presence the veriest hind must perforce pause and bethink himself?

The ethics of ruins—their educational value: what has it not done for Italy of the Renaissance? Petrarca already, and Sannazaro and Boccaccio, have drawn deep draughts of enthusiasm from this source. And all this quite apart from the possibility that these deformed heaps of rubbish may hide some marble head, soiled with

---

* So there is the contorted ruin of a Roman building on the beach at Cantone, below the large tower, not far from a spring which gushed into the sea. The bricks, unfortunately, bear no stamp.

the dust of ages, from under whose stony brow there gleams a look of rare wisdom or sweetness; a revelation—inspiring, compelling.

Meanwhile, what of Strabo and his *desert* Siren islets? This: either the villa here and that on the islet of Isca, of which I will speak later, were only built after his death or, if during his lifetime, he had no knowledge of them. Supposing Mommsen to be correct in surmising that his *Geography* was written as late as the reign of Tiberius, there is still much to be said for the hypothesis of another scholar that it was composed in a distant region of Asia Minor, where it is not likely that the latest information was to be procured.

Be this as it may, one thing is interesting: he says that there were *three* Siren islets. Now if Isca be omitted from this group, as lying too near the land, there is still the large rock of Vetara close to the Galli which cannot be overlooked and which raises their number to four. Can this mean that the three (true) Galli rocks were at that time united into one single block making, together with Isca and Vetara, the three of Strabo? It almost looks like it. Far be it from one who has grown up under the shadow of Lyell to advocate cataclysms: in comparison with other catastrophes which have occurred in these regions the disruption of the Galli rocks from each other would be the merest trifle. We have some historical account of the havoc wrought here during the last thousand years by gales and landslides (ice and earthquakes have done little damage), and it stands to reason that the preceding ten centuries must have been equally fertile in disasters; all the time, too, majestic earth-contortions, they say, have tilted the country up and down, disquieting the works of man.

Where is the house of the poet Tasso, the convent of Revigliano, the town of Marcina, the harbour and arsenals of Amalfi, or the ancient Conca, whose picturesque horn juts into the waves opposite the Siren rocks, and where Richard Cœur-de-Lion halted on his way to Palestine? Engulfed, all of them. A complex study, bristling with difficulties, but full of geological and historical interest. Concerning the "Serapis" temple alone a voluminous literature has sprung up; whether the marshy situation of Pæstum be due to some such subsidence may still be questioned—the deforestation of the mountain slopes, which filled the plains with alluvial soil and dammed up the river beds, might also be suggested as an explanation. So the islet of the Siren Ligeia has lately become joined to the mainland through the deposits of the Calabrian streams.

The Greek period over, ancient life on these eastern shores of the Parthenopean Bay resolves itself into one word—Tiberius. His predecessor, it is true, *discovered* Capri, for no earlier Roman, not even the diffuse Cicero, so much as mentions the island; it was as unknown to the aristocracy of his day as it is to the modern *Romani di Roma*, who would as soon think of sailing to the stillvex'd Bermoothes as to Capri: Augustus it was who landed here time after time, charmed with the convival Greek natives and the mild climate; who built those twelve Imperial palaces. But the court remained nominally in the capital. Of Tiberius we know that he "*insederat*", concerning which cryptic word enough has been written, and that he lived here for ten consecutive years (Plutarch, who sometimes blunders in his dates, says seven); and what this entails may be observed when some sovereign of to-day establishes a temporary residence among the mountains, while country-houses of officials and snobs grow up like mushrooms all around. The Sirens always called Augustus back to them: Tiberius they held fast for good.

This island—Capri—was too small to contain the swarm of nobles and administrators who helped to conduct the affairs of the world; they overflowed and brought life to the mainland, and their names survive to this day in Ceserano, Marcigliano, Mitigliano, and so forth. To this inundation there is the testimony of Sorrentine inscriptions, of works of art like the Aphrodisius statue, and, above all, of the actual existing masonry.

No doubt there was a revival on these shores under Marcus Aurelius and another under Hadrian, but these were men of a different stamp; they were not true Siren-worshippers; they knew what *Weltschmerz* meant. The world had aged frightfully in those few intervening years. Marcus was a conscientious valetudinarian whom the world has agreed to take at his own valuation (that correspondence with Fronto has a sick-room air—the querulous note of expiring antiquity); in Hadrian were summed up all the romanticism and disordered curiosity of a soap-bubble renaissance.

The builder of this sumptuous villa on the Siren rock was no freedman, nor yet a mere worlding. I can conceive such persons establishing themselves in the fat fields of Sorrento, where there was "society" and some business to be done in wine or oil, or among the reeking baths at Baiæ; but it is contary to what one knows of human nature to suppose that an islet like this should appeal to them. No, he was a civilized man, and it is to be imagined that, unlike Tiberius, who could create his own society, bidding men come and go as he pleased, this one returned city-wards in the winter months to stimulate himself with the din of the Forum and the conversation of his town friends, and to test anew the capabilities of his digestion. The hermit's motto, *vixit qui latuit*, was not altogether his, since the man that has the true feeling for seclusion among these scenes will be the last to prolong his stay, though he may well return year after year, as the Sirens call him back. Nearly all the Roman villas on Capri and the opposite mainland face to the north, which proves that they viewed this country as a summer resort. Who can live here in the winter? Only "foreigners" come at that season. From November to April the whole wind-bag of Æolus is let loose; when there is no hurricane, it rains in torrents; Capri, even with modern appliances (such as they are) is often inaccessible, while the Galli rocks are surrounded for weeks by a weltering waste of foam. No sensible person, unprovided with the comforts—as well as the dis-illusions—of Tiberius could stand the uproar for three or four months on end; it is like being on board a boat, and when men come to like that kind of life they are, as Johnson remarked, "not fit to live on land. . . ."

Unavoidably one learns to take an interest in the winds here-abouts, seeing that these Siren regions are fanned by every breath of Heaven. In summer it is a simple matter; sea-breeze by day and land-breeze by night, stepping into each other's shoes with praise-worthy regularity; but later on things become complicated, and the catalogue of local winds swells to a formidable size. The northern *tramontana* which closes the pores (speak not of love to these folk when the *tramontana* blows), and the scirocco that relaxes them, are the best known, but not the most popular; the latter may well have increased since ancient times, perhaps on account of the deforest-ation of northern Africa, else the Romans, who had absurdly sensitive skins and nerves, would have execrated it even more than they did.

Blue-black tints and crisp waves prevail during the *tramontana;* an "honest" wind, because, blowing off the land, it is debarred from becoming dishonest so near the shore. The scirocco's tints are green and yellow, and it has no pretensions to honesty—its wintry con-vulsions are sometimes so violent that the salty spray is carried far inland, and can be tasted in secluded orchards on the last remaining figs. But perhaps this is cloud-work, for when the delirium is at its height, the clouds often descend and join the fun, tempting the waves to meet them half-way. When these water-spouts, careering distractedly over the waste, break, the clouds cling to what they can of the nether element and bear it away with them on their aerial voyages.

The great storm of 1343, described by Neapolitan chroniclers and in one of Petrarca's letters, blew from this quarter; it destroyed shipping and villages, swallowing what little was left of Amalfi (for that town had been reduced to a fragment before Mola da Tramonti wrote his chronicle in 1149), obliterating landmarks all along this coast, and thrusting even rivers, like the Sebeto, from their courses. Intense darkness fell over the land during those awful days, and turned men's minds to thought of prayer.

I can remember a scirocco phenomenon equally unearthly, perhaps, in appearance. At that time, too, our hearts were somewhat perturbed; things had happened; there had been wars and assassinations of kings, and it was feared, by the simpler sort, that retribution was due. A sultry afternoon was drawing to its close, and I had been observing a small cloud that emerged above the sky-line. It was round as a disc, of ruddy hue, and in texture so compact and un-ethereal as to appear solid. Slowly it grew, and never changed its shape; an hour passed; it gradually expanded into a monstrous peony upon the firmament and, instead of drifting as clouds do, seemed rather to be pushed forwards mechanically from behind the scenes. Its uncommon shape and colour, its spasmodic growth, began to attract attention; we herded together and found ourselves watching its movements not without uneasiness. Suddenly, after an unusually vigorous jerk, the cheering sun was effaced, blotted out behind the curtain, leaving the world in a dim roseate fog. The change was disquieting, and there fell upon us the hush of an eclipse. Then it rained in big, warm drops. I looked at my hand—blood!

"*Male pioggia, signore,*" said an old man, hurrying past me. *Male:* that was the word—an evil rain.

Next morning trees and flowers were smeared over with an incrustation of mud, and sprightly white-stuccoed houses splotched with brown. And presently wise men came with microscopes and chemical paraphernalia; they analysed a speck of the deposit of

the blood-rain and found in it plant-spores from the Sahara and
animalcules of a thousand kinds—a whole world in miniature,
fallen in a raindrop from the sky. . . .

It is rather puzzling when one comes to think of it, to conceive
how the old Sirens passed their time on days of wintry storm.
Modern ones would call for cigarettes, Grand Marnier, and a pack
of cards, and bid the gale howl itself out. But those ancient feathered
fowls—did they peck at each other viciously, or content themselves
with shivering in silence among their crags? So have I seen, during
a blizzard, the bedraggled vultures perched among the bleak hills
of Asia Minor. They sat round the corpse of a camel, one of the
unhappiest of its race, that had dragged huge carpets over the
mountain tracks and expired in the performance of a task for which
it seemed peculiarly unfitted. The vultures craned their necks, but
not one of them moved from its stone. They were plainly hungry.
But they preferred it dry.

No; summer is the time to pasture in Siren land. Even Mrs.
Shelley, for whom I entertain no profound respect, could not but
feel the charm of this season. "It seems", she writes from Sorrento
in summer, "as if I had not before visited Italy." The heat is too
considerable for violent exertion, but time passes quickly doing
even nothing, if one does it well. And for studious persons who
desire local information, there is literature galore—histories and
chronicles of the rich city of Massa in the olden days. They read
pleasantly under some vine-clad arbour.

Rich and populous it must have been, for older authors give
glowing accounts of its palaces and industries and great men.
How, then, came it to sink to its present level? The sages will refer
you to corsair raids or to the plague of 1656, quite forgetting that
the writers who describe such a flourishing state of things lived
exactly at the time of these events. I rather think it was another
kind of plague, the plague of a century of Bourbonism, which
reduced these regions to a condition of misery whence they are now,
thanks to a better government and to Argentina, slowly emerging.
For ordinary pestilences and famines and earthquakes are mere
amateurs in destruction whose effects are healed in briefest time:
there may even be witnessed, after occasions when the plough of
affliction has violently disrupted the soil, a strange quickening of
growth. But misrule strikes at the root of things, since the humane

strivings in a people, those of its elements that actively make for good, are so sporadic that their annihilation is wholly different from a haphazard calamity. And there was a sinister thoroughness in the Bourbon system which ensured success. The effects of such a conscientious selection of badness must necessarily endure; it takes longer to rear up that which is humane than its opposite, seeing that there are a thousand wrongs for one right. "There is no town and there is no country", says a Neapolitan historian, "which would not inevitably be impoverished by the loss of so many and such distinguished men." It is this same elimination of progressive elements which has done so much harm to Spain and Russia, and which paved the way, according to Professor Seeck, for the fall of ancient Rome. Medical men are beginning to estimate, with something approaching accuracy, the effect of wear and tear upon the individual organism; experiments on the lines laid down by Mosso and de Fleury may soon enable us to express it in mathematical terms; but its effect upon the organic system of communities—upon their arts, commerce, industry, and all the finer fibres of their social being—who shall compute it? Who shall estimate the vital strain of a century of terrorism?

Those Englishmen, therefore, who complain of certain unpleasant characteristics of modern Neapolitans, might do well to remember that the Bourbons had been incapacitated from further mischief when their saviours from over the sea appeared on the scene and allowed them to continue for another half-century that rule of brigands, monks, *lazzari*, and other vermin which was responsible for this deplorable state of affairs. There had been tyrannies before in Naples, odious tyrannies; but despots, secular and religious, had been powerless to smother the grand traditions of Hellenic culture, the envy and delight of ancient and mediæval Europe. A glance into early literature will show what Naples has done in the domain of philosophy—it was ever the first city of Italy for speculative thought; a glance into the works of pre-Bourbon travellers will afford a description of the inhabitants of Naples, and of the provinces, as *they* saw them. The Neapolitan Academy for the Study of Nature was the first to be founded in the world: it preceded the English Royal Society by nearly a century. One of the brightest pages in human history is the successful struggle of the Neapolitans against the inquisition. This, and much else, might be said in praise of pre-Bourbon Naples. But where philosophical books may not even be imported into a country, much less printed; where the reading of Voltaire is punished with three years' galley-slavery, and that of the Florence newspapers with six months' imprisonment—how incredible it seems, nowadays!—the flower of civilization withers and fades away. Despotism, priestcraft, and proletariat have ever been good friends; a kind of freemasonry, unintelligible to simple folks, has conjoined them from time immemorial against the honest and educated classes. Unable to stand alone, they lean against one another for mutual support, and thus in the mephitic calm of ignorance, the structure remains upright, a marvel of equipoise: like a child's house built of cards, a breath of enlightenment—and it collapses.

We find natives of Siren land involved in all the movements of the capital. Capri, for instance, distinguished itself in the inquisition-frays—a certain Costanzo of that town was one of the three chiefs of the *fuorasciti* who, while numbers of the Neapolitans fled into the country to escape the bloodshed, purposely came to Naples with their adherents in order to support the city against Don Pietro di Toledo and his proposed inquisition. The contest was no laughing matter. It lasted for months; the streets ran with blood; sparks, they say, flew from the eyes of the terrible viceroy, and the notary Grassi, who had been deputed to read the city's protest to him, was so overcome by the ordeal that he took to his bed afterwards and died in three days. As a pendant to this liberalism, the pious Monsignor Apuzzo, Bishop of Sorrento, perpetrated the official Bourbon "philosophical catechism"—an exquisite monument of bigotry. And foreign residents, too, have sometimes come forward with honour. There died at Capri, in 1892, the Englishman Wreford who for nearly half a century, as *Times* correspondent, waged unceasing warfare against Bourbonism and whose report on the ill-treatment of political martyrs furnished the material for Gladstone's letter to Lord Aberdeen of 1851. It is fitting that a man like this, who "did a knight's service for Italy and the world", should not be forgotten, and the municipality of Capri will do well to erect a tablet to his memory.* He came to the island, originally, for an afternoon, and stayed there over thirty years.

The Sirens, says Hyginus, were fated to live so long as they could detain passers-by. Can they be still alive?

And he who really finds time heavy on his hands might do worse

* They have since done so.

than compile a literary *catalogue raisonné* of this region.* By Janus!
A little while ago I found myself recommending the planting of
trees and the unearthing of Roman remains, but now it seems to
me that the compiling of bibliographies is a more respectable
occupation, for in tree-planting there are degrading collisions to be
anticipated with thievish gardeners and workmen, as well as the
painful reflection that posterity will turn into cash the fragrant
groves, chuckling at the old fellow's sentimentalism ("he blundered
into a good thing, now and then"); while the excavation of antiques
runs perilously near the bric-à-brac business, a demoralizing form
of commercialism. How one changes! But *malheur*, says Renan, *à
qui ne se contredit pas une fois par jour!* Around the bibliographer's table
there lies a passionless calm, unruffled by politics or sex-problems;
we all become tender-hearted towards the innocuous enthusiast
who writes for the delectation of one odd lunatic-scholar in every
hundred years. The thing has been done, of course, by various
writers—but in a perfunctory fashion; the ideal catalogue of a
region like this must be compiled *con amore*. . . .

Here meanwhile, is a curious item touching a shipwreck on the
Galli rocks which will be referred to therein. I translate it from a
manuscript entitled *Dies brumales* in the convent of Sant' Anna del
Pertuso. So far as I can discern, the *Dies brumales* seems to be the
product of some monkish pedant-poet who aimed at inculcating,
under the cloak of adventures, moral maxims to youths preparing
for a religious life; somewhat after the fashion of the Jesuit Daniele
Bartoli who published, in the seventeenth century, an edifying
but wholly unreadable "Geography Transported into Morals".

"When Anselmus had done, the Prior told us that this about the
Arimaspians was only an old fable contrived to show the folly of
gold-seeking. For gold and love to aught save God, said he, are

---

* An unmistakably wholesome sign of the times in Southern Italy is the revival
of local historical studies. Societies are formed, libraries collected, and every little
spot has its champion biographer—often busy professional men, who sacrifice their
leisure to patriotic researches. Siren land is no exception; much has been written
of late concerning Sorrento and Capri; Filangieri's new account of Massa is
scholarly and exhaustive and the bibliography of Doria promises well. Works
which used to be picked up for a few sous are now worth as many francs, and the
chief second-hand bookseller in Naples tells me that for the last three years not
one of the rarer writings on Capri has passed through his hands; old monographs
like that of Persico on Massa, Secondo on Capri, or Molegnano on Sorrento have
clean vanished from the market: when found, they can be weighed against gold.
Such facts are as convincing as a good Treasury budget.

the mainsprings of wrong action, and few evils that afflict mankind cannot be traced to one or the other. And he said that long before regular trafficke with the Orient was established by the Vessel of Cava, certain mariners of Amalfi went forth in ships and were often killed by barbarians or shipwrecked for their greed.

"And now a rare tale, quoth he, comes to my mind anent a vessel which foundered in a siroc not far from the Siren rocks, where all hands were drowned save only the captain's son, who was reserved for a worse fate. Him the waves bore to a pebbly beach, as far as might tire a little child to run, whereon sat a maiden singing, who looked up with eyes of friendship. Being a grave lad, he walked aside and, stumbling among the stones, happened upon a heap of decaying human bones, a loathly thing. Yet she followed with endearing words, till he lost reason for her sake. Fair to see was this maiden, and to bespeak—fair beyond all imagining to those she had fooled, and he deemed himself favoured above the angels. A brief infatuation, for soon a change came over her, and while he cherished her more than before, the light of love faded out of her eyes, and there stole into them the look of an hundred generations of tigers. Then ever and anon he would bethink himself of what he had seen among the rocks, and would fear for his life. For he had given his heart, but she had sharpened her teeth.

"And Anselmus said:

"'I conjecture that this was some Siren's mischief.'

"But the Prior held that Sirens are fables of the pagans, and that belike this was an earthly maiden, and what befell between the two is called earthly love."

IV

TIBERIUS

Let us examine this Siren-loving monster, Tiberius, a little nearer.

Broad-shouldered, stooping, and tall above the common measure, slow in his movements and speech, with great glittering eyes and hair falling over the nape of his neck, wrapped in a ceremonious and almost awkward reserve—such is the external impression we gain of him. And if, forgetting awhile his character as ruler of the world, we survey him in a private life, we soon discover what manner of man he was—a specimen of what the French call *la vieille roche*. Courteous and formal, a strenuous cultivator of the "grand manner", a conservative in speech, detesting all slipshod expressions, slang, and Gallicisms (Hellenisms); economical, conscientious, methodical; a scorner of luxury and dissipation and an outspoken enemy of the irregularities of fashionable married life. this old man—he was old, before he became emperor—possessed many of the virtues which, if we are to believe our grandfathers, were far commoner in their days than in ours. Of course his frugality was interpreted as avarice, while a certain invincible shyness, peculiar to many great men, was put down to pride—that celebrated pride of the Claudian house, whose true significance, like that of the democratic Gracchi, it has taken the world twenty centuries to understand. The younger generation of his day hardly appreciated traits like that recorded of him when, one day, only half a boar being served up at table—the other half having been eaten previously—he observed to the embarrassed company that "the half boar has just the same taste as the whole". A particularly fine fish was brought to him; he sent it out to be sold, remarking that some rich fellow like Apicius or Octavius would be sure to buy it. He was right; after some bidding, it fell to Octavius for 5000 sesterces. The profligate youngster Caligula, we are told, was kept very strictly "under the simple and wholesome mode of life" of Tiberius on Capri; whenever he went out for a spree, he disguised himself in a wig and muffler so as to escape unobserved. . . .

Of the military genius of Tiberius, his political sagacity, his assiduity in work: of his wonderful ability for finance and administration, there has never been a question. If the Roman world was able to withstand the shocks of the madmen who succeeded him on the throne, it was due to the stability and prosperity in which he left it. And wherein lies the secret of his intellectual superiority and successes? In this, I think: that he had a conspicuous preference for the able and honest common man. He knew the rottenness of the aristocrats of his day and treated them accordingly. "He was always unwilling to admit them to authority, and it is unquestionably true that, taking them as a class, they were during his long and prosperous reign treated with unusual disrespect. . . . Although he evinced the greatest anxiety to surround the throne with men of ability, he cared little for those conventional distinctions by which the minds of ordinary sovereigns are greatly moved. He made no account of dignity of rank, he did not even care for purity of blood. He valued men neither for the splendour of their pedigree, nor for the grandeur of their titles. . . . His large and powerful intellect, cultivated to its highest point by reflection and study, taught him the true measure of affairs and enabled him to see that to make a government flourish its councillors must be men of ability and virtue; but that if these two conditions are fulfilled, the nobles may be left to repose in the enjoyment of their leisure, unoppressed by those cares for the state for which, wit a few brilliant exceptions, they are naturally disqualified by the umber of their prejudices and by the frivolity of their pursuits."

Is not this an exceedingly truthful account of the aims and methods of Tiberius? Yet it is extracted out of no biography of that emperor; convert the "he" into "she", and the words will be found in Buckle's description of Queen Elizabeth.

Both sovereigns correctly judged that the nobles of their time had played their part—idle, intriguing, and discontented, they were now merely a menace to the peace of the empire. Among the self-made men whom the Roman emperor drew to his court was the senator Lucilius Longus, who clung to Tiberius "in good and evil days" and whose death, we are told, afflicted him as much as that of his only son. Another was the knight Curtius Rufus. To those who reminded Tiberius of this man's lack of pedigree, he was wont to reply: "Rufus, it seems to me, is his own ancestor". The minister Sejanus was also one of these *new men*, as the Romans disparagingly called some of the ablest of their time. The persons who witnessed the testament of Tiberius were "quite ordinary people". He married his grand-daughter to a man whose grandfather, Tacitus regrets to say, "everybody had known as a common knight in Tibur". Like Elizabeth, too, he had little respect for the senate, whose undignified flunkeyism made him sick. "O generation fit for slavery!" he exclaimed to them. And simultaneously he detested —an ancestral trait and one that he possesses in common with refined persons of all ages—the grossness of the proletariat. He never encouraged their cravings for gladiatorial shows. He gave few games. That sufficed to damn him in their eyes and to make them forget all he had done for the maintenance of public order, and all his munificence towards them in moments of public distress. "Into the Tiber with Tiberius!" may well have been sincere, for the common herd of ancient Rome was the same ignoble beast, governed only by its appetites, and as incapable of any generous or even consecutive thought, as that of our day.

The events of his life, a series of sharp disappointments, brought out more clearly with increasing age the characteristic of the Claudian house: cynical aloofness. Embittered in his family and marital relations, thwarted by the intelligent plebeian (Sejanus) in whom he had placed his confidence, he felt all the loneliness of his position.

He felt also—his power.

Modern Europe, grown wise with age, has muzzled its sovereigns. Thus has arisen a race of constitutional marionettes, whose chief occupation—to judge by the newspapers, at least—consists in "swopping" uniforms, rushing about the continent in special trains, and hanging ribbons and decorations round each other's necks. This is all as it should be, and it is well to remember that the muzzling has been done by the class of men whom Tiberius respected and sought to bring to honour. It is also well, now and then, to ask ourselves this question: how many of those who now "govern" Europe would display the magnanimity of Tiberius if they possessed a tithe of his power—how many would follow his example in refusing all external honours, or exercise his clemency towards religious dissentients, caricaturists, and political adversaries? The mind shudders to think of the pandemonium that would break loose if these were allowed, only for a day, the freedom of Tiberius. On that day, there would be more prosecutions for *lèse majesté* in Germany than in the immense Roman world under the whole reign of Tiberius; Austria and Russia would be aflame with the fires of *autos-da-fé*. There is recorded, on this last matter of religious persecution, a remark illustrating the fundamental sanity of Tiberius which cannot be too often repeated. A man was about to be put on his trial for insulting the divinity of the deceased Augustus, but the emperor stopped the proceedings by saying that "gods could avenge their own wrongs"; *deorum iniurias deis curæ*— a genial, golden pronouncement, which deserves to be graven over the portals of every church on earth.

The fact is, he had learned worldly wisdom where our present rulers can never hope to learn it—in the rough school of life. And he had the courage of his convictions. How many men and women of to-day, the slaves of contradictory conventionalities, might take to heart that saying of his: "Let them hate me, so long as they approve my actions." This is monumental. We may place it beside that sentence which Stahr, with great propriety, has cited at the end of his volume on Tiberius, and which shows his real feelings in regard to public opinion. After repeating the words of Tacitus to the effect that "it was not so much that he cared to gratify the present generation, as that he was desirous of standing well with posterity", Stahr quotes the final passages from a speech in which Tiberius deprecates the erection of a temple to himself and his mother: "For myself, conscript fathers, I am a mortal man; I am confined to the functions of human nature; and if I well supply the principal place amongst you, it suffices me, I solemnly assure you; and I would have posterity remember it. They will render enough to my memory, if they believe me to have been worthy of my ancestors; watchful of your interests; unmoved in perils and, in defence of the public weal, fearless of private enmities. These are the temples I would raise in your breasts; these are the fairest effigies and such as will endure. As for those of stone, if the judgment of posterity changes from favour to dislike, they are despised as no better than sepulchres. Hence it is I here invoke the gods, that to the end of my life they would grant me a spirit undisturbed, and discerning in duties human and divine: and hence, too, I implore our citizens and allies that, whenever my dissolution comes, they would celebrate my actions and the odour of my name with praises and benevolent testimonies of remembrance." "And thence-forward", Tacitus adds—I cannot resist quoting this characteristic touch—"thenceforward he persevered in slighting upon all occasions, and even in private conversation, this worship of himself; a conduct which was by some ascribed to modesty; by many to distrust of his merit; by others to degeneracy of spirit"—and by none, it seems (certainly not by Tacitus), to its most natural cause, common sense.

Common sense—that is the mark of Tiberius, and no wonder it was a feature offensive, almost unintelligible, to dreamers who yearned for things that are not, for things to come or things that have been. A destructive flood had overswept some districts of Rome, and there was an outcry that the goblins overhead must be appeased and the Sibylline Books consulted with that object. Tiberius thought it more profitable to appoint a commission to enquire into the causes of the disaster and report upon the measures to be taken for avoiding it in future. Sober talk like this will never win a crowd.* Towards the end of his life he allowed senate and nobles, both equally worthless and effete, to seize each other by the throat; anticipating, probably, that the most impulsive and incapable on both sides would be the first to succumb, leaving the men of moderation to survive. A rugged method, the method of nature; yet a cynical and civilized modern aristocrat like the late Lord Salisbury would have acted in precisely the same manner. Brutality and common sense are not rarely different names for the same thing. There are men who call surgeons brutal, because they amputate limbs.

This firm grasp of general principles never degenerated with Tiberius into coldness. On the contrary, there ran through his nature an opposing current: a strong vein of kindliness and consideration for others which alone can explain many of the enigmas, as they are called, of his life. He was capable both of feeling, and of inspiring in others, deep attachment. He might even be called an idealist in the sense that he seems to have expected more of the world than he found it could, or would, perform; and, as such, his

* When it was announced to him that the skeleton of a giant had been unearthed and his views were asked as to what should be done with it, he replied that "they had better leave the giant lying where he was". How different from Augustus, who possessed something of the curious spirit of Sir John Soane and founded the first palæontological museum in the world, containing "giants' bones and weapons of heroes", which were zealously collected for him on Capri.

sufferings at the blows of fortune were proportionately the more intense. For the calculating individual changes little during life; from the cradle to the grave he pursues the even and not always lovely tenor of his way: the man of heart, as we say, has only to live long enough in order to become something of a cynic. And Tiberius lived to the age of seventy-eight.

Of his kindliness many instances are on record. Such was that little incident at Rhodes. "One morning, in settling the course of his daily excursion, he happened to say that he should visit all the sick people in the town. This being not rightly understood by those about him, the sick were brought into a public portico, and ranged in order, according to their several distempers. Being extremely embarrassed by this unexpected occurrence, he was for some time irresolute how he should act; but at last determined to go round them all, and make an apology for the mistake even to the meanest among them, and such as were entirely unknown to him." By what an accident of history has this charming episode been preserved! When his brother, whom he loved sincerely, died, Tiberius accompanied the funeral cortège, on foot, all the way from the forests of Germany to Rome. Paterculus, speaking from personal experience, has recorded how thoughtful he was, during his campaigns, for the health and comfort of his troops. When any officer was ill, Tiberius saw that everything was done for his well-being and recovery; "for all, who required it, a carriage was in waiting; the use of his sedan-chair was free to all, and I myself, among others, have profited by it." When at last his dissolute second wife Julia, the cause of endless trouble and pain to Tiberius, had been divorced from him by decree of her father Augustus, he "interposed by frequent letters to Augustus on her behalf, that he would allow her to retain the presents he had made her, notwithstanding the little regard she merited from him". His affection for his first wife Vipsania, whom Augustus obliged him to divorce for political reasons "not without great anguish of mind", is recorded by various ancient writers. A chance meeting of the two that took place after this event is thus described: "At divorcing Vipsania he felt the deepest regret: and upon meeting her afterwards, he looked after her with eyes so passionately expressive of affection that care was taken she should never again come in his sight". Observe, now, how so simple and natural a story can be misconstrued. After referring to this passage, Beulé says: "*Peu de mots peignent beaucoup de choses: ce ne sont point des larmes qui*

*jaillissent des yeux de Tibère à la vue de la compagne de sa jeunesse; il
n'éprouve ni douleur ni regret; ses yeux s'enflent, se tendent, s'enflamment.
Les sens parlent donc seuls, c'est le cheval qui hennit devant une belle cavale."*
Truly, the *dernier mot* of Beulé's *odium republicanum.*

Although such flagrant defamations are scarce, there are various
passages where a misinterpretation of some authority, now lost, has
led to far more serious errors. Here is an interesting example from
the classics which I do not remember having seen recorded among
the thirty-odd monographs on Tiberius that have come under my
notice. On the one hand, we have the careful tables drawn up by
Sievers, Freytag, and others, analysing the criminal cases under his
reign, from which it can be seen how frequently he intervened to
mitigate the sentence of the condemned. We have seen the testimony of Tacitus, who records a senator saying: "I have often heard
our prince (Tiberius) bewail the event, when, by suicide, a criminal
has prevented the exercise of his mercy". On the other hand, we
are told that the emperor was so bloodthirsty that he lamented
whenever a criminal "escaped" him by killing himself. "For he
thought death so slight a punishment", says Suetonius, "that upon
hearing that Carnulius, one of the accused who was under prose-
cution, had killed himself, he exclaimed: 'Carnulius has escaped
me!'" The accounts both of Suetonius and of Tacitus may well
have been drawn from the same original source. Now: this pre-
venting—this escaping: what shall we make of it? Does the suicide
escape his cruelty or his clemency? We may decide for the latter
version by throwing into the balance the fine trait recorded of him
to the effect that, although slow in his usual speech and almost
wrestling, as it were, with the utterance of his words, "his language
flowed freely and rapidly whenever he had occasion to succour
(*quotiens subveniret*)".

Can anything definite as to the character of Tiberius be read out
of his busts? I think not. I think we are not yet in a position to
deduce a single mental quality from the features of any human
being, alive or in effigy. Grossly asymmetrical lines will of course
suggest a flawed physical structure and consequent disharmony of
mind; but phrenology, the theory of Gall, and physiognomy, as
expounded by Lavater and his disciples, are still on a plane with
astrology; the modern historian or critic, who builds a hypothesis
of character upon the evidence furnished by such vague speculations,
is no less of a quack than Nostradamus. Like many inexact arts, to

be sure, these tend to become more scientific every day; various currents are converging in that direction; but nothing exemplifies better the worthlessness of present-day authority in these matters than the conflicting characteristics which writers, according to their several passions or prepossessions, succeed in discovering in the busts of the Roman Cæsars. When one remembers with what slavish fidelity the artists of ancient Rome reproduced the original features in these works, it would stand to reason that the character to be read out of any single one of them would be constant. Yet it is no exaggeration to say that a portrait of one of the Cæsars is capable of as many interpretations as a contested passage in Holy Scripture. There is no vice, and there is no virtue, that has not been plainly read out of the busts of Tiberius. His mouth, according to one writer, betrays "indecision"; another discovers that "about the delicate mouth plays a smile of superiority"; a third writes, "probably at no time has nature formed such a perfect diplomatic mouth. Firmly closed, it illustrates Talleyrand's saying that speech was given us to conceal our thought"; while a fourth shudders at "the horrible grimace, which one cannot drive from one's remembrance". And so on, with every other item of the face.

In regard to the bust as a whole, a similar uncertainty prevails. In the Paris sardonyx cameo, Beulé recognizes, admirably portrayed, all the vicious qualities that form his idea of Tiberius, "*la bouche, le menton, sont gras, sensuels, épais, et tournent au type de Vitellius. Le cou est énorme, enflé par le vin, la bonne chère, et comme par un venin secret, etc. etc.*" According to Bernoulli there is no reason for supposing this cameo to represent Tiberius at all! The "veiled head" sold to the British Museum by Castellani is rejected by some of the best authorities as not representing Tiberius, while many persons consider it one of the most life-like busts. As in most of them, the nose, the telling feature of the face, has been restored, and in the present instance by an unusually inferior artist, so as to change its whole expression. The nose of Tiberius was probably moulded after the aquiline pattern of his mother's, with whom he had many points of character and physiognomy in common. The restorer of this "veiled head" has given it a nose of a peculiarly London cast, so that the portrait at a distance looks less like Tiberius than like his family butler. The ears are also restored in conventional fashion —altogether, the bust is a good instance of the unwarrantable liberties that are taken with ancient works of art. And yet if this

London head were placed side by side with that in the Naples museum, the resemblance would appear in a flash, in spite of the disfiguring "repairs". The London portrait represents him fifteen or twenty years older than the other; there are lines of age about the face, and the eyes are more sunk under the prominent orbitals, but there can be no doubt as to the identity of the person. To compare photographs of these marbles is misleading; they must be examined on the spot, for a slight change in the position or height of the camera may affect the entire physiognomy; nor must it be forgotten that the profile differs on the two sides of the face. But what type of man these busts figure forth can only be deciphered by those who have made up their minds on the subject beforehand. Long years will elapse before serious psychological deductions can be drawn from the data of iconography.

After a youth of exemplary virtue, and half a century more of public life, during which the manners and morals of Tiberius were an honour to his age, he retired in his sixty-ninth year to the island of Capri, in order at last to be able to indulge his latent proclivities for cruelty and lust. So, at least, the wisest of us believed for twenty centuries. We have all heard of the reformed rake; Tiberius was the reverse: from being an Admirable Crichton, he became the prototype of the Marquis de Sade. But it is needless to go into this *res adiudicata;* historians like Duruy, Merivale, and Ferrero, however much they may disagree upon other questions, are at one upon this: that no scholar of to-day, with a reputation to lose, should stake it upon the veracity of Tacitus and Suetonius. That is a great step forward. Napoleon called Tacitus a "detractor of humanity": he seems to have arrived at this opinion upon purely *à priori* reasoning, but critical researches have borne it out. The Roman historian has been tumbled from his pinnacle, and there is poetic justice in the fact that Tiberius, whose memory he succeeded in disparaging for nearly two thousand years, has been the cause of this revision of judgment. Nor need we call this stately writer hard names; it suffices to say, what no one will deny, that he suffered from a constitutional dislike of the obvious; his mind was involuted; he worked with a fixed idea, and that fixed idea was diametrically opposed to the fixed ideal of Tiberius.

We often observe that an individual who is not fully bred exaggerates all the peculiarities of the race to which he desires to

belong. Thus a German Jew, domiciled in London, will eat his
plover not only putrid, like the rest of us, but putrid and raw. Even
so Tacitus, as an aristocrat of the lower order, was extreme in his
aristocratic tendencies, he was *plus royaliste que le roi;* for no one save
really great people, like the Claudians of Rome, can afford to treat
their class at its true value. According to Boissier, Tacitus "resigned
himself" to the empire; it seems to me that he resigned himself
with sufficiently bad grace, and if, like Tacitus himself, I could
claim the gift of knowing the inmost thoughts of men, I should say
that the anti-oligarchical leanings of Tiberius appeared reprehensible
to this reactionary who yearned, in his heart of hearts, for turbulent
days of immature political development, which every Roman of
sense rejoiced not to have witnessed.

He took his pen in hand and wrote. All ancient literature of this
class is what the Germans call a *Tendenzschrift:* we must ever remember that such a thing as truth is neither what authors endeavoured to write, nor what readers cared to read; the extent to which
the whole world was tainted with the rhetorical spirit is not easily
appreciated nowadays. And beside this love of simple veracity,
another recent product of human growth is that of scientific
psychology. The "great psychologist" Tacitus, who imposed upon
ancient and mediæval Europe with his childlike and subjective
method of approaching these problems, with his sublimely artful
manner of reading imaginary characteristics into historical personages in order to draw puritanical conclusions therefrom, will find
himself ill at ease among men who have outgrown scholastic
morality, and think themselves quite moral enough when they try
to discover a plain answer to this plain question: Is it true, or is it
false?

The shrewd Montaigne seems to have been the first to doubt the
sincerity of Tacitus; Schedlbauer cites a German pamphlet of 1646
in favour of Tiberius; but it was reserved for the French sceptic
movement to shatter eternally the faith hitherto reposed upon
Tacitus and Suetonius. As with other authoritative writings, it was
little suspected how rotten—once touched—they would prove to be.
Previous to that time, these tales were blindly believed. So Gilles de
Raïs, who was executed in 1440 after having murdered eight
hundred children, confessed in his defence that he was led into
these excesses through reading Suetonius' life of Tiberius. Strange
to think that, but for Suetonius—are we never to have an annotated

modern translation of him?—we might not have heard of Blue-beard.

Then followed the inevitable reaction, a wave of sentimentalism and general obfuscation from which we are, at this moment, emerging. During this long and dark period, Tiberius again put on his old character; he was a "deified beast"; his court was composed of "pale and trembling slaves, dissolute women, and executioners". In this exhilarating company the old gentleman is supposed to have lived from the age of sixty-eight up to his death ten years later. That sane people could be found to listen to such nonsense, proves what a systematic education in "believing the impossible" can accomplish. What would they now say of Monsieur Bacha, the last of a succession of conscientious scholars who have dissected the fables of Tacitus, who consistently refers to the once revered historian as "*le poète*"? "*Dans l'invention de ses contes, Tacite s'est incessamment préoccupé d'intéresser le lecteur.*" I suspect that the chief reason why it pleased us to dislike Tiberius arose from the fact that Christ was crucified during his reign; the culpability of the emperor in this matter is not obvious, but when religious feelings come into play, the mind ceases to trouble itself with cause and effect. The logic of the emotions, says Ribot, does not acknowledge the fundamental principles of the logic of the intellect. One point is noteworthy: with this recent revival of rationalism has gone, hand in hand, an increased feeling of decency. The obscenities which charmed our pious forefathers of the Grand Tours, who would muse for hours over the *Sellaria* of Capri, and sell their last shirt to buy a sham sphinctrian medal, have ceased to absorb a generation fed upon healthier mental fare.

If we knew exactly why Tiberius, as a young man, shut himself up in Rhodes, we might understand the reason of his retirement to Capri. This departure for Rhodes may be regarded as the key to his character, and a great diversity of motives—fear, disgust, cunning, hatred of Julia, ambition, self-abnegation, disappointment, pride, general moroseness—have been assigned by various writers for this step. Family reasons, the eternal intrigues of the women of the Julian and Claudian houses, and his own mother's behaviour towards him, probably weighed heavily in the case of Capri; but, as Mr. Baring-Gould points out: "Throughout life that passion to be away from the stir of life, and to be alone with his thoughts and with his books, manifested itself spasmodically."

It is quite likely, too, that, convinced of the impracticability of republican and despotic systems of government, his friends and helpers all dead, he attempted the experiment of constitutional rule, interfering as little as possible in the machinery of the state, while reserving to himself the last word upon all graver matters. Above all, he was weary after a public life of nearly sixty years of incessant toil.

The idea of retiring from the cares of government may seem absurd to us. But we must consider the kind of work which confronted Tiberius. Modern sovereigns, whose most violent physical exercise takes the form of shooting tame pheasants or leading a drowsy state-ball quadrille, would be killed outright by a single one of his many campaigns: the economic problems with which he grappled day after day would permanently liquefy their brains. The labour of government is taken out of their hands by persons who are fitted to perform it; not one of them could say, with Tiberius, that "he found in work his only refuge from cares". Unlike him, therefore, they remain ever delightfully young, and it is hardly to be expected of them that they should bid good-bye to the world in this heyday of perennial youth. Our rulers never tire from the cares of government: they never feel them. Tiberius, at the age of sixty-eight, felt them, and this retirement to the rock-islet of Capri is of grave significance in the world's history, inasmuch as then, for the first time, the centre of the world was displaced, the spell of the Eternal City broken and, in the words of J. R. Green, "never thoroughly restored. If Milan, Ravenna, Nicomedia, Constantinople, became afterwards her rivals or supplanters as the seat of empire, it was because Capri had led the way." And small wonder if these closing years of the tyrant have appealed to the imagination of poets from early times, for he looms grandly in his majestic and mysterious isolation; there is pathos, too, in that ruined family life, and a tragic note in his hopeless endeavour to stem the rising flood of irrationalism and slave-spirit that were soon to overwhelm the great Roman world.

Where did all these Tiberius-legends arise? I question whether they were actually manufactured in Rome; they were probably a local product that found its way into the memoirs of the younger Agrippina. To the Greek population of Capri the personality and habits of this emperor were hardly sympathetic; no doubt his presence made them feel uncomfortable, especially when contrasted with the easy-going conviviality of Augustus. A certain sycophantic spirit of ancient lineage (the Romans would have associated it with their conception of *græculus*)—a certain hellen-istico-political tendency to anonymous letters and misrepresenta-tions, may have laid the foundations upon which Tacitus and the others erected their surprising fabrics. Dion Cassius, who ought to have known better, since he warns his readers of the general untrustworthiness of all Augustan history, was yet too much of a Greek not to enjoy a little gossip of this kind. We all know that *les absents ont toujours tort* and that, as Bacon says, "mankind is possessed of a natural though corrupt love of the lie itself"—particularly when it is told of the moral shortcomings of great people. Some escapades of Caligula or other youngsters may be responsible for the origin of a few of these tales, all of which, if related of Tiberius, are improbable, and some impossible—a fact which did not strike his biographers, who, like our own earlier historians and painters, were less anxious about veracity than about making as fine a picture as possible. As Mr. Huidekoper justly observes, the persons whom Tiberius selected to accompany him to Capri were all good men, and the last to condone any form of vice. But the strongest evidence lies not in the praises of Paterculus. It lies in the silence of Seneca, who is outspoken enough as regards the irregularities of other emperors. "What necessity", asks G. M. Secondo, the contem-porary of Voltaire, "drove Tiberius to indulge his lusts on Capri, when nothing hindered him from doing so at Rome?"

Among the many explanations of these Capri orgies that of Wiedermeister must not be omitted. He seriously suggests that the thoughtful entourage of the old man merely carried out the precepts of the contemporary physician Celsus as to the stimulating effects of sensuous pleasures upon the declining health of Tiberius. The tortures of prisoners and the nautch-dances were only nerve-tonics, scientifically applied. Perhaps the *gerocomic* method, not unknown among the ancients, was also attempted. Celsus probably drew his knowledge of it from the Orientals who still practise it; a certain old king in the Bible derived strength from it; as late as 1700 the great physician Boerhaave (according to Hufeland) was in the habit of recommending it for the infirmities of old age, and I am told that it is not yet altogether out of fashion in good society.

Wiedermeister is a good illustration of the evils of writing history on the *Leitmotif* system. Even as Pasch—to my thinking—perverts some evidence and omits the rest in order to show that "ambition" is the mainspring of every action of Tiberius, so this writer finds everything to agree with his preconceived theory of "insanity". Tiberius at Capri is supposed to have suffered from the mania of persecution, ending in senile dementia. In proof of his madness is adduced the fact that *he complained of the debauched habits of his (adopted) grandson Nero.* As if Tiberius had not been making complaints of this kind, and with perfect justice, all his life! We can understand Tacitus considering that a man who lives outside *la ville* must be a lunatic or a desperate person; the Emperor may well have been an enigma to republican bourgeois, but a modern writer, surveying this period of Roman history, might have noticed that the gift of self-control and sanity is precisely what distinguished Tiberius in a world that was rapidly losing the faculty of dominating its reflexes. The empire was breaking up from psychical disorders. Hysterical and otherwise mentally deranged individuals are apt to distrust the saneness of those who are placed in charge of them, and this, I think, accounts for most of the "madness" of Tiberius. In retiring at the close of an arduous life to enjoy the beauties of nature on fabled Siren shores, he was only doing what any civilized person might be expected to do.

Even at this distance of time it seems not easy to write of this man, as Tacitus claims to have done, without passion or partiality. Of the prodigious literature which has sprung up around his name, one of the best surveys will be found in Professor Gentile's interesting monograph. Happily it cannot be said of this controversy, as of many others, that it has produced more heat than light. I would express the opinion that the Tiberius question has been practically settled; nothing more, at least, can be learned out of books; the material at our disposal has been sifted in a perfectly satisfactory manner. Yet the record is far too incomplete to allow us to form a final judgment. To do this, we require the memoirs which he wrote himself, as well as the lost historical works of Pliny the Elder, Cremutius Corda, Paterculus, Seneca, and others. Of this ancient literature, which would complete our picture of Tiberius, a great portion is lost for all eternity; some of it remains, in all probability, within a few feet of our reach.

Whoever wishes to consult it must wait till a generation, which really possesses the civilization it vaunts, shall rescue it from the lava of Herculaneum.

V
THE PHILOSOPHY OF THE BLUE GROTTO

To-day the north wind, the *tramontana*, is blowing. A glance out of the window suffices: the sea is deep blue, with ruffled face; mountains and villages are standing out in clear-cut sunshiny reality. And yonder goes the steamer conveying six hundred foreigners for their day's visit to Capri and its celebrated Blue Grotto. Unhappy mortals! They are packed like sheep, although they have paid untold sums for their tickets.

But—in parenthesis—if the foreigners were not constrained to travel first class and at exorbitant rates, how could the steam-boat company pay its expenses? For the natives of the country are divided into two great sections: those who travel with third-class tickets, and those who travel with no tickets at all. And of these two sections the latter is by far the most numerous, comprising, as it does, every one who claims to be a friend or patron of the company, such as: all persons connected with marine service in any part of Italy; stationmasters, engineers, signalmen, soldiers, and so forth, as "colleagues"; hotel proprietors and their families and servants, because, if there were no hotels, there would be no foreigners for the steamers to carry; village fishermen, because they can handle an oar, and their wives and sisters who cook fish which comes out of the sea; certain privileged shopkeepers who once sold a piece of soap or a cigar to a patron; greengrocers, because the captain is fond of vegetables; pastry-cooks and confectioners, because the second stoker has a large family of children—in fact, almost the entire population of the country is exempted, for one reason or another, from purchasing tickets. Eight days ago a grimy house-painter, travelling in the "foreigners'" steamer, informed me that he always voyaged gratis because he lived in the same street as the captain.

Only the poorest of the poor, those who command no respect from either captain, crew, or agents, are obliged to buy third-class fares.

On board, however, the company makes no invidious distinction between these two great sections of natives: they are all accommodated with seats in the first cabin.

And occasionally it arranges for a public example *in terrorem*. Only a short time ago I listened to a stately old gentleman protesting, with tears in his eyes, that he was a prince of the blood besides being mayor of ——. But on that day the official was obdurate. It was "tickets or stay behind". Loudly grumbling, the venerable one extracted a few sous out of his pocket for a third-class fare, and presently I found him seated at my side, explaining to a sympathetic audience that the company had lost what little reputation for honesty it ever possessed. . . .

The *tramontana* generally blows for three days, and is followed by a spell of halcyon calm. Then is the time to visit the Blue Grotto, as an English poet of the thirties has very correctly pointed out—

> The day must cloudless be to visit it,
> The brilliant skies of Italy should pour
> A flood of radiance o'er the tranquil deep,
> And zephyrs even should be hushed and still, etc.

But not in the tourist crowd, although Augustus Hare tells us that the magical effect is enhanced by the rush of boats, the general confusion, and impassioned shrieks that burst forth on all sides. Nor yet in the morning hours, whatever the guide-books may say to the contrary, for it is only later in the day that the roof and sides of the cavern begin to clothe themselves with that quivering violet sheen due to the low position of the sun. This fairy-like bloom more than compensates for some lack of intensity in the blue of the water.

Dear Ouida! Is there really nothing to be said for the full-blooded generosity, for the passionate blend of realism and idealism of her earlier work? However that may be, it was these afternoon hours which her heroine Idalia, with her usual good taste, selected upon a memorable occasion for a visit to this "temple not built of men".

"Passion was stilled here; love was silenced; the chastened solemnity, the purity of its mysterious divinity, had no affinity with the fevered dreams and sensuous sweetness of mortal desires.

. . . The boat paused in the midst of the still violet lake-like water. Where he lay at her feet he looked upwards at her through the ethereal light that floated round them, and seemed to sever them from earth. . . . Would to God I could die now!"

This was the Blue Grotto of the last generation.

"When I entered it," says Gregorovius, somewhat more articulately, "I felt myself transported into one of those fairy-tales so real to childhood. The world and daylight have disappeared suddenly, and one finds oneself in the over-arching earth and in the blue twilight of electric fire. Gently the waves lap and the bubbles rise sparkling, as though flashing emeralds, ruddy rubies, and countless carbuncles were shooting up through the depths. The walls are of phantom-like blue and mysterious as the palaces of fairies. It is a glamour of strange nature and strange effects, quite marvellous, at the same time weird and familiar."

Plainly, the Blue Grotto must be one of the wonders of the world. Yet I question whether, if it were discovered to-day, it would attract the attention it once did. For it appeared on the crest of an immense wave of cavern and ruin worship that overswept Northern Europe—the reaction after the hard and brilliant sceptic movement of the preceding century. It was part of the return to nature; of the revolt from reason. Mankind was weary, for the moment, of straight thinking. Shelley warbled of odorous caves so tunefully that men were almost tempted to become troglodytes again; Rousseau raved of noble savages: he showed us how to discover beauty in Switzerland—the beauty of a coloured photograph. Yes; and long may Switzerland with its sham honey, sham wine, sham coffee, sham cigars, and sham Wilhelm Tell—with its inhabitants whose manners and faces reflect their sombre and craggy mountains—long may it continue to attract, and wholly absorb, the superbly virile energies of our own upper-better-middle classes! Thanks, Rousseau; thanks for not living in Italy.

Others did. Flaxen-haired dreamers, like Hans Christian Andersen, began to sing the praises of the Blue Grotto to a generation reeling with emotionalism. Says Speckter, another sentimentalist: "A melancholy, dreamy effulgence irradiates all things, and in this Blue Wonder are blended Love, Art and Nature. The Blue Grotto is the full, the over-full, nectar-goblet of Phantasy." They who wish to know to what depths of inanity this kind of talk can be carried, should read *Fiormona*.

The South Italian, constitutionally more sober and familiar with things of beauty, cannot wind himself up to this pitch of rapture over natural objects, besides being quite deficient in that pathetic fallacy which sets up a bond of communion between ourselves and the inanimate world. There are wondrous tints of earth, sky and sea in these regions—flaring sunsets and moons of melodramatic amplitude that roll upon the hill-tops or swim exultingly through the æther; amber-hued gorges where the shadows sleep through the glittering days of June, and the mad summer riot of vines careering in green frenzy over olives and elms and figs; there are tremulous violet flames hovering about the sun-scorched limestone, sea-mists that climb in wreathed stateliness among wet clefts, and the sulphurous gleams of a scirocco dawn when fishing-boats hang like pallid spectres upon the sky-line: there are a thousand joys like these, but the natives do not see them, although, to please foreigners, they sometimes pretend to.

The Blue Grotto belongs to that multitudinous class of objects whose connotation is uselessness and whose full charm is not to be perceived by the bodily eye alone. If the beauty, even of landscape, were to be perceived solely through the medium of the optic nerve, the myopic Hearn would assuredly not be the best describer of things Japanese. This is clear from the way Northerners used to write about this cave; it is not only intensely blue, but it also reminds them of things quite immaterial—of the fairies of their childhood, of the fabled blue flower of romance, of the legend of Glaucus and Elysian skies. Its beauty, therefore, lies partly in suggestion; there is something behind the blue—the mystic's spiritual associations. To a delightful Frenchman, on the other hand, its colour suggested a very material object: a candle held at the back of a bowl of sulphate of copper.

The old theory that the Greeks were insensible to the romance of scenery is exploded; apart from the testimony of the anthology and other literature, a single building, like the temple of Bassæ, proves that they were a-tremble in sympathy with the milder voices of nature. And what we may call the indifferent attitude of the South Italian in such matters results, I think, from two causes: the influence of the Romans, whose chief idea of beauty was some snug villa remote from politics and bores; and of mediæval movements, that destroyed certain finer emotional fibres and sundered the connection with the mythopœic lore and nature-gods of olden days.

The coils of muscle about the shoulders of some stripling as he strains himself to raise a heavy limestone block; a young girl whose swelling form gives promise of fruitful maternity; a waving corn-field, a shower in May, a dish of fat roasted quails—all this is still legitimately *bello:* but mountains are mere hindrances to agriculture, unsightly protuberances upon the fair face of earth, as the pre-romantic Englishman Burnet also called them (no ancient trait of ours, this fellow-feeling with nature: the very word "romantic", as applied to scenery, occurs for the first time in Addison)*; land-caves are useful for storing hay; sea-caves, blue or green, for sheltering boats in rain; the sea itself, with all its choral harmonies, is merely a place where fishes are caught. The war of elemental forces, stimulating to complex modern minds, has never laid aside for them the terrible and anti-human character with which Greek poets and artists long ago invested it, and which seems to have exceeded their limit of romantic beauty because of its destructiveness to man's life or handiwork. But while the native is beginning to understand, though not to share, the Northerner's passion for storms and cliffs and solitude, he still remains hopelessly at a loss to comprehend those recondite ideas of the beauty of pathological states, of suffering and disease which, creeping in from the East, have affected even us, the children of Goths. In short, it seems to me that the South Italian's notion of beauty is never disassociated from that of actual or potential well-being.

It is therefore hardly surprising that the Blue Grotto appealed so slightly to the inhabitants of Capri that they never succeeded in discovering what there was to discover in it. More than three-quarters of them, at this present moment, have not entered it. Those who have been there express no desire to behold its marvels a second time.

And are we not coming round once more to this old pre-romantic point of view? To the romanticists who flocked hitherward in such shoals that their writings and engravings still flood the market, Italy—her landscape, literature and art-relics—was a teacher, *the* teacher, the very crown of life. What is Italy now? I open a catalogue of travel publications and find, on three consecutive pages, a list of sixty-eight new books describing every corner of the globe, three of which deal with Italy: three out of sixty-eight,

* Addison in 1705, but John Evelyn in 1654.

and one of them a belated translation of old de Brosses' gossip (1739).

If we now go to Italy at all, we go not to learn, but to compare. Horizons undreamed-of, intellectual and geographical, have recently dawned upon us. Greece was discovered; then Egypt and Babylonia and the Sanscrit regions, and—to take only the case of antiquarians—men whose sole idea of research has been to excavate statues for decorative purposes and who, if they ventured to theorize at all, confined themselves to searching for ordered designs of Providence among disordered accidents of history—these men are now engaged in building up, out of mounds of Asiatic kitchen-refuse and such-like trash, a plan of man's early existence upon earth which their ancestors would have deemed the height of folly and blasphemy. Everything has shifted since *homo sapiens* himself shifted and ceased to be the hinge of the universe; life, once the gift of a jealous god, has become a mere series of readjustments, and "nature" the summary of our experience of them; it is hopelessly old-fashioned, nowadays, to read benevolent intentions out of, or into, a movement of things of which we ourselves, together with all the gods and devils we ever created, are only an aspect—an emanation; and which, though it displays neither good nor evil, has yet taught us an entirely new code of morality: the code of truthfulness. We are no longer men of a book, like the Turk with his Koran or the ancients who ended in being hypnotized by their Homer—things that may be a strength in early stages but that lead to ossification; if we now die of a kind of national arteriosclerosis, it will not be the fault of our teachers.

The attitude of a present-day visitor to spots like the Blue Grotto is unintelligible unless one remembers this change in the world-spirit—unintelligible often to himself. I have heard people lamenting that they cannot feel its beauties as acutely as they think they ought. And yet there is nothing to grieve ourselves about; we receive as much sensuous stimulation from the landscape as is good for us and, to atone for lack of sentimentality, we are probably interested in many things of which our grandfathers never dreamt. A sincere zest in diverse facts of life—an opening of moral pores: this is the result of the new departure. Man's field of inquiry used to be limited, while his credulity was unlimited: it is now the reverse in both cases.

Who of us nowadays writes in language like that of Speckter?

Alas, we are tired of dreaming; we have become materialistic once more, like those horrid Frenchmen; we will read our Haeckel over and over again, but none of us—no, not one—visits the Blue Grotto twice. And yet it has made Capri. It has slowly but surely routed the rivals of this island, Ischia, Sorrento, and Amalfi, who are bursting with envy; it has created hotels, steam-boats, and driving-roads; it has stuffed the pockets of the gentle islanders with gold, transforming shoeless and hatless goatherds into high-collared Parisian cavaliers; it has altered their characters and faces, given them comfortable homes and a wondrous fine opinion of themselves. *Viva la Grotta Azzurra!* It has lately built the funicular railway; it has dappled the island with the villas of eccentric strangers; it has studded the lonely sea-shore with caves fancy-tinted like Joseph's coat. For hardly was the Blue Grotto discovered and the meaning of the word "blue" explained to these children of nature before other gorgeous caverns, hitherto unnoticed, claimed attention. The foreigners liked colour in caves. The foreigners brought money. Colour in caves is cheap. Let them have it! Therefore, in a twinkling, the two-mouthed Grotta del Turco became the Green Grotto; the venerable Grotta Ruofolo put on a roseate hue sufficient to justify the poetic title of Red Grotto, and the Grotta Monacone (*vide* the relation of Kopisch) was discovered to be white—actually quite white! The stranger had his wilful way, and the metamorphosis had cost the Capriotes not a *soldo*. It was a blessed time: every one beamed with joy. But what will the future bring? The gentle islanders have grown rich, rich beyond the dreams of avarice, and almost turn up their noses at *soldi;* while travellers are beginning to turn up their noses at Capri caverns, whose odours, to tell the truth, are not always of violets.

If the Green and other grottos had ancient names, what was that of the Blue? It used to be called Grotta Gradola: a pleonasm, inasmuch as Gradola, or Gratula, is merely a corruption of Grottola (grottola, gruptula, grupta, crypta), and the district overhead bears the old name to this day. I know no earlier proof to show that the Italians were acquainted with the Blue Grotto than that contained in Coronelli's *Atlante Veneto*, which includes an interesting map of Capri, whereon it is marked as "Grotta Gradola". Coronelli was cosmographer to the Venetian Republic, and his work is dated 1696. In the face of a document like this, how absurd it is to say that the cave was unknown to the natives and discovered by a foreigner! It was Landor, I believe, who said that people who talk loudest are always in the right. This was exemplified only the other day when some Germans once more "discovered" a new cave above the Grotta Bianca and filled the newspapers with reports of their achievement, which consisted in using the rope left there by a previous party and effacing an inscription by which they had recorded their visit. The true facts are preserved in the *Geographical Journal*.

The poet Kopisch took a swim in the Blue Grotto in August, 1826—it was not "inaccessible", for he entered it, a few days later, in a boat—but to Andersen belongs the merit of drawing the attention of Europe to its beauties. If *The Improvisatore* had not created such a sensation—who can read it nowadays?—Kopisch would not have thought it worth while publishing, at a later period (in 1838), his well-known account of this exploit, which he calls a discovery, though he admits that the grotto was known to the islanders at the time. The fame of the Blue Grotto was the cause, not the result, of this publication. And another proof of Andersen's moral claim has just come to light in the recently printed diaries of the poet Platen, who spent a few days on Capri in 1827 with Kopisch, sailing all about the island, and not so much as mentioning the marvellous grotto found by his friend in the preceding year. These two romanticists—Kopisch and Andersen—beat the drum. And it strikes me as characteristic of the Northerner that he should suppose that "superstitious dread" prevented fishermen, during long centuries, from visiting this particular cave. Little they know these folk who imagine that superstitious dread plays any part in their daily lives or that supernatural beings, devils or saints, are allowed to interfere in the main objects of existence! Every nook of the shore had been searched by them from time immemorial, and Beelzebub himself could never keep a Capri fisherman out of a sea-cave if there were half a franc's worth of crabs inside it.

Nor was Kopisch the first person to disport himself in this enchanted pool. Long ago, as the islanders will tell you, the Emperor Tiberius and the fair nymphs of his harem did the same, as is plainly proved by ancient masonry about the cave; indeed, seeing that nearly every sea-cave on Capri bears traces of old walls, all of which were built by Tiberius for bathing purposes, it may be imagined what a clean old gentleman he must have been. The only question that remains to be solved is how he entered the cavern; volumes have been written to show that the sea-level is not what it used to be in his time, and it is therefore hotly disputed whether he walked, dived, swam, drove, or flew into it. There is even something to be said for the hypothesis that he crawled on all fours. For at the back of the grotto is a mysterious and narrow passage opening westwards into the bowels of the earth, which certain sages, who have assuredly never explored it, declare to be an artificial tunnel leading from the imperial villa at Damecuta to the cool waters of the grotto. Tiberius and his frail cortège, after scrambling on their stomachs for half a league through this dank and dismal drain, certainly deserved, and perhaps needed, a bath. Let the sages decide these matters: if we do not arrive at the truth, it will not be for lack of theories. Like every one else, I have my own views on the subject, but nothing would induce me to set them down here, for I dread controversy, and there is no more fearful wild-fowl living than your historico-physico-geologist. Another of these tunnels, near at hand, is said to connect the *Palazzo a Mare* with the villa of Jupiter, about three miles distant! It is nothing but an ancient cloaca, even as that at the Blue Grotto is a natural crevice supplying in former days the water which helped to erode the cavern.

There was a confusion at one time between the Blue Grotto and a huge sea-cave called the Grotta Oscura, which lay on the south side of Capri underneath the Certosa convent. This Grotta Oscura used to be one of the sights of the island, and many writers have left us descriptions of its magical twilight effects and drippings of water. The locality is now covered by earth and rocks, a landslip having taken place there in 1808 which closed it up and carried down two donkeys who happened to be grazing overhead at the critical moment, as well as a stout martello tower which the monks had built as a refuge from pirates. The hour was well chosen for this catastrophe, for the days were at hand when the corsairs ceased to threaten these shores, and when a rival cave was to become world-famous which would have eclipsed the beauties of the old. New institutions, new attractions, had made them superfluous; they were swept away at the right moment, and no trace of them remains save the still fresh scar on the hill-side which affronts the traveller's eye as he sails past under the shadow of *l' Unghia Marina*.

The shade of Tiberius, which used to haunt the Grotta Oscura, forthwith emigrated to the new cave, where it has since resided.

This is one of the many myths invented by the *Cicerones* of past days, who understood the value of quoting historical authorities and of showing pseudo-historical sites to the credulous traveller of the Grand Tours. Thus there is also a "Grotto of Polyphemus" both at Sorrento and at Capri, and at the latter place an appropriately chosen "Point of the Sirens" which, seeing that it is not mentioned in any old deeds, maps, or books of travel, must be taken to be of modern manufacture. At a certain period, Neapolitans began to take a keen interest in their Siren origin; a large literature sprang up on the subject and the name *La Sirena* has been popular ever since: witness the ill-omened palace on the Posilipo.

On Capri the greater part of these legends are woven round the name of Tiberius. When one remembers that no serious antiquarian researches have been carried out on this island for the last hundred years, during which the science of excavating and interpreting ancient relics has been not so much revolutionized as created, one can understand the prevalence of this Cicerone-archæology. The "Villa of Jupiter" itself, which every tourist visits, is a purely modern fiction; old writers never describe it by that name; and so is the "Salto di Tiberio", where he threw objectionable people over the cliff, and the *Sellaria*, where other things occurred which are best left in the obscurity of a learned tongue. Yet to what outpourings of virtuous indignation have they not given rise on the part of our travelling forefathers, who were hugely interested in the misdeeds of Tiberius.

"May the memory of the monster vanish in the presence of this *wunderschöne Naturscene!*" exclaims the pious Stollberg, who became still more pious later on. "*Quoi!*" echoes a Frenchman, "*cette terre souillée n'est pas devenue stérile?*" An English author improves upon the Salto-legend by causing the spot to be artificially levelled "in order that the condemned might be made to take clean and flying jumps in his presence", while an Italian laments the "rocky promontory from which he was wont to cast his poor, innocent girl-victims". Such are the fruits of Cicerone-archæology.

It is a mistake, I think, to suppose that the various legends of Tiberius which now form part of the mental equipment of the Capriotes and constitute a profitable source of revenue have remained vivid in their memory ever since his day. This is the common belief: but I would hazard the statement that for more than a thousand years—before Italy began to be visited by tourists—

every reminiscence of the old Roman had faded out of the popular mind. Be this as it may, from Ben Jonson onwards a long succession of imaginative writers have chosen this theme. Byron meditated a play on the subject. Some of these stories are good, but many are sad drivel—there is whispered talk of grottos and weird abominations;* artless Anacapri maidens, Oriental slaves, Caligula, and other familiar figures enliven the scene, with an occasional *pas de caractère* (decidedly so) by the ladies of the ballet.

Meanwhile, it is really fitting that the inhabitants of this island, who owe to Tiberius more than to all the saints in the calendar, should put up a memorial to their benefactor. For *Timberio* is still a name to conjure with: to conjure things out of the foreigner's pockets. He is no dim memory, but a clear-cut personality who becomes more distinct and tangible in proportion as these gentle folk conceive themselves of his commercial uses. Several of the former generation knew him quite intimately, and found him most condescending and amiable—*un vero galantuomo*, one old man used to describe him. It is curious, too, to observe that the bloodthirsty aspect of the tyrant is becoming effaced, the popular mind having always a sneaking fondness for a genuine devil or Don Juan, who is never so black as he is painted. Even Timberio, every one knows, had his little traits of gentlemanliness. He was rather too fond of a pretty face, but Lord! so are our priests and a good many others as well. And then he was a real *Signore*, not like the people who come to the island nowadays and who are worse than any Neapolitan for haggling about small change; he paid for everything just what we liked to ask, he built deuced fine cisterns, and he was the only man who could afford a carriage and pair on Capri before there were driving roads. Fine sprees in the Blue Grotto: Ha, ha! As for that Salto of his—why, if that were put into working order again, it would be the best thing possible for the place; Timberio knew what he was doing, he knew! . . . Has His Excellency perchance a cigar about him? Ah! . . . And he had electric light in his bathroom, the scoundrel! Yes, signore, it is a pity Timberio died so young—those infernal women. . . .

_____

* Old Ausonius evidently had something of this kind on his mind when he wrote that third tetrastych—

> *Frustra dehinc solo Caprearum clausus in antro*
> *Quae prodit vitiis, credit aperta locis.*

VI

BY THE SHORE

IT was on a cloudy morning in the days when I still suffered under the delusion that one could come to South Italy in winter-time, that I made my first acquaintance with the shores of the Sorrentine peninsula in Ciro's fragile barque. His surviving parent, a stalwart peasant woman, a veritable mother of the Gracchi, forcefully pressed his claims; he was the chief support of a large family, the perfection of qualities, and strong to handle an oar. He did not even smoke "like these vagabonds here", pointing to her other four male off-spring, "who smoked before they were born"; in short, a *figlio di giudizio*, meaning that he possessed tact and politeness combined with attention to personal advantage, a Homeric quality which calls for high praise among a people who admire a man in proportion as he thinks for himself.

I looked at the lowering sky and demurred on the ground of his inexperience. His age, yes; who could tell what his age was? Soon enough they would pounce down on him for military service, and then we would find out all about it. A blessed country, where women never know their ages, and men only for a brief month or so. For why keep track of one's years? Is it not like remembering one's infirmities? Wise men have enough to do, remembering those of their friends.

"Very well, then," she said. "You shall have the little Matilda as well. She is *appassionata* for her brother."

It was more than I had bargained for to take a squalling brat of four in a small boat as a guarantee that the weather would be fine, and I was casting about for an objection that should be unanswerable and yet not offensive to maternal feelings, when Ciro settled the matter by seizing the child with one arm and rowing off with the other. There was nothing more to be said. He quieted its fears with the tenderness of a mother and the resourcefulness of an experienced grand-aunt, and I must confess that, as infants go, she behaved with exemplary tact. They like babies, these boys. On subsequent occasions the little Matilda was left at home.

I asked him, as I have asked many others since, about the Sirens who sang among these rocks. But Ciro's only Siren was an imaginary *innamorata* who still loomed far ahead, though he would have me believe she was waiting for him round the next corner. And the other Siren stories I have heard all bear a modern stamp, thus: that there are three Sirens, young girls, but accursed (*maladette*); that there is one Siren, whom nobody has ever seen and who lives on the Galli islands, where she "calls the weather"; and lastly, that "the English caught the Siren and took her away with them". I am not sure to what this may refer. The English surveyed the coast in Bourbon times and drew up an excellent map of it; they left certain diabolical marks upon the cliffs which are still pointed out with awed respect. The rape of the Siren may date from those days.

Nor could he, or anyone else, give me information about the legend recorded by K. A. Mayer to the effect that "about the Siren islets a huge spectral ship, called *nave di Papa Lucerna*, sails by night; it dates from Roman times and is manned by Roman sailors. It blocks up the straits from Cape Campanella to Capri." This story seems to have faded out of the popular mind.

He knew all about quail-catching and how to snare the red-legged partridges on Mount San Costanzo, which are now, perhaps for that reason, as rare as the dodo; he had also killed some of the wild rock-doves that haunt the *Grotta delle Palumbe*, a yawning sea-cave which throbs with an emerald light-reflection not unlike that of the celebrated Green Grotto at Capri. You will do well to pay it a visit. It lies between Recomone and Isca, close to the rock-needle of Scopolo (locally pronounced Scrofolo)—a word of ancient Pelasgic origin, signifying cliffs in or near the sea, and recurring on Capri and on Ischia.

It is something of a coincidence that two out of the five Siren rocks should bear the names of Isca and Vivara, like the larger islands of Ischia—it used also to be called Isca—and Vivara on the other side of the Bay of Naples. The derivation of Isca is not quite certain; there are Iscas all along the coast; the other means a vivarium (of rabbits). Yet the Siren islet Vivara, though spelt thus on maps, is pronounced Vetara, and I cannot help thinking that this is a corruption of its mediæval name Avetaria. On Vetara there are quails and grass which are rented for about thirty francs a year;

a few ancient bricks, probably imported in post-Roman times; an open cistern; and a race of lizards darker than those on the sister-rocks and approaching in colour the well-known Faraglione breed of Capri.

Isca, which lies like some brooding, round-backed sea-monster within a hundred yards of the shore between Crapolla and Reco-mone, is a far more interesting place. For here are the remains of two Roman buildings, one at either extremity; the best preserved facing eastwards with a couple of rooms still intact, and marbles and fragments of pottery lying around; the other at the sunset end. At both points are rock-cut steps climbing up from the sea; those at the western corner wind past a roofless Roman chamber clinging to the hill-side which the fishermen—by way of giving it an expia-tory name, at least—call the chapel of Saint Anthony, though it clearly never served that purpose.

The most suggestive relic of paganism on Isca is a small grotto which Ciro showed me, and which lies about a yard above sea-level beneath this "chapel". Its entrance has been artificially heightened by chiselwork; within, is a dim and irregular rock-chamber, lined with Posilipo tufa. The builder or proprietor seems to have been dissatisfied with his original design, for new walls of the same period have been constructed across some of its angles, hiding the old ones and making the grotto smaller but more pleasing in shape. The masonry is still covered, in patches, with a fanciful incrusta-tion of limestone pebbles, presumably to heighten the quaint effect. Perhaps it was painted within, or partially inlaid with shining *tesseræ* of blue glass, like some of the caves on Capri.

What deity dwelt here? The water that now oozes from above, fashioning bosses and ridges of translucent opaline stalagmite upon the old flooring, may well have been collected in those days into a shapely marble basin which now serves, for aught we know, as font in some village church. Fully to enjoy this chill retreat one must escape into it, as I have sometimes done, on a breathless July after-noon and listen to the water dripping musically in the twilight and look back, through the narrow opening, upon the burning world beyond; then indeed one feels that its Haunter, whoever he was, deserved worship, and deserves it still. Ciro suggested that the "gentiles" used it *per pranzare*—for dining purposes, which is likely enough; they were fond of taking their pleasure in cool grottos, as we know from that accident at Spelunca where Tiberius nearly lost his life. At the water's edge is a diminutive harbour with what looks like an artificial entrance for a skiff; it reminds me of the Grotta Arsenale at Capri, which has also a small rock-hewn basin of ancient origin at water-level for the convenience of visitors: all of which would go to prove that the sea-level was approximately the same then as now.

Not far away is another semicircular cave with Roman walls and pavement. It lies about ten metres above the sea.

Did these two villas on Isca belong to different families? I like to think otherwise: Isca is too small for two families; too small, almost, for one. I like to think of some solitary Siren-worshipper here, spending a brief summer month amid his vines and books and flute-girls, and flitting from one end to the other of his microscopic domain according to the posture of the planets or his own ephemeral moods; or perhaps a pair of them who, in moments of misunderstanding, would separate awhile, each wending to his own abode, there to meditate upon words and actions misconstrued and the frailty of all human concerns, and how the thing called friendship, once that blithe communion of boyhood is past, is but the gossamer bond of the disillusioned or a frankly utilitarian speculation, seeing that most of us, but chiefly the noblest, are shaggy solitaries growling distrustfully, each in his own cave.

In Roman times the two villas may well have been embowered in trees and connected by a shady arbour. The islet at this moment is utterly bare, and it is hard to believe that only a few years ago it was partly covered with vines, potatoes, and melon-plantations, and partly with timber: six thousand bundles of firewood were taken from it. It is at present on the market; two or three thousand francs are asked, and I would be glad to think that it fell into the hands of one who would renew its forgotten charms. It has the great advantage of being easily rendered inaccessible, for the cliffs, though not high, are nearly unbroken all round the island.

A ship was wrecked here not long ago in a wintry storm; the sailors were cast ashore, where they lived for four days on grass and lizards till the gale subsided and they could be taken off. Such disasters are not invariably accidental. There was one on the south coast of Capri lately; the crew escaped as usual, but the boat was shattered to pieces and the sea covered for miles with its floating cargo of corn. The vessel was old and heavily insured, and the captain received the congratulations of all sensible folk. . . .

There are spots on this southern shore, as at Ierate, where the precipices are wondrously beautiful, descending into the waves, with mysteriously shaped openings in their smooth walls. One of these fissures, under the lighthouse at Campanella, passes clean athwart the rock and out at the other side, the sky looking through the rift like a passionless eye of blue. Clouds of swifts emerge from these rents and oval recesses, skimming the water with rapid wings.

Cliffs, sunny and bird-haunted. . . . How true is this old language? If a man took thought for never so long, could he devise two happier epithets for these sheets of southern sea-rock, flashing in the sunshine and enlivened by wild cries and flutterings?

What are these Æschylean birds? The grey swift and its harsh-screaming northern companion; swallows of more than one kind; the two kestrels. These are ubiquitous. Then: peregrines and other falcons; rock-doves; the Mediterranean herring-gull with its jocular laughing-note, and the azure-tinted thrush, whose cunning brings tears to the eyes of the native sportsmen. It contributes little towards the general commotion, but its loud and tuneful song re-echoes among the clefts. In the breeding season it makes a long roundabout to approach its nest, with counter-marches and stealthy diversions, a piece of *malizia* which extorts the fisherman's approbation. Sometimes, too, you may see the exotic wall-creeper hovering among the ledges with jerky butterfly-movements, or the kingfisher picking its way southward from rock to rock, when the streams in the north have begun to freeze over. They call it *uccello di San Martino*, because it generally appears on that saint's day in November. It is strange to see this bird, which we associate with dim forest pools and reedy streamlets, darting like a blue meteor along the open salt-water beaches. Eagles and ravens, sea-fowl in Greece, have deserted Siren land; the latter used to be so common in Anacapri that one of the reproaches levelled in olden days at its inhabitants was to the effect that they had learnt their harsh dialect from the raven's croak. No doubt an ornithologist would find much to interest him here during the spring and autumn migrations, for a number of rare birds alight at these seasons. But the country will wait long for its Gaedke, since every feathered thing is shot and eaten, irrespective of size or species.

It is not good to be a bird in Siren land.

On the mainland opposite Isca is situated a miniature Blue Grotto, which can be entered at low water or viewed from above through a hole in the rock—whence its name *grotta perciata* (cloven). It is a favourite abode of the *bove marino* or hooded seal, an amiable monster which used to frequent the caverns of the Tyrrhenian but will soon be extinct. In severe storms this huge creature sometimes takes refuge among the rocks, emerging with half its body above the breakers: the face and cowl-markings are human enough to be mistaken by simple folk for those of a monk, and wherever there is a cave or promontory along these shores called Monaco or Monacone, it refers to the apparition of this sea-monk in days of old. The *monstrum marinum monachi forma* was a ceaseless source of marvel to the learned Aldrovandus, Olaus Magnus, Pontoppidan, Maiolus, and other sages; in 1531 there was even captured, in his full vestments, a sea-bishop, *vir marinus episcopi forma*—he was presented to King Sigismund. Of this race must have been the triton sounding a conch in a cave, concerning whose discovery ambassadors were specially despatched from Portugal to the Emperor Tiberius, and that other one, six cubits long, which was caught in the waters of Posilipo in 1660, with a trumpet in his mouth and a crown on his head. Like the Sirens, these male sea-dignitaries became so common in the Middle Ages as to lose much of their consequence. And, like them, they were generally mute: De Maillet reports that one who was kept alive at Sestri used to sit in a chair all day long, sobbing and refusing food, and could not be induced to utter a syllable.

Ciro told me how the *bove marino* lives here and at the point of Campanella, and now and then, on moonlight nights, swims over to the Galli rocks to eat the celebrated *frutta di mare* there, or to the Red Grotto at Capri to visit "certain relations"; which visits, he added, were always scrupulously returned. I imagined that these animals, familiar to me from the Ægean, had nearly vanished hereabouts. Not a bit of it, says Ciro. They are only sly—infernally sly.

"Why, only two years ago," he told me, "I caught one myself on this beach. I heard its voice: it was calling for its mother. And soon enough the old woman came up, but—! you should have seen how she made off when she saw me. It had no teeth and was as gentle as a little puppy-dog, a most delectable beast."

"What did you give it to eat?"

"Bread and beans. But it died all the same. One day they killed a very, very old one. He was the grandfather of the whole family, and he had a tremendous moustache as white as the sky. We all had compassion on him—he was so like the old general at Sant'

Agata. But the fish he had eaten! And sometimes they climb into the vineyards at night to steal the grapes, just like a confounded *cristiano*. Many people have had their grapes stolen that way. And when they have had enough, they fold themselves into a sort of ball, like an orange, and roll back into the water, and drink, and drink. . . ."

"Don't you think someone else might steal the grapes?"

"Boys' tricks," he replied scornfully.

You will not hear folklore from the girls of Siren land. They are not going to be caught talking nonsense, like their brothers. They are quicker than boys in perceiving why a foreigner asks after such things, and can cast off old memories of the race more easily, having worked on them, I suppose, less thoroughly. Besides, for a stranger to converse for any length of time with peasant girls or married women is one of those things which are tolerated (foreigners are queer people, anyhow) but not viewed with pleasure, and he will be respected in proportion as he avoids the familiar tone with women. Old crones, of course, who have concluded their duties towards society, are to be considered as outside this convention. They are often perfect mines of animistic lore.

Wandering among the people here are also certain fairy tales, *conti di fata*, reminiscences of Bidpai and *The Arabian Nights*—the Hashish Eater, Sindbad, and about twenty others—some dull, others humorous, many of phenomenal indecency. But when they are told with an open, frank countenance, amid hearty peals of laughter, they go forth naked and unashamed, like Adam and Eve; and far more amusing. Hard to catch, these Milesian ghosts—the men have no time for such trivialities, the boys are growing sophisticated and self-conscious, and old women of the right sort are becoming rarer every day. I have sometimes thought of collecting them for scholars and doing them into monkish Latin, a sonorous tongue allowing of tergiversations and *double entendres* and a mock dignity peculiarly adapted to this kind of literature; not omitting, in certain parts, some of those magnificent verses which are chiefly associated with church music, but would serve a worldly purpose equally well, such as—

> *O iuvamen oppressorum*
> *O solamen miserorum*
> *Da contemptum supernorum*
> *Dixit custos rotulorum.* . . .

The Romans may have invented Latin and the Moors rhyme, but it was reserved for Christians to contrive this happy blend of both, these full-blooded cadences that crash through the thin troubadourish squeakings of mediævalism like some purple-nosed abbot elbowing his way to the refectorium.

Projects!

Some of the men are good raconteurs, but they are apt to know too much; they are overlaid with recent experiences, and so they overlay their tales. Even as the young blackbird best displays the ancestral thrush-like markings of the race which become over-coloured in the adult, so here the younger generation portrays most clearly some of the traits and feelings of the past—of that incomprehensible, lawless, and terror-stricken past of which the individual child-mind is no mirror, but only a distorted reflection. For children begin by being older than their parents, and end in being younger, and the recesses of their minds are inaccessible as that Hercynian forest of old.

Compared with that of northerners, the mental outlook of these boys is restricted, and a narrow frame will hold the picture of their hopes and fears. But this picture has all the directness, the naïveté, of what is called the youth of the world; a very ancient youth, since it already bears the impress of uncounted generations of anti-lawlessness. It is not praising them unduly to say that their minds, like their limbs, grow straight without schooling, and that they possess an inborn sobriety which would be sought in vain among the corresponding class in the North. It is the quality which the Greeks called σωφροσύνη. Inured to patriarchal discipline from earliest childhood and familiar with every phenomenon of life from birth to death, they view their surroundings objectively and glide through adolescence without any of the periodical convulsions and catastrophes of more introspective races. Their entire vocabulary consists, I should think, of scarce three hundred words, many of which would bring a blush to the cheek of Rabelais; yet their conversation among themselves is refreshingly healthy, and many subjects, popular enough elsewhere, are tacitly ignored or tabooed. Not Puritans, by any means, nor yet the reverse; they will bend either way, but, the strain relaxed, they forthwith straighten like a willow wand: if this be not virtue, according to Aristotle's definition, what is? Emigration is unfortunately producing a very different crop of youths; gamblers, wine-bibbers, and flashily dressed mezzo-signori.

The environment, to be sure, to which these people are so well adapted, is one of archaic simplicity, and every one of its social and ethical problems has long ago been solved and codified; amid the wilderness of our ever-changing worldly circumstances they would be hopelessly lost; indeed, they regard our whole civilization as a vast perambulating lunatic asylum.

Small wonder, considering the exemplars of septentrional culture which occasionally stray hither: elderly females that wander by the sad sea-waves, distributing Protestant tracts to illiterate pagan fishermen; beetle-collectors; pale youths who fix up a hammock in which they live night and day, declaring that such was the way of the Christian Fathers, then suddenly vanish, leaving their bills unpaid; or downright lunatics like that batch of men and women who arrived the other day *vom lieben Schwabenlande* in apostolic garments, which they proceeded to doff in the market-place, till the population rose up against them. (They said it was the newest fashion in religion, which is quite a mistake, because it is the oldest—that of the pre-Adamites and gymnosophists. Francis of Assisi endeavoured to revive this sunshiny method of adoring the Almighty, to which Krafft-Ebing has given a new name.) To minds accustomed to militarism and the "Thing In Itself", there is something intoxicating in the purity of the atmosphere and the comparative freedom from police inspection—your Teuton loves being supervised—to be enjoyed here: it prompts them to improbable deeds. . . .

"Do you see that old house over there?" Ciro once asked me, pointing to a ruined tenement. "A *male sito*—a bad place, signore. Strange things come flying out of that window; bricks, and pieces of cloth, and lightnings, and God knows what. And sometimes—sometimes one can see a light burning inside. Ugly things."

"Would you be afraid of living there?"

"Afraid? Not likely! But they carried away everything years and years ago. Why, the carpenter alone said he would not do his part of the job for less than three hundred francs."

"The *munaciello*?" I suggested.

"Who believes in the *munaciello*!"

A good many people, apparently. Or perhaps they only pretend to; it is hard to say. He is quite a useful domestic spirit, if you know how to deal with him; he gives lucky numbers for the lottery and shows where money is buried. But you must keep the information to yourself, and not imitate the foolish woman whose oil jar he filled up day after day till she confided the secret to a neighbour, which spoilt everything. Sometimes he guards the house in the shape of a snake, or appears to the terrified wayfarer as a ghoul—a bodiless head.

More often he is simply spiteful; he throws people about. They re-furnished a certain resort of his, a decayed tower, thinking to drive him out: on the very first evening, he tumbled the proprietor out of bed. If you look up from the sea at Cantone you will observe to the westward, under the cliff of San Costanzo hill, a yellow* house, solitary, among olives; it is called "Grale"—a name I cannot explain—or *casa degli spiriti*, and it used to be a summer residence of the monks who lived below: its subsequent history is also curious but not edifying. This "house of the spirits", then, is a chosen abode of the *munaciello*—he threw a woman off the roof and a child out of bed; disguised as a pig, he actually tempted a man to cast himself over the precipice and so perish.

I lived in it for two months, but never caught sight of him.

A volume could be filled with the local legends of the *munaciello*, who is sometimes accompanied by one or more cats. It is the malicious and sly monk, with one foot in hell; but what makes him interesting is that around this rather plump modern contrivance have grouped themselves many fragments of ancient and mediæval beliefs, floating dispersedly adown the stream of time: the witch-element, Sabazius, Queen Mab, Poltergeist, the Familiar, Proteus, and so forth. A heterogeneous accretion; like those wanton islands of the South that are formed of multifarious river-debris lingering around some insignificant nucleus.

The Mammone, though he only frightens children, has a far purer pedigree, being the lineal descendant, they say, of Mormo, the terror of little Greeks and Romans. But perhaps this is a mistake; perhaps he is Mammon, one of the many heathen idols who become a demon. There is something of the *beetle* in Mammone which is not clear to me: beetles, great and small, are often called by this name, and if you ask why, the answer will be: "Because they are so ugly." It stands to reason that gnosticism and suchlike observances were more hateful than downright paganism to the early church, and I sometimes ask myself whether this *mammone*, this god of the heathen, was not identified in a manner with these cults and with

* Now painted pink. This is the house where *Siren Land* was begun in May 1908, at the section (p. 177) "The summer is fast drawing . . ."

the scarabs which poured into Italy during the later Empire, or
were found among its ruins and worn, here as elsewhere, as amulets
for their occult virtues. If you show a scarab to a child he will
always call it "Mammone". However that may be, the beetle-
charm, which differs from the ancient scarab shape, still survives
and is credited with great efficacity: the Neapolitan murderer
Erricone, when arrested recently in New York, was wearing one of
them round his neck.

It is a singular parallelism, by the way, that the Mammone, a
beetle, should be useful for frightening purposes, even as we talk
of a bug-bear: bug signifying both a beetle and a fright. . . .

Many other caves and inlets we explored together in that craft
of Ciro's, and much he told me of their wondrous lore: far-off
memories now, flashing like sunny gleams across the intervening
gulf. . . .

What Ciro's ambitions were, I never learned. Or perhaps I have
forgotten. Doubtless they were modest and well within range of
realization, for the improbable had no place in his worldly calcu-
lations. On him Athene had set her seal of temperance; that want
of self-knowledge, the greatest sin of the Greeks, could never be
laid to his charge. Maybe he dreamed of some white-domed cottage
among vines and olives, not far from the sea, with a boat near at
hand, and five or six children as amiable and simple-minded as
himself. His dreams, whatever they were, remained unfulfilled, for
he lies buried in an alien land, under a flaming sun. So his mother
told me some years ago, merely adding, with antique resignation,
that he was a good son.

Requiescat.

VII

THE COVE OF CRAPOLLA

ONE of the quaintest spots in Siren land is the inlet of Crapolla on the south coast. A rugged path, frequented by fishermen who bring their produce over the ridge to Sorrento and by a few bathing enthusiasts of Sant' Agata, leads down the incline, becoming more precipitous as it breaks away, perforce, from the stream which flows alongside, and which ends in a cascade at the back of the inlet. This is no walk for a summer morning when the glare from the shadeless limestone rock is terrific, and one wonders how those old monks who lived in the abbey of San Pietro di Crapolla close by the sea were able to endure it. Likely enough, the road was shaded in those days by oaks, single groups of which may still be seen along this slope in isolated spots where it has been found too troublesome to cut them down. These Theocritean vales are fast disappearing, since oaken timber is in great request for shipbuilding at Piano di Sorrento and Castellamare—though not for purposes of furniture, as it grows too fast to be solid; the chestnut takes its place in this respect.

The monks were of the Basilian order, and documents relating to the abbey go back to the twelfth century: in fact, all along these shores, at Nerano, Sant' Elia, Capri, and elsewhere, were small monastic establishments, generally of Franciscans or Benedictines, who spent calm and godlike days in these abodes of peace, content with what vineyards and houses and ducats the pious inhabitants gave them in exchange for spiritual consolations. No doubt the corsairs are responsible for the abandonment of some of these convents. This one at Crapolla must have remained fairly intact till the thirties, except that it was unroofed, for Marianna Stark describes the mural paintings and the interior of the church, which was separated into three aisles by a double row of columns, eight in number; six being of Parian marble, the others of granite. It is an utter ruin now. Some of the columns are supposed to have been taken from the great Minerva temple at the promontory of Campanella—Donnorso, who wrote in 1744, is one of the first to make this assertion, which may well be true. The grey granite ones are still there, lying among the debris, and undoubtedly antique; the others, the white ones, were carried away from Crapolla about thirty years ago and sawn up, I was told, into window-sills, mortars for pounding sugar, and other domestic implements. *Sic transit!* At the entrance of the so-called Abbazia in Sant' Agata are two small marble columns* which are said to come from Crapolla— they are grooved in a spiral whose centre depression may have been overlaid with mosaic.

A hermit lived among the ruins of the ancient abbey so long as visitors went there to supply him with donations, solving the problem which ever confronts these holy men: how to *mangiare franco* (eat gratis).

Everyone knows who took away the wealth of Crapolla and other sacred buildings all over Italy. It was Napoleon.

"Come here, Don Gioacchino," he said one day to one of his scoundrel friends, "and let me see what advice you have to offer. Listen: I must make war with Moscow, a paltry half-year's job, and—well, I have no money. Now?"

"Half a year, your Majesty?"

"Not a day more."

"Make money with the church plate of these Italians and buy cannons with it. That will suffice for exactly six months."

"An excellent suggestion, *caro mio*. And you shall be general in my army."

And so it came about that the convents were raided and a new sort of money, called Napoleons, coined with their proceeds. But the war lasted seven months instead of six, and everybody was killed except Napoleon and his friend, who had sewn themselves up in the belly of a horse. Even that did not humble Don Gioacchino, for he afterwards tried to be governor of Naples, and the king was obliged to have him shot at Pizzo in Calabria.

Some say that the ship which took the wealth of Crapolla was so laden with gold that it foundered just outside the islet of Isca. *Chi lo sà!* If so, it will be fished up again when the blessed Bourbons return to power.

There was one thing which Napoleon overlooked when he sacked

* Now carried away.

this abbey: its *tesoro*, or buried treasure. It was a hen and six chickens of pure gold, and it was raised not so very long ago. A boat arrived late one evening with three men, who stepped out and walked up to the ruin; the first man carried a sack, the second a pick-axe, and the third—*the book*. That looked suspicious. . . . They hammered all night long, and when the sun rose they were gone. How it was found out? Why, a short time afterwards a small boy went to look at the excavation they had made and picked up a golden chicken which they must have lost or forgotten—he took it to the tax-collector at Sorrento, who gave him a few sous for it. (Lucky tax-collector! It was worth many hundred thousand francs.) Then other people looked more carefully, and soon discovered the exact spot where the hen had been sitting in the earth, with three chickens on each side of her.

The country is full of these treasure-legends, but the natives are not prone to supply information on the subject, fearing that the stranger may be versed in *l'arte* (magic) and thereby enabled to unseal the enchantment for his own benefit. This same "chicken-motif" occurs in many parts of Italy. It all depends upon the proper use of "the book"; few people, naturally, understand it, else the hoards would all have been raised long ago. At Campanella there is a golden lamb hidden in some crevice; at Pastena, too, in the subterranean passage of San Paolo, lies a fabulous treasure. A man crept in one day and filled his pockets with precious things, but on turning to go home he found, to his surprise, the tunnel barred with an iron gate. Then a Voice said—

"Disgorge your gold!"

He did so and the gate vanished. But he had shrewdly kept back a few coins and was creeping away well pleased with himself when, suddenly, the passage was blocked again.

"Out with the rest of it!" thundered the Voice; whereupon he reluctantly emptied his pockets and was allowed to escape into daylight again.

I, too, once crawled into this tunnel, but discovered nothing more valuable than the skeleton of a goat. . . .

And the legend of Campanella is interesting because, instead of the magic volume of Virgil or what not, the explorers entered the caves armed with a talismanic ring (Oriental influence). There, a monstrous figure on horseback issued from the darkness, saying that unless they succeeded in raising the treasure by the third attempt their lives would be sacrificed. They failed; and an immense wave of the sea rose up to drown them, which they appeased, in the nick of time, by casting the ring into the foaming gulf.

From Crapolla you can be rowed eastwards to Sant' Elia, the Ultima Thule of Siren land, where another treasure lies buried. It can also be reached by walking down from Torco, along a stony path skirting the cliff, with incomparable views over the Salernitan Bay and the Galli rocks; or again—an easier route—from the Colli di Sorrento past the once famous limestone arch, *Arco di Sant' Elia*, a portentous freak of nature. It is a sad wreck now, this one majestic portal opening upon the blue wonderland of sky and sea; the wind, which fashions the arches and pinnacles and melon-shaped grottos and all the bizarre accoutrements of these coasts, gnawed at the keystone till the span yielded. Richard Burton climbed over it in 1835—in 1843 it is described as "shattered".

There used to be a theory, still popular, that all these natural features had been eroded by the sea, a curious delusion, which postulated a frequent rising and sinking of the land and took no account of the fact that similar structures exist in limestone regions hundreds of miles inland. Subterranean threads of water, and rain, and wind, are responsible for them. The water filters through the rock in minute channels, disintegrating it by chemical action and, later on, by sheer mechanical force; where it issues, a cave is formed, with the help of winds and rain. This is the origin of nearly all the land-caves of the district such as the *grotta dell' Arco* and *del Castello* at Capri; in some, like that below the "Villa Jovis", the old water-course, now dried up, can still be plainly seen. Where the elements attack a rock which is softest in the centre, a natural arch is formed: a pinnacle, where it yields at the sides. The force of the wind is incalculable; even on apparently calm days, a terrific current may be rushing upwards from the sea, as on that fateful occasion in September, 1902, when some wood gatherers on Monte Lauro at Capri, throwing away a lighted match, suddenly found themselves enveloped in a conflagration and perished miserably all but one. The accident was witnessed by many fishermen from their boats, but nothing could be done for them; one by one they dropped down the awful six hundred feet of cliff into the sea, whence the charred bodies were afterwards recovered—their shrieks could be heard as far as the opposite mainland. Which, by the way, is not as wonderful as it seems; in this air, persons can sometimes carry on a conversation across half a mile of land or a mile of water.

I often find my way to Sant' Elia. It is a steep olive-covered slope trending seawards, and in former times may well have supported a few families that fled away when a cataract of rocks descended from above, among the debris of which their ruined houses are still discernible. Two shattered gateways against corsair-surprises, built at precipitous points on the paths leading east and west, also testify to the existence of a population at this remote spot, as do the mouldering remains of a once fair chapel by the water's edge. The place is sufficiently venerable, as its Byzantine name indicates; and a few fragments of antique marbles among the masonry of this sanctuary show that, in still earlier ages, some Roman villa may have stood near this site. An ancient land. . . .

The jewel of Sant' Elia is an old farm-house which lies out of the track of descending stones and, though uninhabited, is still in use. It is a sturdy little building and simplicity itself as regards architectural ornament and inner arrangement; a genial simplicity, born of rustic needs and corrected, and re-corrected, by ages of steady thought, which discarded all superfluities and culminated, at last, upon a note dignifying the lowliest things: fitness. There is a beauty in fitness which no art can enhance. This structure displays nothing of the prettiness, the mazy irregularity, of many Southern peasants' houses—much less the Giulio-Romano stateliness of sleek Lombardy farms: you enter into a rectangular loggia opening, in bungalow fashion, upon a row of rooms that shelter animals and implements and a ponderous oil-press and piles of glowing lemons; then, climbing up to the next floor, where the *famiglia* once lived, you find exactly the same pattern repeated. What more simple? But the site has been correctly chosen; the exposure duly calculated; the arches of the loggia are well proportioned, so are those of the rooms, whose vaulted ceilings are solid and high: in short, of ten thousand chances of wrong-doing, every one has been avoided and, like some smooth river at the end of its course, it now displays no trace of the torments and struggles which accompanied earlier stages. Such a dwelling marks the survival of the fittest—the coincidence of efficiency with economy *thus, and not otherwise*: the justification of yonder falcon floating, a speck of gold, in the empyrean; or, for that matter, of some humble beast that, trusting to immobility and a mottled pelt, even now evades his eye.

This *masseria* is utterly deficient, of course, in the comforts of civilization: it was built for no such purpose. Yet I have memories of certain impromptu luncheons—quails and cream cheeses and succulent raisins preserved in vine leaves—on that upper loggia with a civilized and charming companion; memories of blue sea shimmering through a silvery network of olive branches, with talks, over coffee, of far-away things. . . .

Less innocent conversations have also echoed within these walls. Here was a favourite meeting-place of the brigands who infested the peninsula up to the seventies—here they caroused and discussed their plans of operation, climbing up afterwards, by break-neck paths, to the heights of Marecoccola, where they separated. The great Pillone was the most celebrated of them—you can read about him in Bergsoe's *Italian Novels*.

An old woman, who witnessed their last stand against the *carabinieri*, told me how it befell. They were bivouacking on a hillock below Termini called *La Chiunca*, which in those days was covered with immense oaks; their enemies silently encompassed them and demanded a surrender. They refused, and a sanguinary fray began—the brigands shooting from behind the trees with deadly precision upon their unprotected assailants. But their ammunition was soon exhausted and they all fell fighting, save a few who managed to escape. Not a man of them was taken alive; a wounded one crawled away as far as Monte Faito, where he was afterwards found dead, with a crucifix (probably stolen) upon his breast. Such deeds of daring are over, for the present, in this country; the brigands of modern Italy have deserted their ancient fastnesses; they recline in the Chamber of Deputies, where no one molests them.

When I first heard this story the Germans were engaged in testing their new bullets upon the natives of Samoa, who thought themselves safe behind trees, and I imprudently told the venerable dame that her brigands would stand a poor chance against modern weapons such as these: bullets that pierce an oak. She said nothing—she was far too polite to contradict; but she thought a good deal, and I saw that I had sunk considerably in her estimation, not so much for trying to foist a fairy-tale upon her, as for believing it myself.

And the treasure of Sant' Elia? It lies buried under a tower near the sea. A workman's spade one day encountered an underground marble slab which bore the lettering: BEATO CHI SCAVA (Blessed who digs). Wild with excitement, the man delved lower and presently struck another one inscribed "Blessed who digs deeper", and after some hours of frenzied toil the third tablet was at last revealed. It was inscribed——. No, I cannot possibly pen that inscription; suffice to say, it was not very explicit as to the whereabouts of the treasure. Whoever is interested in the matter, must make a pilgrimage to the spot; the peasant who works the land is called *figlio del malpensiero* and will doubtless supply the desired information. It was his own father to whom the adventure happened, which proves that it must be true.

On Capri, at Veterino and in other parts of the island, there are a variety of treasure-legends; perhaps the best known is that of the equestrian statue of Tiberius, which a boy is said to have seen in a chink of the rock—the *motif* recurs in that of the Suabian Barbarossa, of Gyges as narrated by Herodotus, in Plato's *Republic*, and no doubt elsewhere.

All these hoards are guarded by spirits of the gentiles (Romans)— evil genii that have sought a refuge underground from the effulgence of Christianity. So it is all the world over: Minos creeps into the earth, into the universal Venusberg, and when the time is accomplished, great Jove, at Demogorgon's call, will descend and follow him down the abyss. Each deity becomes a demon in his turn, and his adherents pagans or provincials; to argue a common origin for those religions which possess an underworld is surely a mistake, for if the rulers of the moment are overhead, and the man on earth, whither shall the devils betake themselves save down below?

The Sirens, too, have suffered a sea-change; once earth-powers, they have now retired into the dim purple depths of ocean—a transmigration which necessitated some structural changes in their anatomy. Euripides already spoke of them as dwelling in Hades with Persephone. So gods and demi-gods go the way of men— *eodem cogimur.*

Strange, by the way, this startling metamorphosis of the Sirens in mediæval days. How came it about? According to Schrader, the first mention of the fish-tailed ones occurs in the *Liber monstrorum* which was written towards the end of the sixth century. He calls them a "Frankish invention". It seems to me more likely that fish-tailed mermaids existed from time immemorial all over the North, and that the compiler of this early work, being naturally puzzled what to make of the classic Sirens, brought them into the category of shapes familiar to him. Saint Isidore, a contemporary of the *Liber monstrorum*, and the Byzantines all invest them with the ancient bird-attributes.

Below the old abbey is the cove of Crapolla, a tiny beach dotted with fishing-boats and hemmed in by mighty walls of orange-tawny limestone. A colony of Roman fishermen lived here; their ruined abodes cling like bee-cells to the rock, and the conduit they built to regulate the cataract still serves its purpose. This is a lively place in summer-time, at sunrise when the fish are brought in, or in the late afternoon when you may contemplate the preparations for the coming night's work and watch the boats as they glide off severally, like sea-gulls taking flight from their nests, till the last one has vanished round the rocks, and you suddenly find yourself alone, quite alone, on the smooth, warm pebbles. Then is the time to dream awhile.

In winter Crapolla is uninhabited; the boats are drawn up out of reach of the waves which thunder in between the encircling precipices. Only one white-bearded fisherman, with a face like Father Christmas, lives here throughout this wild season. His name is Giuseppe Garibaldi,* and no one knows better how to catch the wary *cernia* as it lies hidden among the rocks; if he wished, he could be as rich as a king. But money slips like sea-water through his fingers and, when he makes a good catch, he prefers to treat his friends. For forty years he has known no other life than this, though he can tell of stirring times when he lived at Naples before turning his back on the world and carving out a quiet existence for himself in this secluded nook, where he now potters about, blithe and loquacious, in his leaky black tub. So he lives, this *cigale* of seventy summers, reckless of to-morrow and often gaily fasting for days together when his purse is empty. All too soon, I fear, he will be found lying lifeless upon the stone floor of his hut (his bed was pawned thirty years ago and never redeemed) and there will be one gentleman less on earth.

Several deaths have occurred at Crapolla owing to the rapacity of the country folk who lose their lives in scrambling upon the face of the cliff in search of firewood. Not long ago, the spirit of the last of these victims began to be troublesome by haunting the place, but the priests compromised matters by erecting a wooden cross on the spot where he fell, which satisfied everyone. Near at hand, at

* His real name was Persico, like that of the old historian of Massa. He died September 6, 1914.

Recomone, something of the same kind ought to be done, for it is a *male sito* in spite of all its natural charm. A shingly beach, solitary, overgrown with slender rushes and the strangely beautiful sea-thistle and other uncommon plants which have clambered down the hot gully overhead, Recomone is the chosen abode of a spectre, an *ombra* which does an infinity of mischief, such as throwing down stones and loosening the ropes of boats moored to the shore. The fisher-folk *fanno l'indiano*, they play the Indian—feign complete ignorance of the matter.

"How, signore?" they will say, "you believe in ghosts?"

The peasants are more communicative. There are two or three variants of the story, but the most generally accepted version is that, some years ago, a certain woman who had made much money by adulterating wine, died, and the sin preyed so much upon her spirit after death that it left her no peace. She used to wander dolefully about her former home, scaring old and young. At last it became such a scandal that they got a "strong" priest to talk to her. It was on this wise—

PRIEST. Now then, what is this they tell me? Prowling about the village, eh?

SPECTRE. I can't help it; I watered the wine.

PRIEST. You ought to have thought of that sooner.

SPECTRE. I did. But I always forgot again.

PRIEST. *Peggio per te.* I shall now banish you to some lonely spot, where you may do what you please.

SPECTRE. Oh, oh. . . .

PRIEST. Let me see—there is Fossa di Papa.

SPECTRE. Not there—not there! Rather to Recomone.

PRIEST. To Recomone then, and off with you!

This story is interesting, as an *ex post facto* explanation of some forgotten incident: this beach was in bad repute long before the present ghost was born. So the traveller Swinburne writes, in 1780, that "Nerano is famous among mariners for being haunted by evil spirits". Whether they really believe these tales is quite another matter. I think they merely derive from them a certain emotional shiver, an echo out of their own past, such as some persons obtain from a spiritualistic séance or from a creepy story well told.

These spirit conjurations are not invariably successful, and a

priest of questionable reputation should never attempt the task, for
spectres see things invisible to mortal eye and are notoriously
recalcitrant and plain-spoken. "And who the devil are *you*?" said
one of them the other day to a fat *canonico* who was threatening him.
"I know! A drunkard and a thief! You doctored your father's will;
you had four and a half litres of wine yesterday, and last Wednesday
you cheated sixteen francs out of your uncle. And what are you doing
to-day? Looking for a new cook, as usual. And why? Because——"
But the *canonico* suddenly remembered another engagement.

It is chiefly the young priests who are chosen to constrain these
rebellious spirits; chastity, and chastity alone, can rivet their
obedience, and the people are hopelessly sceptical as to the asceticism
of the older ones. . . .

The name Crapolla has been derived from "akron Apollinis",
as though a temple of Apollo had stood here. But this is pure
Cicerone-etymology—the origin of the word is the same as that of
Capri, and in old deeds it is actually called Capreola. What Capri
means is not quite certain; it is neither Greek nor Phœnician; there
are places with similar names all over Italy and half a dozen
Capri's and Caprile's within a few miles of here. Quaranta deduces
it from a Tyrrhenian root signifying rocky or stony. Why not?
When, nearly two centuries ago, Greek etymology could no longer
explain all local names and traditions, the enlightened took refuge
in Semiticism, and thus there grew up the ponderous Shem-Ham-
and-Japheth literature of Martorelli and his disciples, which we
have outgrown in its turn. Nowadays, the conveniently obscure
Tyrrhenian language helps to solve old difficulties. But it makes
new ones.

This Cicerone-etymology which has infected the whole of this
region—the whole of Italy, in fact—is a legacy left us by the *à priori*
scholarship of past generations which worked with fixed ideas:
it was pleasant to make learned assertions, and to believe is always
easier than to doubt or to deny. There is Nerano, for instance,
which has become fancifully connected with Nero—*Re Nerone* they
call him—who plays approximately the same part here as Tiberius
does at Capri. These are his baths; yonder, in those caverns, were
celebrated the orgies of which we have all heard. There are three
of these caverns under the crag of Mount San Costanzo; the largest,
a noble grot, distils limpid water which is collected into a small

reservoir. In one of these three lies the treasure, a golden statue of a child, but only one man had the *book*, and that was the old hermit of Capri who promised over and over again to come and perform the necessary adjurations, but somehow or other never kept his word; and now he is dead. He was the last person whom the Capriotes would have suspected of being versed in necromancy, an ex-shoemaker and a great simpleton, but the men of Nerano knew better: a prophet is of no account in his own country.

And how curious is the Cicerone-etymology which derives Citarella, the breezy hermitage upon Monte Solaro on Capri, from Venus Cytherea. Ever since it was wrongly reported that an antique pavement had been found here, learned local writers had elaborated visions of a snowy temple on this height, Eryx-fashion, with roses and doves and grave youthful priests—wisely omitting, however, the chief part of such temple equipment. The medical baths of Citara on Ischia—which is the same name—have also been brought into connection with this Venus and are therefore recommended as a cure for sterility. Here we have an instance of a serious custom growing out of wrongly derived etymology. These baths, which Iasolini also recommended for baldness and elephantiasis, are no longer taken by women. Perhaps waters with a contrary effect would not have lost their popularity so soon.*

I do not know the meaning of Nerano (it is also called Anarano, Donerano, Inerano, and Inderano in old deeds), but Citarella is one of the many names on Capri which wandered over during the Amalfitan domination—the result, I suppose, of overcrowding in the days before the Republic received its death-blow in the war with Pisa, when the Pandects were carried off. Says Edrisius: "The island of Capri is inhabited by men of Amalfi who keep flocks there." The family of Citarella is a well-known one; they were nobles of Ravello and patricians of Amalfi, and no doubt drew their name from the town of Cetara (Cetarelli) on that coast. Now what does Cetara mean? I cannot say. All kinds of origins have been suggested for the names of such places in Italy; perhaps it also means *rocky*, for Hecatæus has a "Kyterion polis", which is now Cirisano, on a

* The strangest of all these derivations are those invented solely *for the sake of symmetry*—the above-mentioned Veterino is derived from Vitellius because near at hand lies a "Timberino"; the islet of Vervece, near Massa, signifies a *sheep* (vervex) because Capri, just across the water, means a *goat*. The real origin of Vervece is *verruca*, a wart, an isolated protuberance; it is the same root as that of Eryx.

rocky height; Cetraro in Calabria is similarly situated; citarella, the rock-haunting bird, is the same as our kestrel; Bérard derives it from a Hebrew word signifying high spot, mount of sacrifice. The islet of Kythairon, whence Venus took her epithet of Cytherea, is notoriously stony and bare; Phœnicians founded her temple there, and her cult spread thence over Cyprus and Greece to Campania. And so we arrive, as the result of this philological disquisition, at a most unexpected conclusion: the name Citara (Citarella) is not derived from Venus Cytherea, but *vice versa*.

Let us never visit Capri without climbing up to Citrella, for it is a fair spot. It was a Dominican foundation and up to a short time ago a hermit used to dwell here, but the hermit business has decayed all over Western Europe, and of the six or more devotees who used to haunt the rocks and ruins of Capri only one has survived—the successor of that over-talkative Consalvo who, in 1528, as Gregorio Rossi relates, was in large part responsible for the defeat of the Spanish fleet and the death of the viceroy at the hands of Doria in the sea-fight near Conca. This cloudy abode used to be surrounded by a grove of wild Aleppo pines, but they have now been cut down as fuel and to supply the newly imported craving for Christmas trees: an amazing custom, when one thinks of it—to load a tree with lighted candles and other incongrous trumpery—which might well have remained in the land of its birth.

Here, at Citrella, were buried the victims of the cholera of the thirties, many foreigners among them, and it would be hard to find a pleasanter resting-place for all eternity, unless it be the crater-meadow of Monte Rotaro on Ischia where, simultaneously, the cholera victims of that island were interred. What a contrast between the two! On Rotaro the volcanic earth with its hoary mantle of vegetation and, within the deep funnel, a green woodland calm, as though seas and storms no longer existed upon earth: Citrella, poised like a swallow's nest upon its windswept limestone crag; far below, the Titanic grandeur of South Capri and the dimpled ocean, strewn with submarine boulders that make it look, from such aerial heights, like a map of the moon enamelled in the matchless blues and greens of a Damascus vase.

Citrella, of course, has its treasure. Some men saw a heap of gold and silver lying in a cleft of the rock, but a tremendous thunder-storm broke in upon their operations, the torch they carried was blown out three times, and . . . certain other things occurred; one of them died the same evening; all of which did not prevent the others from resuming the search next day. It is truly astonishing to hear educated natives, who have visited the university, speaking of these things in a hushed whisper. An occasional discovery of real value may have fostered the growth of these legends; in Campania, as in parts of the Orient, the ruins of an ancient civilization, with its subterraneous passages and marks of vanished pomp, gave them verisimilitude and a *locus standi;* Naples is half-way to Baghdad, and no one quite understands the native character who has not lived in the East.

This Oriental trait, if such it be, is only one of many that have been gradually superimposed upon one another. Whoever rightly deciphers the human palimpsest of the Parthenopean region will perceive how faint are the traces of Greco-Roman schooling, how skin-deep—as regards primitive tracts of feeling—the scars of mediæval tyranny and bestiality. And Christianity has only left a translucent veneer, like a slug's track, upon the surface; below, can be read the simple desire for sunshine and family life, and a pantheism vague and charming, the impress of nature in her mildest moods upon the responsive human phantasy. Our Gothic gloom and the sand-wastes of the East beget fearful gods and demons; those of Campania, though equally well accredited, are all in a manner sunny and humane, for the atmosphere is too limpid to permit the formation of terrifying spectres like those of Nurcia or even Beneventum.

There are witches hereabouts, *giannare* (from Diana, now queen of witches), but they are rather like ordinary women; there is nothing mysterious or malefic about them. As for the devil—did I tell you of the man who saw the devil last week? He was walking up this very road, about sunset, and there was the devil sitting on a ∙ stone in front of him. What he looked like? Oh, horns and hoofs and all the rest of it—nothing out of the way—just the devil, you know. The people will tell stories of the devil, popularly known as Saint Pantaleone, because foreigners like to hear such things, foreigners being rather simple folk in some respects; but though they speak with fervour and conviction, they do not take him seriously. Dozens of houses are haunted by him and his imps but, unlike many in our civilized England, the rents do not fall, and *cristiani* live in them all the year round.

How came the revered Saint Pantaleone to be identified with the Prince of Darkness? Because he gives lucky numbers for the lottery; therefore he must be in league with him; therefore he is the devil himself—an example of the rhetorical figure we learnt at school: "the part for the whole".

It is the same with the saints. Every one of the heavenly host may be cheated at a bargain; the Virgin and her infant Son—the adult Jesus is practically unknown here—are adored with feasts and flowers; they are *tanto belli;* but to endeavour to imitate either of them would be deemed a most unprofitable speculation. A Greek fashion of regarding the gods.

Saint John alone is an exception to the rule—he is positively vindictive in seeing his bargains carried out to the letter and has become quite unpopular for that reason. I cannot help thinking that this is because he represents to the common mind some ancient and ferocious heathen shape, whose midsummer fires are lighted to this day in many places: inexorability being the proud attribute of all the older deities. "'Tis hard to reach the heart of Zeus."

I picked up a curious local legend which amalgamates this ancient shape with the more recent Adonis and the still later Christian saint. Here it is:

They say that Saint John had a purse of money. And there was a mother and a daughter. Said the daughter: "How shall we manage to take away his purse?" Then the mother answers: "We must cut off his head." They say that the daughter took a sword and cut off Saint John's head and took the purse. When the *festa* of Saint John comes round (midsummer) he sleeps the whole time, because, if he were to wake up, the world would come to an end. On that day, the mother and daughter are always running across the sky, the mother with a beam of fire in her hand, to burn the daughter for having cut off Saint John's head. When Saint John wakes up, he always asks Saint Peter: "I say, when is my *festa* coming round?" And Saint Peter answers: "That's past long ago!" The old men say that if one puts a plateful of water outside the balcony and looks into it, one can see in the sky the mother with the beam of fire in her hand and the daughter running before her. Says the daughter: "Mother, Mother, why did you say it?" Says the mother: "Daughter, daughter, why did you do it?" And all that day long they are running across the sky.

That German divine who lately traced, with some little exacerbation, Catholic institutions to their pagan origins, forgot to discover, or perhaps to mention, that his own pseudo-rationalistic
creed is far more deadly, since it infects those who lead the march of
culture. If Italians are ever to have that reformation of which they
talk so much, it is to be hoped that they will go a step further than
the Germans, who pulled up at the first *Wirtshaus*. Even now,
Neapolitans shrug their shoulders at Saint Januarius, whose
periodical liquefaction is a fine pretext for fireworks and military
music, and while the world is astonished at the nuptials between
the lord of a great *Kulturstaat* and the Antique Fraud, Catholicism
in Naples, ever serene and infantile, is gracefully expiring; its
venerable frame suffused, dolphin-like, with all the myriad hues of
the rainbow-tinted paganism whence it sprang. All this must be a
matter of climate. New names will supplant old names, but so long
as the climate of Campania does not change, its religious beliefs—
ceremonies, rather—will always cluster round radiant elemental
powers of sun and ocean.

We have wandered far, too far, from Crapolla. But there is
nothing to hinder us from returning when the mood fits. And let us
choose the sea-route on a night of full moon, for all discords dissolve
in the mellow sheen of a Southern night and blossom forth, if you
care to look, into new and ghostly harmonies. Peasants and bourgeois may sleep in their beds; your Siren-worshipper has this in
common with Arabs and other primitive folk, that he knows the
uses of night. (How often do the sensuous needs and pleasures of
civilization coincide with those of wilder stages!) At such an hour
the twin rocks guarding the entrance to Crapolla might well be
mistaken for the portal of some Ossianic realm—the representation
of it, rather; for stereoscopic vision being annulled, all depth and
distance, rents and ravines, are merely indicated by mauve shadows
upon a plain surface.

Have you never sailed under one of these precipices by moonlight? It is a picture that you see, not a palpable cliff of limestone;
a picture that floats past you; some enormous, silver-tinted cartoon
conceived by William Blake, in the mad moments betwixt sleep
and waking. Those ancient, seared rocks, so familiar at noontide,
have put on strange faces since the moon rose. Their complexion
has waned to a livid splendour, and their wrinkles and bosses
resolve themselves into unsuspected designs—designs of spears and

shields and bastions and all the pomp of heraldry that melt away, under incessant showers of gentle light from above, into other combinations of form, ever new and so convincing, that at last the mind, weary of riddles, surrenders to the stony enchantment and drifts along in a calm disdain of reality.

Such, maybe, was the spirit that swayed those blameless seekers of the Holy Grail.

VIII

RAIN ON THE HILLS

A MOST unusual occurrence, this steady summer rain. The sky is thickly overcast; it pours in sheets. A month ago, it might at least have done good to the country. But what is the country to me, weather-bound in a small village far from my base, with every prospect of spending the night half-supperless among strange folk and in a strange bed? What demon guided my steps this morning?

There is this at least to be said in favour of a region denuded of trees, that a summer rain cools the air. England, with its dense vegetation, exhales a steamy heat after a shower at this season, and the sodden fields, with their sleek round trees, make the wanderer feel more than ever as though he were some caterpillar crawling about an interminable bed of lettuces. Yes, English nature is too green, and that green too monotonous in shade and outline; it is (*entre nous*) a salad landscape; you may find pretty vignettes of the sugar-water type, but London alone is picturesque in the large sense of the word—London and Newcastle-on-Tyne.

This rain will produce a short-lived crop of grass, to be scorched again in a few days. The year of Siren land has only three seasons: the cloudless summer of brown fields, cicada-days; the green spell of rain and storms; three months of flowery spring. Summer melts into winter by bland transition, without hectic tints of death and castings of leaves, and when, in May, the grass begins to wither, the vines take up the joyous refrain. One fact must have struck all who have spent a summer here—the difference in temperature between the cultivated and barren lands. The latter are perceptibly warmer. The coolness of Sant' Agata is due not so much to its height above sea-level or to its exposure to the refreshing mistral as to the fact that it lies in an ocean of fruit-trees and leafy walnuts and hazels; nor is it their shade, but rather what Professor Marsh calls the "frigoric effect of leafy structure" which brings about the chill.

To step from sunshine into shadow is naturally cooling, but whoever enters this cultivated zone even at midnight will shiver involuntarily.

A few hectic tints there are, but one must know where to look for them. If, in the early days of December, you happen to glance down some of the gullies clothed in ilex, you will be surprised to see the uniform green surface flecked with alien markings. This is the flowering ash, companion of the ilex, about to cast its leaves; each tree has a particular tint which it reproduces year after year at this season; some are spectral grey, others straw-coloured, but the most beautiful are the deep crimson whose effect, among the sombre holm-oaks, is exactly that of the red spots upon a blood-stone.

A month before the cicada strikes up, the last firefly has already extinguished its candle. Ischia is as full of fireflies as the Sorrentine peninsula, but there is not one on Capri; too little verdure, perhaps, or too much wind. I have never watched the brilliant tropical night-luminaries with greater pleasure than these humble ones, for there are sounds in the jungle at all hours of the night, but here the attention is unconsciously riveted by what seems an anomaly in nature—the noiselessness of so much commotion. They call them *fuochi morti,* with reference to their flickering lights; other nations connect them with Saint John, the midsummer saint, which would be inappropriate here, as they are all gone by that time. On the other hand, the common wood-louse (*oniscus*) goes by the name of *porcello di San Giovanni,* and the naturalist Latreille seems also to have been struck by its resemblance to a little pig, for he dubbed another kind *porcellio.* How this diminutive beast came to be connected with the great saint is past my finding out; in point of pedigree, at least, it is not unworthy of him, for if Saint John goes back to Attis and Adonis, the "little pig's" ancestors were already great people in Siluria.

And still it rains. . . .

Wild and exhilarating perfumes will arise as soon as the clouds disperse. As volatile oils, they start from the ground; afterwards, when the sun has warmed the withered plants, each one begins to breathe out its characteristic odour. It is rather hard to analyse this fragrant multi-herbal emanation: I suspect that the dried fennel-stalks are the *Leitmotif* in the symphony. The cistus bushes, whose frail purple and white roses would enchant a Japanese artist, give forth a pungent aroma when the sun beats upon them; other spots are dominated by the honey-sweet savour of scorched thistles, of the wild juniper which, nowadays, can be seen to full perfection only on the inaccessible crags of Montalto, or the common fig. Those persons who are so curiously insensible to this last odour should go to a certain mossy court-yard overshadowed by gnarled fig trees and heavily permeated by their cloying scent: pleasant were the November hours spent here long years ago when nothing to the purpose was said, and every now and then a dry leaf, falling upon the pavement with a metallic clang, startled the tongue-tied ones into a full consciousness of their own thoughts. . . .

And far away can be descried, on clear days, a tall building, firm-seated upon a rocky eminence above Amalfi: the Torre di Orlando. This place is associated in my mind with the scent of wild thyme, for its terrace is, or was, overgrown with it. General Avitabile, an Italian adventurer and vice-governor of the Punjaub during the Indian Mutiny, whose life has lately been written by an Englishman, built this noble palace, intending to end his days there with a young wife whom he adored. Hardly had they settled down before she murdered him. 'Tis wonderful—to paraphrase a saying of Thackeray's—'tis wonderful what a woman may do, and a man yet think her an angel. But the general appears, from all accounts, to have been also something of a scoundrel. The house is at present to be sold; the bidders are many, but I am told there are sixty-two heirs to the property, and as soon as sixty-one have agreed on the terms of sale the odd man raises objections. So it crumbles to pieces, day by day.

And what more? Shall I tell of certain plants abhorred by the peasants? There is the asphodel, the flower of the Elysian fields, which became the English "daffodil", and whose derivation from *a-sphodelos* (unburied) may be fanciful, but is none the less appropriate, as can be perceived by anyone who tries to keep the stately roseate blossoms in a room. They call it *borro* or *cefalia*. Harmful to cattle, it multiplies incredibly and the roots insinuate themselves into the rocks with such demoniac tenacity that only dynamite will dislodge them permanently. "*Assai terribile, questa figlia di putana,*" I overheard a farmer saying the other day as, with pick-axe and crowbar, he endeavoured to clear a patch of ground of them for cultivation. Next comes the bitter sea-quill, known as *cipollana*, from its immense onion-shaped bulb. In winter a bunch of juicy green leaves crowns the root and nothing would be easier than to extirpate it at this season. But the peasant has other things to do just then; besides, he is waiting for the flower to appear in spring. Spring comes, but no flower; on the contrary, the leaves die away and the *cipollana* sinks into the earth and is forgotten. But in the heat of summer, when every other plant is withered and mankind walks as little as possible about the parched fields, detached spires of silvery blossom start in breathless haste from the ground. These are the flowers of the squill, beloved of Egyptian she-mummies as symbols of generation; the seeds are scattered broadcast in the nick of time to catch the first rain and the mischief is done. A sly plant. By the time the tell-tale leaves again sprout forth, the flowers have vanished; the peasant once more waits for the spring; and so on, *in sæcula sæculorum.* Unscrupulous Neapolitans import cart-loads of the leafless bulbs into the city, where the plant is unknown, and hawk them about the streets as "Californian lilies".

The ivy-leaved smilax is another pest; its inconspicuous blossoms smell sweetly for a few days and the red berries are pretty enough to see, but it is armed with poisonous claws and, once established among trees or walls, there is no ejecting it. They call it *raie* from its white roots (*radici*), which are sometimes boiled into a medicinal broth and which travel underground in all directions and at any depth, coming up to the surface whenever they feel inclined to make a fresh tangle of thorns for the discomfiture of optimistic cultivators. A friend of mine employed a man for a few months in eradicating them out of a small piece of land, paying him for the roots by weight; after an absence of two years, the smilax returned smiling from Tartarus.

Detested also by man and beast is the tree-euphorbia; even the goats sniff at its venomous secretion. But it is worth while strolling over these hills at the end of May to observe this plant before it sheds its leaves. Green all through the winter, it now takes on every shade of colour in its annual death-agony. No two bushes are tinted alike, not even when their roots are intertwined; earthy and ghostly white, orange and brown and vermilion, from coral pink to a rich burnished copper, from palest saffron to tawny gold. The red kinds are visible from afar and often shine with a lustrous iridescence, a rare freak of coquetry, like the *reflet métallique* of Oriental pottery. Ten days—and all is over; the gaunt stalks only begin to clothe themselves anew in autumn. Its acrid milk was formerly put to a singular use—the boys, in order to escape military service, injected a drop into their eyes, provoking inflammation and greatly puzzling the good doctors, till the trick became too popular.

Whereas the asphodel, owing to shallow soil, never attains any great size here, the "totomaglia" (euphorbia) seems to fatten on air and sun-scorched rock; one, a perfect monster of about sixteen feet in height, was lately cut down near Campanella: it yielded three faggots of wood, weighing, approximately, fifty kilograms apiece. Such giants are becoming scarce.

Other plants, rare and beautiful, grow in abundance on these limestone hills. The flora of Siren land has been better studied than other departments of natural history, particularly that of Capri; old Paolo Boccone already, in the seventeenth century, named certain plants peculiar to this island; others were engraved by the wise and lovable Cirillo, whose work remained incomplete (the first volume is dedicated to Sir Joseph Banks) because he was strangled by the Bourbons in 1799; Capri flowers have also been collected or described by Giraldi, Graeffer, Tenore, Gussone, and such a large number of recent botanists that a respectable literature exists on the subject. No one can fail to notice the red lily on the higher grounds, the gentian-hued lithospermum which fills up the crannies of the rocks, the wild stock, the brilliant vetch, the large purple anemone, and the blue thistle* (not so blue, however, as its representative on the African hills). It is astonishing that this plant, so common on the mainland of Italy, has not found its way to Capri. But the orchid tribe is particularly numerous there, twenty-eight species having been found. There is the sweetly smelling kind which is the last to blossom; bee orchids and butterfly orchids and birds'-nest orchids; the weird *homme pendu* orchid from which dangles the effigy of a man; others with monks' faces peering from under dusky cowls.

The little rock-islet of Monacone has a species of narcissus all to itself.†

And still it rains. . . .

It will be some time before the picture of this room is effaced from my memory. It is vaulted in the old style and the white walls are adorned with American calendars and advertisements; under foot, a richly tinted pavement of Vietri tiles, broken yellows and

* It is not a true thistle.
† Now considered problematical.

blues, dating from the days ere the modern Neapolitan ware, with its undignified patterns and anæmic coloration, was exported hitherward. The massive furniture gives an air of well-being to the place; upon a commodious wardrobe stands the inevitable *lar familiaris*—the infant Jesus—under a glass case, and a fine selection of *caccio-cavallo* cheeses, suspended from iron hooks in the ceiling, reminds me of the dinner awaiting me at home.

Patienza!

The good folk have retired into the kitchen region, leaving me in sole possession here; the rain seems to have chilled their wonted communicativeness; an uncle, too, has lately arrived from over the sea and certain family questions, I understand, are likely to become acute. Every ten minutes a polite young girl thrusts her head within the doorway to ask if I am comfortable. Incomparably more comfortable, I reply, than out of doors. Perhaps the signore would prefer to write with a *calamaio*? No, the signore will continue to use his pencil, having learned long ago that neither pens, ink, nor blotting-paper can be procured in the kingdom of Italy.

"A long letter," she ventures to remark.

"To my *sposa*—at Naples."

"My bridegroom," she informs me, "is twenty-two and has been twice to New York. The last time he returned with three thousand francs, and the next time we go together."

"Is that your engagement ring?"

"Yes; it cost him thirty-five francs. And this watch and chain, a hundred and fifteen francs. And now he has bought me twenty pairs of silk stockings and says I must put them on, all twenty, when we go through the American Custom-house, else the officials will steal them. I think it will be difficult."

"The *sposo* might wear half of them."

"Oh, he! He could wear forty, but he won't."

Of course she will marry him; they all do; the old maid, so familiar to lovers of English landscape, is practically unknown in Siren land. But the husbands seldom take them to America, contenting themselves with sending money home and returning every now and then. Like the women of Lemnos, these sit manless among their rocks, doing a little laundry work and an infinity of chattering.

The Italian field-labourers wash their clothes but never their bodies; the Russian, their bodies but never their clothes; ours—neither. . . .

Dirty clothes, says Saint Jerome, are a sign of a clean mind. Saint Bernard, if I remember rightly, lays down a contrary maxim. . . .

"Perhaps the signore would like to read? I have brought a book." Ariosto!

God forgive me; I cannot read Ariosto on a rainy day, and when the sun shines, he always contrives to make himself invisible. A very retiring disposition these heroic poets have.

Such modesty would ill become the present generation, and accordingly I find, in my very pocket, a modern trade circular—not always the worst kind of literature—Felix Alcan's catalogue. A pleasant sound, that name of Alcan; it smacks of—I know not what; of alcoves—alcohol. . . . It seems to me that the Jew is now doing more towards civilizing the West than he ever did in the past; he spends as liberally as we do, but more wisely, having a saner conception of charity: in short, he has learnt his lesson. And when the day of reckoning comes, the services rendered to the cause of enlightenment by Hebrew publishers and journalists will also not be forgotten. A nation fed upon Monsieur Alcan's pap has grown out of its infancy; it may well smile at bogies like *Jupiter tonans*, or *Vaticanus fulminans* with his attendant swarm of tonsured anachronisms. How we change! Here is a nation of Christians thanking Jews for their enfranchisement from the most odious tyranny on earth, that of the mind, engendered by a creed in defence of which they once persecuted them with fire and sword. The irony of history, with a vengeance.

What firm can show a list like this? Even if one wished to learn about things English, one could hardly do better than consult all these works on English trade unions, logic, psychology, free trade, ethics, and so forth. And our Anglo-American writers are represented in translations: Bagehot, Bain, Balfour Stewart, and all the rest of them. Have we anything approaching this widespread desire for knowledge; does our public ever hear of corresponding French authors, like Féré, Fouillée, Guyau? Would they care, moreover, to read abstruse works on *Éducation de la volonté* or *Solidarité morale*, many of which are here in their tenth, their twentieth, editions? And our publishers would not swoon away at the suggestion of bringing out those translations from foreign monumental works that figure here—at half the original cost? A poor student lamented to me some time ago that he was charged eighteen shillings for Shipley's *Invertebrata* and thirty-two shillings for Weismann's last book. "Young man," I said, "learn French—you are never too old to learn—and buy all your books, even those by English authors, in French translations; the balance saved, send home to your aged mother." "By Jove," he replied, "I never heard of anyone teaching French. The very thing! And as for that balance——"

Altogether—Alcan's catalogue: what a text for a lay sermon, if the preacher were not rather in the mood for edibles than ethics. Such, however, being the case, farewell, good monsieur! On some later occasion, perchance, I shall desire you of more acquaintance. Meanwhile, *Felix esto*. May your shadow, the *bulletin annuel*, never grow less! May it outlast the Bo-tree's in miasmic Anurajpura; may it outspread that of world-ash Ygdrasil, whose boughs encircle heaven and earth and in whose branch-charmed twilight the deathless gods revolve our fates.

"Can you supply me with something to eat, fair Costanza?"
"How not? Whatever you command."

Whatever you command. Fairy-like bubbles of Southern politeness which, when pricked, evaporate—as a friend of mine used to say—into indifferent macaroni. Yes; not even macaroni can be correctly prepared here; what goes by the name of parmesan being a compound containing ninety per cent of potato flour, while of butter, edible butter, not an ounce is made in all Siren land; statistics reveal a disquieting importation of margarine. Were those early authors, the Swiss Rehfues, the *junger Deutsche* of the *Fràgmente*, De Blainville, Portarelli, William Russell, and a dozen others—to say nothing of Boccaccio—were they dreaming when they praised the cow-products of Sorrento and Massa and Capri? No. But the vineyards have hunted grass out of the land; the timber-cutting has dried up all the hill-sides and watersprings. Fifty years ago the slopes of Monte Solaro on Capri were so thickly overgrown that the cows which pastured there used to wear bells round their necks in order that they could be traced in the dense shrubbery; three hundred head of cattle were exported yearly; nowadays, a single dyspeptic calf could engulf the whole island in a day, so far as normal fodder is concerned. May I never live far from a cow! A real cow, I mean—not a tottering, scrofulous phantom that skulks in dank cellars; a cow that eats grass and not bitter walnut twigs and sulphate-of-copper-bespattered vine leaves; a cow whose natural functions culminate in butter, not in lard. Oh that I had the framing of the laws! How I would broil certain respected merchants in their own margarine tubs—ay, and their wives and children—how I would broil them!

"We have a fish soup; *guarracini* and *scorfani* and *aguglie* and *toteri* and——"

Take breath, gentle maiden; the while I explain to the patient reader the ingredients of the diabolical preparation known as *zuppa di pesce*. The *guarracino*, for instance, is a pitch-black marine monstrosity, one to two *inches* long, a mere blot, with an Old Red Sandstone profile and insufferable manners,* whose sole recommendation is that its name is derived from *korakinos* (korax = a raven; but who can live on Greek roots?). As to the *scorfano*, its name is unquestionably onomatopoetic, to suggest the spitting-out of bones; the only difference from a culinary point of view, between the *scorfano* and a toad being that the latter has twice as much meat on it. The *aguglia*, again, is all tail and proboscis; the very nightmare of a fish—as thin as a lead pencil. Who would believe that for this miserable sea-worm with verdigris-tinted spine, which an ordinary person would thank you for not setting on his table, the inhabitants of Siren land fought like fiends; the blood of their noblest was shed in defence of privileges artfully wheedled out of Angeoin and Aragonese kings defining the *ius quoddam pescandi vulgariter dictum sopra le aguglie;* that a certain tract of sea was known as the "aguglie water" and owned, up to the days of Murat, by a single family who defended it with guns and mantraps? And everybody knows the *totero* or squid, an animated ink-bag of perverse leanings, which swims backwards because all other creatures go forwards and whose india-rubber flesh might be useful for deluding hunger on desert islands, since, like American gum, you can chew it for months, but never get it down.

These, and such as they, float about in a lukewarm brew of rancid oil and garlic, together with a few of last week's bread-crusts, decaying sea-shells and onion-peels, to give it an air of consistency.

---

* Its ridiculous airs and graces have struck even the unobservant natives, and small boys may be heard singing, among other *guarracino*-songs, the following ditty which I will transcribe phonetically for the benefit of the Ollendorff student:

> *Guarracino che ghieva per mar*
> *Ieva trattando di s'insudar*
> *Belle scarp' e ben pulit'*
> *Nu capiello a cannonat'*
> *E Nannina lo porta al lat'.*

This is the stuff for which Neapolitans sell their female relatives. But copious libations will do wonders with a *zuppa di pesce*.

"Wine of Marciano, signore."

"Then it must be good. It grows on the mineral."

"Ah, you foreigners know everything."

We do; we know, for example, that nothing short of a new creation of the world will ever put an end to that legend about the "mineral".

How unfavourably this hotch-potch compares with the Marseillese bouillabaisse! But what can be expected, considering its ingredients? Green and golden scales, and dorsal fins embellished with elaborate rococo designs, will satisfy neither a hungry man nor an epicure, and if Neapolitans pay untold sums for the showy Mediterranean sea-spawn, it only proves that they eat with their eyes, like children who prefer tawdry sweets to good ones. They have colour and shape, these fish of the inland sea, but not taste; their flesh is either flabby and slimy and full of bones in unauthorized places, or else they have no flesh at all—heads like Burmese dragons but no bodies attached to them; or bodies of flattened construction on the *magnum in parvo* principle, allowing of barely room for a sheet of paper between their skin and ribs; or a finless serpentine framework, with long-slit eyes that leer at you while you endeavour to scratch a morsel off the reptilian anatomy.

There is not a cod, or turbot, or whiting, or salmon, or herring in the two thousand miles between Gibraltar and Jerusalem; or if there is, it never comes out; its haddocks (haddocks, indeed!) taste as if they had fed on mouldy sea-weed and died from the effects of it; its lobsters have no claws; its oysters are bearded like pards; and as for its soles—I have yet to see one that measures more than five inches round the waist. The fact is, there is hardly a fish in the Mediterranean worth eating and therefore: *ex nihilo nihil fit*. Bouillabaisse is only good because cooked by the French, who, if they cared to try, could produce an excellent and nutritious substitute out of cigar-stumps and empty matchboxes. But even as a Turk is furious with a tender chicken because it cheats him out of the pleasure of masticating, so the Neapolitan would throw a boneless *zuppa di pesce* out of the window: the spitting and sputtering is half the fun.

"There is a fine *palamide*, too, from Mortella, brought in this morning. . . ."

It is the misfortune of Siren land to have been celebrated, since centuries, for these noble-looking fish, which are exported in thousands to the epicures of Naples and whose flesh tastes like shoe-leather soaked in paraffin. The natives, and not the foreigners, keep up the price of fish hereabouts; they are all icthyophagous, like the Athenians of old, and it is nothing short of a miracle that any kind of swimming or crawling creature continues to frequent these coasts, considering the way they are persecuted.

It is not good to be a fish in Siren land.

Hundreds of fry, which in a month or two would have weighed half a pound a piece, are caught to make a single dish; dynamite is also used, as well as the juice of the euphorbia and the roots of the cyclamen—locally termed *spaccapiatti*: split-plate—which poison the water and bring the fish to the surface. How admirable are the Italian fishery laws and how admirable it would be, for the little fishes at least, if they were obeyed, now and then! Latterly, too, acetylene has been substituted for the old-fashioned pine-torches at night, and with tremendous effect: the startled creatures collecting from far and near and thrusting their noses out of the waves to see the grand illumination. I have counted two hundred and eighty of these lights gleaming upon the dark waste of waters—they look like stars fallen upon the deep.

At this same Mortella (it lies near Cantone on the south side of the peninsula and the name derives from its myrtle-thickets) a tunny fishery was formerly established, which paid a yearly rent of four hundred ducats, and another one further along the coast at Sant' Elia; but the municipality, they say, taxed them so disproportionately to their gains that they emigrated to Conca. In these *tonnare* everything is caught except the tunny, which has wisely ceased to visit these regions. There was another establishment of the same kind on Capri, near the Palazzo a Mare, long ago.

From the summit of Mortella, too, you can often watch the dolphins playing, this stretch of sea being one of their favourite resorts. It is easy to conceive a liking for this sportive and classical beast, even if one disbelieves both the theory of Professor Schubert of Munich, who, in the nineteenth century (A.D.), wrote a treatise to prove that the human race was descended from a dolphin, as well as those old fables concerning his affection for mankind—how he helps them to catch fish, how he loves their arts and music, and has often saved the noblest of them from a watery grave. . . ..

And still it rains.

The window where I sit would afford a fair view upon vineyards and distant sea, if the panes were not streaming with the downpour, which can be heard rushing like a cataract into the cistern at the back of the house. It has converted the roadway beside the door into a water-course—sticks and straws and nondescript objects careering downhill on its yellow flood. . . .

That is a humane conceit, too, of the dolphin's piercing the armour of the crafty crocodile as it lies hidden in the muddy African river, enticing to death the compassionate traveller with mock groans and tearful complaint; and a pretty story is told by Aulus Gellius or another of the ancients about a friendship between a boy and a dolphin. Let me see if I can remember it.

Hermias lived with his father, a fisherman, and of all the boys who learned letters at the gymnasium none was blither of heart or comelier of limb, and none excelled him in those manly sports which were so highly commended in those days. Swimming was his chief delight, and so it came about that one day when he was far from land, having outstripped all his fellows in a race, he was hardly surprised to see a dolphin plunging alongside of him. It played about him in fondest fashion, hiding its deadly fin as in a sheath—for the smallest wound from a dolphin's fin is death to man—and, as soon as the boy grew tired, took him gently on its back and bore him to the shallow water. It was plain that the sea-beast had conceived an attachment for him, for the next day and on all the following days, when work was over and the lads ran down to bathe, Hermias found the dolphin waiting for him. Whenever he wished to play with his new companion, he used to call out, "Simo, Simo!" and the dolphin instantly swam to the shore to meet him, vaulting in glad wheels over the surface of the water. Why did he call him Simo? He never thought about it; it seemed to be his natural name.

The news of this friendship soon spread about the town, and crowds of folk used to collect on the beach to see the fun. Stranger things were done in those times than nowadays; nevertheless, it was so remarkable that even Octavius Avitus, a mighty great lord and governor of the province, came down to see the boy and ask him questions. The old fisherman alone hated Simo, for he knew that the merest scratch from the dolphin's fin would be fatal to his son.

"That fish-friend of yours", he used to say, "mislikes me.

Beware, my boy, of his terrible fin." Sooner or later, he feared, some mischief would happen.

Even so it fell out.

"Ah, Simo, you have hurt me!" Hermias suddenly cried out. He had jumped too heavily on the dolphin's back and scratched his breast on the sharp point. Then he laughed again and thought it a small matter.

Simo saw the waves stained with blood and guessed the truth. He carried him to the beach and watched him slowly limping homewards; he even tried to rise out of the water, so as to follow his boy-companion, but could only struggle a few paces up the dusty path. And there he lay, panting on the hot earth. He could hear the waves behind him, lapping on the sandy shore and inviting him to glide back into his cool home, but he thought only of Hermias. Great tears dropped from his lidless eyes.

"I am hurt, father," cried the boy, as he fainted on the doorstep. The fisherman laid him on the couch and looked at the wound.

"That is the dolphin's work!" he exclaimed with anguish. "My poor child—my poor child!" Hermias never spoke again.

Then the father took down a brave axe that was hanging over the couch, and nets and other implements, and a lusty pair of oars, and strode seawards to reach his boat, determined to battle with the murderer of his son. Suddenly he staggered backwards and the axe dropped from his hand: his enemy, the sea-beast, was stretched across the sunlit path before his eyes.

The old man stared in wonderment at this prodigy.

Simo lay in the agony of death. His eye was glazed, and colours of every imaginable hue chased each other over his smooth body, while now and again the flanks heaved, as though a sigh had escaped his heart. All at once his skin became wrinkled and ashen grey. The dolphin had died out of love for his lost playmate.

The townsfolk, when the heard the news, took counsel how best to honour the memory of this strange and strong attachment. They laid the two friends in one tomb, and over it they reared a marble statue of a fair lad astride upon a dolphin, in order that all who passed that way might learn that loving affection is still in repute upon earth. And Octavius Avitus, the governor, was not content even with this, but caused medals to be struck, with an effigy of the two comrades upon them, and therein showed not only his kindliness but also his understanding, for the tomb and the statue have long since crumbled away, but these coins are still scattered all over the world, bearing into distant ages the report of their happy friendship and unhappy fate. . . .

No tales of this kind are in circulation among the people here; still, they certainly regard the dolphin with no hostile feelings, probably because they have observed its reckless, death-scorning love for its offspring, which appeals to their own hearts. Regarding the fabled play of colours before death, I have also inquired: they know nothing. This may be due to lack of observation, for they have little eye for such things. But, so far as it goes, it coincides with my own experience, which I cannot claim to be extensive, since I only once had an opportunity of watching a dying dolphin. It had been harpooned and dragged on board, where it lay shivering and breathing hard. A youth was then seen to sharpen a long knife: he was a student of physiology. Turning up his sleeve, he plunged the blade swiftly into the dolphin's breast, whence he drew forth a quivering something, which he examined carefully. There was no iridescence—not the faintest trace of it; perhaps the death-stroke had been too rapid.

The fishermen here have elaborated what seems to be a myth for excusing this animal's ravages among the fish. It is not the common dolphin, they say, which is responsible, but a rarer kind called *ferone*. The *ferone* never travels in schools, but by himself; he destroys the nets out of sheer spite and makes a point of killing more fish than he can eat. When the *ferone* appears on the scene, all the common ones, the *fere*, take to flight. In short, he lords it over the others, he is guileful and malicious, and no death is bad enough for him. This reminds me of "bull-elephant" stories in India, and may possibly have the same foundation in fact.

A much more mysterious monster is the *gatta marina*, or sea-cat. It raises its head above water to see where the nets are, and then dives in that direction to eat the fish in the meshes. It has four feet with prodigiously long claws and only comes at certain seasons, and then not always. Its colour is black—that is, not altogether black; and it weighs less than a hundredweight, but often more. It is covered with a sort of fur, rather like the dolphin, but a little different. Nobody eats the sea-cat except some people, who do. . . .

Inexhaustible is the fish-lore of Siren land; they have a firm belief that everything which creeps and flies on earth has its counterpart under the waves. Shall I tell you of the sea-turtle and how, every now and then, a "marine flea" crawls under its flapper, which makes it very angry, because at such times, it can only swim sideways in an absurd fashion, and all the other fishes laugh at it and pull its tail, till at last——

"Perhaps the signore would prefer a hen?"

No, thank you. I know those hens and how they are caught. This is the manner of it. The careful housewife singles out the scraggiest of her fowls, which forthwith stops eating and watches her steadily with one eye, doubtless aware of her intentions. The preliminary coaxing being of no avail (it is merely done for form's sake), five small boys are despatched in pursuit with sticks and stones. They begin by liking the job, for their prey, sure of victory, marches straight in front of them without deigning to look round, an easy mark for projectiles. One stone grazing its tail, it takes flight and settles in the vineyards on the hill-side, amid howls of execration from the boys. Other pursuers are roused and join in the chase; a cloud of missiles envelopes the bird as it gallops and flutters over stones and up trees, into gullies and thickets; the rabble vanishes from sight—you can hear them shouting a mile off.

An hour or so having elapsed, the hen is seen, a speck on the horizon, flying down from the mountains in a straight line, pressed hard by an undaunted knot of pursuers. *Sant' Antonio!* It is going into the water like last year! And, sure enough, it glides into the waves about three hundred yards from the shore and begins to preen its remaining feathers. May its mother be barren! May its children die unblest! The boat—the boat! It is launched, and at the very moment when the oar is about to descend with a crash upon the muscular frame of the victim, it rises like a lark and perches upon the roof of the church. *A chi t'è morto!* Out with the ladder! All work ceases in the village, the school is closed for the day; the priest and the tobacconist, mortal enemies, are observed to exchange a few breathless words. Bedridden hags crawl into the piazza and ask whether there is an earthquake. No, the hen! The church! The signore! The foreign signore wants the hen—the hen on the church! Just as the nimble *figlio di Luisella* has placed his foot upon that last rung of the ladder—*Ah, Santo Dio!* It has flown away, away into the brushwood, where none but the swiftest and surest-footed can hope to follow.

Towards Ave Maria it is carried in, vanquished. The conqueror, streaming with perspiration and attended by the entire populace, proudly holds it up for your inspection by one leg—the other is missing. A small boy, reluctantly, produces it from his pocket.

Is this a hen?

There is not a vestige of feathers on its body; the head, too, seems to have come off in the heat of the fray. The conqueror tells you that he could have shot it, but was afraid of spoiling its plumage. The careful housewife asks whether you will have it boiled or *al cacciatore*?

What is left of the bird looks as if it were already half cooked. . . .

IX

THE LIFE OF SISTER SERAFINA

A N authoritative, religious biography of Sister Serafina di
Dio, the Christian ornament of these regions, was published
at Naples in 1723, and further details concerning her can
be gleaned from certain *Positiones super Dubio*—ecclesiastical writings
printed at various times with a view to procuring her beatification
and containing statements as to her life and habits made by eye-
witnesses under oath. From these sources, and from them alone, I
cull the following facts, so far as they concern her. And inasmuch
as these documents prove her to have modelled the incidents of her
birth, life, and death in a truly amazing manner upon those of the
more celebrated Spanish nun, Saint Teresa di Dio (born nearly a
century earlier), I will occasionally refer—for a reason which will
become apparent later on—to the latter saint, whose biographies
are in the hands of all scholars. . . .

This remarkable woman, foundress of seven convents of the
Carmelite order, whose influence extended beyond the limits of
Siren land, was born, the third in a family of six children, at
Naples on October 24, 1621. Her father was a Neapolitan man of
business, and her mother—she was the man's second wife—
belonged to the noble family of Strina, which is conspicuous in the
mediæval records of Capri. She was baptized, on the day of her
birth, in the church of Saint John at Naples, receiving the worldly
name of Prudentia; and it was observed with surprise that the
infant did not weep during the ceremony, but kept her eyes gravely
fixed upon the officiating priest.

Saint Teresa's mother was of nobler stock, too, than her father.
She was, moreover, the mother's third child, and likewise the offspring of her father's second marriage. And furthermore she was
baptized on the day of her birth, in a church dedicated to Saint
John.

At an early age, the child Prudentia was taken to Capri, where

she lived with her parents at the foot of the Castiglione hill, and at
a remote house which is still pointed out in the district Moneta as
the "house of Sister Serafina". In this rural solitude, as it must have
been in those days, she soon began to read the *Lives of the Martyrs*,
and to brood over their past torments and present bliss—fervent
dreamings, which were strenuously fostered by her mother, as well
as by her maternal uncle, who, as her confessor and parish priest,
had been able to discern in the infant all the elements of future
holiness. Doubtless this compilation, that has produced many saints
and ascetics, profoundly influenced the unfolding of her childish
mind, but her mother had simultaneously hit upon a second and
equally effective device for working upon little Prudentia's emotions:
she used to take the child into churches and chapels* and allow her
to gaze, wonder-struck, upon the marvels within. Flickering lights,
odours of incense, sternly resplendent images, grave and wondrously
clad priests, swaying censers, and rapid torrents of exultation from
the organ overhead: all these contrivances, so strange, so purposeful,
so different from the green and sunshiny fields of Moneta; and all
of them moving to the glory of Something still more wonderful,
still more mysterious, that hovered around and above the altar—
how indelible an impression must they have made upon the fabric
of her young senses! When adults, with fairly developed reasoning
powers, cannot withstand these sensual allurements, what shall be
expected of a child? Without understanding a jot of the meaning
of all this golden pantomime, her thirsty youth drank it in, and with
such effect that in later years Sister Serafina could never retain full
control over herself at the sight of a holy object; her trances were
of so peculiarly an automatic form that at the sight of a crucifix,

---

* Among these, the hermit chapel on the summit of the "Villa Jovis" is
particularly mentioned, and the picture of Madonna del Soccorso which she there
worshipped exists to this day; it is the oldest of its kind on Capri; the type is semi-
Byzantine and of that dark tint (*bruna, nera, schiavona: nigra sum, sed formosa*) which
is credited with peculiar efficacity. Many of these miraculous pictures, like that
of Monte Vergine or the "brown mother" which was imported to Naples from
Mount Carmel, were painted by Saint Luke, but some are unquestionably of later
date. So the managers of the Pompeii sanctuary have wisely acquired a genuine
"black" madonna, which was manufactured not long ago by a Neapolitan artist.
Black idols are also adored in Russia and Greece—the idea goes back to Pessinus
and the Kaaba, to lingams, meteorites, and what not. This chapel, by the way,
used to be dedicated to Saint Leonard, one of the many saints of Siren land who
have faded away before the effulgent humanity of the Mother of God, whose
picture was then appropriately "discovered under a mass of old masonry": a
common motif all over Italy.

for instance, she would at once fall into an ecstasy, thus learning to believe implicitly and devoutly what most of her fellow-Christians can but dimly hope to understand: the Real Presence. The crucifix which *spoke to her* (like that of Saint Thomas Aquinas) is still preserved at Massa.

Saint Teresa was very remarkable for her crucifix worship.

The penances which this infant imposed upon herself reached the number of twenty a day. In order to cleanse her tongue for the reception of the Eucharist, to which she had been accustomed since the age of eight, she would lick the ground; she disciplined herself with chains, poured hot wax upon her skin, and was advancing fast, by these and similar outrages upon her body, in the favour of God, when the devil was permitted to make use of certain light-hearted girlish friends in order to bring about, as he thought, her destruction. She was then a lively and beautiful girl of fourteen, and the following avowal to her confessor reads rather seriously: "To put it shortly, plainly, and truthfully, I have committed all the sins that can be committed in this world." In point of fact, her earthly cravings had merely manifested themselves in a reprehensible desire to see the carnival like her friends; a desire that was providentially not gratified because, finding in her pocket a copy of the *Legends of the Holy Virgins*, she glanced into the book and was led to see the error of her ways before the masks appeared on the scene. A severe reaction followed upon this irregularity, and further diabolical attempts by seductive or terrifying images were victoriously repulsed.

A more important matter, and one that marks an epoch in her development, was the determination of her father to have her married to a Neapolitan acquaintance. This father, although pious enough (two of his brothers were Jesuits), strongly disapproved of what he called his daughter's religious excesses and, judging a rich and happy marriage to be a sound counter-irritant, pressed the matter forcefully, and would doubtless have gained his point but for the wiles of the uncle, the parish priest, and of a certain Sister Ippolita, a Dominican nun, who played, at this period, the rôle of spiritual intermediary between Prudentia and Jesus, her Elected Spouse. Sister Ippolita, a shrewd woman, understood that this was no time for half-measures. She cut off Prudentia's long and beautiful hair, dressed her in some of her own oldest clothes that were absurdly too big for the girl, and induced her to present herself in this garb before her enraged father, whose exact words the biographer, perhaps wisely, fails to report, though their sense may be inferred from the statement that he heaped threats and maledictions upon his disobedient child. After this defeat the father yielded, like a sensible man, to the importunities of his household, and was thenceforward left in peace. He had done his best, and failed. We are told that throughout life he had been little more than an instrument in the hands of the devil, so far as Prudentia was concerned, and it was not without significance that he should die early, confessing his errors and imploring the pardon of his virtuous daughter who was now left, at the age of twenty-four, to indulge her genius without fear of contradiction.

Saint Teresa, it will be remembered, was also led into an excess of childish piety by the *Lives of the Martyrs*. She too, as a comely girl of fourteen, was tempted by the devil, who made use of certain youthful friends to compass his end. And, exactly like Sister Serafina, she was re-converted through the instrumentality of a nun and a pious uncle.

What that genius was, may be read in the life of Saint Catherine or any of her innumerable prototypes in mediæval or still earlier Christianity. It was an uninterrupted rhapsody of love to Jesus, her Spouse. She was "consumed, burned, maddened, suffocated, intoxicated, liquefied" with Love; she "desired to turn to ashes by reason of the Fire of Love, and then arise in order to become ashes once more out of Love". Her voluminous writings (an enumeration of their titles and contents fills nearly five printed folio pages) breathe an atmosphere of intensest passion—of love, warm and palpitating; they are essentially non-theological, personal lucubrations. For she had all the mystic's impatience of dogma; when touching, at the suggestion of her confessors, upon themes like the Procession of the Holy Spirit or the Incarnation of the Word, her speech at once becomes obscure; how indeed—as Professor Maudsley asks—how speak ineffable things save in unintelligible language? Like Teresa, she merely coquetted, if I may decently so express myself, with the mysteries of the Trinity, that tremendous doctrine which exerts, from its very incredibility, a magnetic attraction upon this class of persons, affording the simplest test of what constitutes religious mystic, whose mind, attuned to improbabilities, discovers to be plain, necessary and beautiful, what others describe as—somewhat puzzling.

Saint Teresa's epigram on this subject, "the greater the absurdity, the more I believe", finds an echo in Sister Serafina's pious exclamation: "O luminous obscurity, so clear to all who love you!"

And what may be called the Gothic or Hell-fire sub-species of Christianity, with its charnels and skeletons, inspired her with peculiar and proper disgust. She could not bring herself to think upon these gloomy aspects of her faith, the bottomless pit, the wailings, fiery torments, and gnashings of teeth; convinced, like many other charitable Christians, that the threat-and-bribe system was incompatible with a pure and spontaneous love to God. "A strange thing," she says, "that one should love God out of interest or out of fear." For this reason, she "wished to abolish Hell and Paradise alike".

Even so, Saint Teresa desired to "blot out both Heaven and Hell".

Nor did her religion lack that typical roseate complexion which demonstrates that *naturam expellas furca, tamen usque recurret*. Her numerous letters and poems to her Divine Lover would shock the ears of Northern Puritans; they resemble the languishing Celestial Amours of Saint Gertrude—amorous plaints, couched in language that might be addressed with equal propriety by some terrestrial Juliet to her Romeo. The very name of Jesus was of so sweet a taste in her mouth that on uttering it she frequently swooned away, and was therefore obliged to deprive herself of this joy in the presence of others "till she was given sufficient robustness of spirit to repress these external movements". In this respect she resembled a certain bishop of Saluzzo who, according to Saint Alfonso di Ligurio, perceived such a pleasant aroma in his mouth each time he pronounced the sacred word *Maria*, that he invariably licked his lips afterwards.

She had been subject to ecstatic conditions ever since the age of eight. She distinguished, during these trances, four principal modes of perceiving the presence of Jesus: the student of psychology will find them highly interesting, as they are defined with the pseudo-scientific precision of the Spanish nun.

Saint Teresa also speaks of four modes, though later on, in the "Castello Interior", she raised the number to seven.

This is how her trances appeared to others:

"One evening she retired into her cell so liquefied with love that she seemed actually to die, and she began to say: Do you not see

Jesus Christ? making signs towards the altar, which was visible from her cell; and became so liquefied that she fainted away, so that we could hardly hear the words she was saying. Sometimes she said: "*Dio bello, quanto è bello Dio!*" and whilst uttering these words she seemed to die, and then suddenly laughed aloud, and cried almost at the same time, and seemed deprived of all strength. . . ."*

It was not long before her Divine Spouse gave token of His particular affection for her. He told her, in visions, "Thou art my bride—I wish to remain ever with thee"; indeed, He loved her, we are told, more than she Him, and thus spake He to the angels: "Behold how fair is My bride, how she resembleth Me; yea, she is altogether My image"; and she, on her part, would remain convulsed with joy on hearing the word *Amami* (love Me) softly uttered as she partook of the Celestial Food. In order to render herself more worthy of His affection she indulged in an orgy of mortifications such as would have killed a more grossly constituted individual. Her very chastity became a form of voluptuousness; never was maidenly modesty carried to a more frenzied pitch. As an infant at the breast she had already felt uneasiness when a man entered the room, and never ceased crying till he left, and such was her sensitiveness in later years that on discovering that one of her pupils secretly cherished a portrait of her brother, a male, she fainted with grief and surprise, and would have died outright "had not Christ, compassionately appearing to His bride, fortified her soul". She refused to sit in chairs that men, even priests, had previously occupied; suckling infants of the male sex were not tolerated within the precincts of her convents, and her eyes were so well trained in a downcast look that, walking one day in the streets of Naples, she accidentally collided with her head against the feet of a criminal who was hanging from a gallows in front of her, to the intense astonishment of passengers.

Earthly womanhood was even more distasteful to her, for while she regarded men, exclusive of priests, as a necessary evil, a beast by nature, whose only *raison d'être* in this world—Saint Jerome held the same view—was the procreation of female children for conventual purposes, women were grievously to blame, if they chose the wrong path. After an unavoidable visit to her convent of the wife of the governor of Capri, who came in somewhat fashionable

---

* Whoever wishes to understand the true nature of these seizures will find ample materials in the works of Havelock Ellis and other modern scholars.

attire, she addressed her pupils on the appalling example of vanity displayed before their eyes and, as a humiliation, set the example of taking a skull and licking it with her tongue in every part. Her infectious zeal fired them to cut off their hair and torture their bodies with a variety of instruments which the biographer describes as "horrible to behold", in spite of the protests of the parents, who reminded Sister Serafina that hers was an educational establishment, a *conservatorio*, and not a nunnery—claustral confinement was not inaugurated here till nearly a century after her death—all this, "in order that they might render themselves more attractive in the eyes of God", whose taste, on the subject of female beauty, would seem to differ considerably from ours.

More repulsive to her than all was any manifestation, or even hint, of the natural functions of womanhood. The *Life* speaks relatively little of her love to the Mother of God, and, reading between the lines, one gains the conviction that even the motherhood of the Madonna, so touching and sublime to many, was hardly congenial to her ultra-virginal mind. Thus, when the Virgin and Son appeared to her simultaneously, she was always in a dilemma whom to adore, and finally she prayed the Virgin not to bring the Son, as He attracted her so strongly that she feared to be wanting in due reverence towards her. "She was so ravished by the incomparable beauties of the Divine Son that she reverently prayed the Virgin Mother to excuse her if in His presence she lacked due respect for her"—a frame of mind which the Mother of God, we are told, benignly appreciated. This is what we should expect, for even holy men cannot escape from the toils of their organic nature. So male saints, in all times and places, prefer the milder charms of female divinities, and the greatest panegyrists of the Madonna have always been of that sex.

Nothing but the ideal youth, spotless and eternal, of Jesus or Saint Michael appealed to her heart. This may be purity. But it is the purity neither of Nausikaa nor of the sage ("The purity which proceedeth from knowledge is the best."—*Mahabharatha*).

The same comparative lack of veneration for the Mother of God was a marked trait in the Spanish nun, who, like Sister Serafina, wrote innumerable love poems and letters to Jesus and was finally adopted by Him as bride.

I will not weary the reader with a list of the torments which

Sister Serafina underwent in order to please her Spouse: the catalogue of her cilices and other machinery for self-torture is a truly
formidable one. She would pray for hours, extended in the attitude
of crucifixion on the stone flags of her cell; she starved herself, and
her girdle, to prevent her from satisfying hunger, was so tightly
drawn that it was found at her death imbedded in the flesh; being
forced by the physician to eat meat, to which she had been un-
accustomed, she experienced a double joy—the joy of swallowing
what was pre-eminently unpleasant to her palate, and the joy of
immediately vomiting what her stomach refused to contain. Her
modesty forbade her to take a bath, but when this became urgently
necessary on account of her health "she discovered a manner of
enjoying an heroical suffrance by sitting in it when too hot, so that
all the skin came off her body". Many of her penances are devised
in apparent emulation of Elizabeth of Hungary and far too nause-
ating to be printed; disorganized, indeed, must be the mind that
thinks to please its Maker by such refinements of nastiness that even
an enthusiastic religious eye-witness, beholding these things, is
obliged to confess: "Which when I saw, I grew sick, and reverently
vomited." Instead of ordinary food, she lived on the Eucharist. Its
Mysteries had become Realities and she saw through the veil of its
earthly allegory into the bright realms of truth beyond. Her confessors were perpetually forced to interpose their authority to
restrain this luxury of self-maceration, and her implicit obedience
to them is all the more remarkable in one who, by her hourly
personal communication with the Powers of Heaven, could well,
one might suppose, have dispensed with any mediation on the part
of man. Can obedience go higher than this?

"One day having been forbidden to approach the Sacred Table,
she perceived Jesus coming towards her after the consecration of the
Host and kindly inviting her to partake of it; Whom nevertheless
this child of perfect obedience repelled. . . ."

The confessors of Saint Teresa were likewise obliged frequently to
moderate her excessive love of penances. Like Serafina, she worshipped obedience, regarding it as the greatest of the virtues.

One result of this godly mode of life was the inevitable impair-
ment of health. Sister Serafina was infirm throughout life; one ill-
ness alone lasted for ten years and brought her to death's door. She
suffered from chronic feeling of heat, while hallucinations of all the
five senses were everyday occurrences; she was declared to be

"hectic" and inwardly consumed to cinders, though free from all organic disease.

Even so, Saint Teresa was delicate throughout life and near death's door at one time; she had the same hallucinations and feelings of heat; she was likewise declared to be "hectic" and inwardly consumed to cinders, though of a naturally vigorous constitution.*

Yes; they were all "burnt", these spouses who approached so near to the Most Highest; for God is a consuming fire. . . .

But another result was an increase of favours showered down upon her by the Divine Lover, who now openly avowed His predilection for her. The stigmata appeared on her hands; her heart was wounded with a dart borne by an angelic child of about twelve years of age, "presumably Jesus Christ"; she enjoyed ecstatic raptures of Heaven and Hell, and wrote, under spiritual guidance, upon the different methods of prayer.

How miraculously parallel is the career of Saint Teresa! She had the same visions of Heaven and Hell and wrote similar treatises upon methods of prayer; the stigmata likewise appeared on her hands, while an angelic child, belonging to the highest order of cherubim, transverberated her heart with God's spear. (See Bernini's monument in the church of S. M. della Vittoria in Rome.)

Sometimes Sister Serafina wrote at the inspiration of Jesus, and it is with surprised regret that the reader of the *Life* learns that a dissertation on Divine Love, *taken down at the immediate dictation of Our Lord*, has been deliberately discarded from this work. Why has the author neglected to publish this treatise? "On account of its length!" Surely this, in a book of seven hundred and forty printed octavo pages in double columns, filled with so many irrelevant details and repetitions, is an unpardonable oversight! Her influence in celestial spheres was such that the patron saint of Capri used her as a vehicle of communication with the Pope, and the Pope, in his turn, besought her intermediation with Heaven. She was furnished with the services of two guardian angels (Saint Teresa had but one), and with what amounts to almost the same thing, namely, the enviable gift, common to many pious persons, of a vision which decides on all occasions of doubt what is to be done. This comfortable faculty, indeed, if the matter be regarded aright, does

* A recent author, A. Marie (*Mysticisme et Folie*, Paris, 1907), discovers traces of constitutional hysteria in the Spanish nun.

constitute the piety of pious people and contradistinguishes them from ordinary mortals, who have only judgment and experience to go upon; for how shall they whose every action, down to the most trivial of life, is regulated by divine orders—how *can* they go far wrong? She performed many miracles, such as appearing in two places at once, foretelling the deaths of friends and others, curing diseases by touch, and instinctively detecting priests who had led immoral lives.

These are among the very miracles of Saint Teresa.

The laws of nature were frequently "suspended"—to use a phrase popular both with Gibbon and the late Duke of Argyll—at the request of Sister Serafina; she allays a storm at sea; quiets an eruption of Vesuvius; like Saint Anthony of Padua, she preaches to animals who understand; like Apollonius of Tyana or the *flying monk* Saint Joseph of Copertino, she is levitated and suspended in air with her head almost touching the ceiling; like Sixtus V and General Manhes, but unlike anyone else in ancient or modern times, she succeeded in extirpating brigandage in the kingdom of Naples; she is useful for childless families, and undergoes a variety of flaming transformations: all of which things are seen and vouched for by devout persons, whose testimony needs must fortify those who possess any belief in the value of witness to the miraculous. But, in my opinion, the most useful wonder that she performed was by liberating in September, 1683, through her intercession with Saint Michael, the beleaguered town of Vienna, the bulwark of Faith, from the Turks. Little did the inhabitants of that city think that they, and thousands of their fellow-religionists, were saved from a fate too awful to contemplate through the supplications—more effectual than those of all Christianity combined—of the humble nun of Siren land. This act alone, if her biographer is indeed not mistaken, might be thought to entitle her to that honour of beatification which fell to the lot of Saint Teresa.

These peculiar graces provoked not only the envy of man, who is ever ready to persecute with his calumnies all that emerge above the common herd, but also of the devil. Throughout life Sister Serafina had frequent visitations of the prince of darkness, and her behaviour in these embarrassing moments may be commended to all who undergo similar experiences; for instead of proceeding to Luther's lengths of undignified personal rudeness, she tried rather conciliatory methods, and once actually induced him to pray and adore

the Saviour. For the rest, his insinuations were not always character-
ized by the astuteness with which he is commonly credited. One
day she observed a young man seated in the corridor of the convent,
guitar in hand, who informed her that he was tempting the nuns—
a transparent device, which she had no difficulty in confounding
("The Devil as Troubadour" is a common apparition all over
Christianity—cf. Lermontoff's *Demon*.) Such was her reputation in
the infernal regions that the devils were heard complaining angrily
that she would not let them settle even upon the roof of the monastery.

Saint Teresa, too, had life-long conflicts with devils.

Altogether, there is an astonishing uniformity in the lives, miracles,
penances, temptations, and deaths of the ten thousand saints that
have sprung up from the fertile soil of the South. Many of their holy
idiosyncrasies, such as self-mutilations, devil-visitations, odour of
sanctity, etc., will be found to be already the property of pagan
predecessors in every part of the world. Is this due to wilful plagiar-
ism? Surely not. It is due to the small range of their mentalities,
for in proportion as materials are limited, so will their permu-
tations and combinations be limited. Like some great writer on
human affairs, who fails to express his rich and varied thoughts in
the restricted medium of a provincial dialect through sheer de-
ficiency of adequate words and phrases, even so the Great Contriver
of all things, harping, for His or our pleasure, on the same few
strings of these His poor defective instruments, can coax forth no
fresh sound, but ekes out lack of novelty by reiteration of monotony.
Nor let it be forgotten that the merit of Catholic saintship belongs
by one half, at least, to the confessor, to whom these willing creatures have surrendered body and soul for the glorification of himself, his Order, or his God.

With the approach of the seventh climacteric an immense change
comes over Sister Serafina: it is nothing less than a psychic revolution. From being an ascetic dreamer, a trembling Spouse of
Christ, a writer of visionary colloquies and poems, she is transformed into a practical woman. There are convents to be founded.
Her friends and relations fostered the scheme; the apostolic injunction *virgines castas exhibere Christo*—what anguish would have been
avoided if that phrase had never been written!—was interpreted
as implying a command, and a timely vision in a Neapolitan church,
during which the Virgin and her Son gave minute instructions

as to the order of the monastery to be founded, and the colour and cut of the clothes of its inmates, naturally left her no further choice in the matter. She at once went to Capri with seven Neapolitan girls who were to become the first inmates of a convent which was dedicated to the Saviour, but is generally known as Saint Teresa. We are told that the building of this establishment cost about 150,000 ducats; this will give some idea of the energy and resources of its foundress. Where had she found the money?

The fearful plague of 1656, which crept over from the mainland, they say, in a lock of hair sent by a maiden to her lover on Capri, had claimed among its victims Sister Serafina's mother, as well as her pious maternal uncle and confessor, the parish priest, who made a will on his death-bed leaving his wealth to his niece on condition that it should be employed in the erection of a convent. This was a very humble start, but a divine vision promised further help, which presently arrived, contributions flowing in from her new confessor, from the Archbishop of Amalfi, the Viceroy of Naples, and other devout friends and relatives. The convent was completed in 1678 and festively inaugurated by Cardinal Orsini, afterwards Pope Benedict XIII, who was Sister Serafina's firm friend throughout life. (It was about this time that she permanently discarded her worldly name of Prudentia.)

It had been a fierce struggle. So much local opposition had been raised by the clergy and populace of the island that the work was nearly abandoned at one time, though it proceeded rapidly towards the end. The devil, too, with characteristic malice, endeavoured to raise an obstacle at the very moment of inauguration: he delayed, up to the day preceding the ceremony, the despatch from Naples of a large slab of marble destined for the high altar, and as it arrived nevertheless in time, he caused it to break in two pieces during its transport; but the crafty cardinal, determined not to be outdone, discovered a block of antique travertine, which served the purpose equally well.

Saint Teresa, too, underwent a complete revulsion of character at the approach of the seventh climacteric; a new epoch begins; the mystic is transmuted into a shrewd and active woman. She had a divine vision in church which commanded the foundation of her first monastery. The work began like that of Sister Serafina, in humblest fashion; but another vision promised help, which presently arrived. Yet she had to combat so much local opposition that the building was nearly abandoned: later on, it proceeded rapidly, though the devil took a personal interest in the matter and contrived a variety of obstacles.

Meanwhile other convents were being built by Sister Serafina; one at Massa Lubrense in 1673; another one, two years later, at Vico Equense. A fourth grew up at Nocera in 1680, while the large one in Anacapri was constructed, in 1683, in accordance with a vow made during the Turkish siege of Vienna to the Archangel Michael, who, having performed his share of the bargain, insisted politely, but firmly, upon the fulfilment of hers. Next, a convent was reorganized at Torre del Greco in 1685, while the seventh and last was consecrated at Fischiano near Salerno in 1691. Thus, in a remarkably short space of time, these establishments were begun and ended.

One of the chief peculiarities in their internal organization was that they were nearly always recruited from the first convent of Saint Teresa on Capri. This, in its turn, was filled by girls from Naples, as the islanders, acting probably under orders from their bishop and clergy, looked askance at her schemes from the outset. The inmates were all of good families, and in Anacapri most of them had two rooms and a servant. From Capri, where they learned the rules from the lips of the foundress, they were transplanted, as occasion arose, to her other institutions, and such was their discipline that even after her death the nuns of Capri were held in great request for reforming convents. It is not reported in full how far those rules differed from those of similar houses; they are described as "veritable distillation of the finest perfection of Christianity", and elsewhere as "those of Saint Teresa, but accommodated to various circumstances of time and place, some things modified, others added, whenever she thought them necessary for the improvement of souls".

It may be well to enquire what gifts enabled Sister Serafina to carry forward these great works. She possessed a dominating personality, a wholeheartedness and zeal, the vehemence of which swept all opposition before it. What persons animated by one single idea, and that grounded on pure emotionalism, can do, may be seen in the life of Mahomet or Joan of Arc or, for that matter, of Saint Teresa. She would have allowed herself to be hewn in pieces rather than yield in her conviction, and all who came under her influence—children, paupers, bishops, workmen, sinners, politicians

—were swayed to think as she did. Of her power over the female mind, a pathetic example occurred when a young girl, who loved her home and had long resisted all temptations to be won over to a more saintly life, yielded at last to the torrent of Sister Serafina's golden eloquence and confessed that "the *disordered love to her parents*, by which she had been previously blinded, had left her heart". Another instance of this hateful destruction of the most sacred ties of humanity is afforded by the history of a nun of Saint Teresa convent. As a vain young girl, she had been persuaded to kneel down before a crucifix by Sister Serafina who then, with great fervour of spirit and in a loud voice, exclaimed to the Symbol: "God of Abraham, God of Isaac, God of Jacob, illumine this creature", and hardly had the girl heard this terrific invocation (for the strange-sounding Semitic names must have been less familiar to her than to Protestant Bible-readers) than "she saw five rays of light issuing from the five wounds of the Crucified, which, uniting together, formed as it were a dart which came towards her and perceptibly wounded her heart, making her feel as though she had entered from a great darkness into the Light", whereupon Sister Serafina joyfully called the others to embrace the new nun. This account is curious, as it illustrates the artificial production of an illusion under the contagious influence of what Murisier calls *expectant attention*: doubtless the identical form of deranged vision that manifested itself to Sister Serafina upon every provocation.

Pious eloquence alone will not build convents. Unlike many enthusiasts, this one, in her worldly relations, kept well within the bounds of sanity, and her calm self-restraint and business capacity in the presence of man affords a striking contrast to her self-abandonment towards God. The analogy with Saint Teresa instantly occurs to the mind. How useful this gift must have been during the construction of her various convents, in reconciling the conflicting interests of workmen, architects, and landowners, in steering her path through the inevitable social intrigues of priests and private families that are connected with all such undertakings, may easily be imagined. It was these practical talents, inherited, no doubt, from her much-despised father, that commended her to the notice of the high ecclesiastical dignitaries who employed her for these various tasks, and in this respect she may not inaptly be compared to Swedenborg, who had likewise inherited from his father a judgment in earthly affairs that was often surprisingly sane. But here the likeness ends. The Scandinavian dreamer speaks from celestial heights as the friend, nay, the instructor, of angels, and his hysterical utterances, that reflect the violent climatic changes of his home, are always expected to contain some hidden allegory which his disciples must unravel if they wish to save their souls: Sister Serafina is only an occasional visitor to Heaven, not an *habituée;* she is humble in the presence of the heavenly hosts, and there is no misinterpreting her central, narrow, but intense creed of love, for it glows as the bland and steady sun "under the roof of blue Ionian weather".

In her own department she was a born administrator. She would take no child over the age of thirteen years, and preferred them still younger, even four years old. This surprised others, but she knew, from personal experience, the importance of perverting the senses ere reason awakes; to seduce the enemy's outposts while the main body of his troops is yet distant—what general will not admire these tactics? She was particularly severe in not allowing intimacies between girls, well aware of the truth that it is evil communications, and not evil examples, that corrupt good manners. She disapproved of their undue affection for confessors; their love should be all for God. Widows and others who had been in contact with the world were not encouraged to enter her convents, and this, again, is true wisdom—of its kind. . . .

No significance need be attached to the fact that the rules of Serafina resemble those of Teresa, as she deliberately set herself to copy them, which can hardly be said of involuntary things, such as hallucinations, visits from celestial personages, and miracles performed after death. Yet the reader of Teresa's life cannot but be struck by her surprising similarity in traits of character to the other: she had the same passion for making nuns; she was equally severe in not allowing friendships; like Serafina, she did the humblest menial work in her capacity of prioress; she made the discipline harsher than many nuns could bear, etc. etc.

A life so active was not without tribulations. Her independence, her originality, and, in one word, her success were provocative of no small ferment on the island of Capri, for a woman enjoying familiar converse not only with cardinals and other exalted members of the Church, but also with supernatural powers, exposed herself to much friction with the local clergy who could claim no such distinctions, and who resented her influence upon the family life

and general social condition of Capri. This lurking grudge sometimes broke into open conflict; she was often on the worst of terms
with the bishops who, for the rest, were not always distinguished
by appropriate pastoral virtues. Thus, in 1652, Saint Costanzo
was obliged to appear in a vision to Sister Serafina, requesting her
to draw the attention of the Vatican to the unsatisfactory conduct
of the bishop, in consequence of which the offending ecclesiastic
was suspended from his functions and an apostolic vicar appointed.
Nor was she the only person who had difficulties with these prelates:
the prior of the Carthusian monastery on Capri obtained an order
from Gregory XV "that the monastery may not be molested by the
Bishop of Capri", and, at an earlier period, a papal injunction had
been issued against the local secular clergy "who, with armed
hands, robbed the farms and live stock of that monastery at the
instigation of their bishop". Stirring times. . . .

She had also her competitors, if such a word can be used. A small
island like Capri, which contained at that time only two thousand
inhabitants, would seem to have had its spiritual needs sufficiently
supplied by a saint like Sister Serafina, two monkeries and two
nunneries, a bishop and a staff of about fifty priests, to say nothing
of innumerable errant religious teachers of various denominations,
two archbishops and half a dozen bishops within a few miles,
and at least six permanent resident hermits as examples of holy
life.

And yet we learn that about 1695 "the islanders had little assis-
tance in spiritual affairs" and that it had therefore been deemed
advisable to send out for their guidance and consolation the Father
Bonaventura da Potenza, then a young man. The biography of
Sister Serafina makes no more mention of this incident than the
biography of the male saint makes of her. He lived in the ancient
monastery of San Francesco, and though he performed miracles and
penitences after the manner of his kind, yet he seems to have lacked
the *éclat* of the mystic nun, and his stay on the island—doubtless
merely an anti-Oratorian demonstration—was cut short. He left,
after three months, for Ischia; convinced, probably, that Capri
was not large enough for two saints at a time.

There were more serious matters. She was accused in her younger
days of immoral relations with her uncle and confessor, the parish
priest, an affair that gave rise to a "horrible scandal", and the
Bishop of Capri, without inquiring into the matter, punished both

severely, but afterwards relented. There is no reference in her biography to this story, which I refuse to believe, though the Devil's Advocate (whose duty it was to reply to the above-named *Positiones super Dubio*) doubtless made good use of it by designating the priest's legacy for the construction of the convent as an "expiatory" one.

She was called a hypocrite, witch, drunkard, liar, lunatic, thief: all of which things she bore with Christian meekness. She was accused of consulting twelve books of necromancy and, strangest of all, or adorning herself with lace undergarments. Here we see the foolish lengths to which human malevolence will go. Lace underwear! Will calumniators never learn that there are limits to what can be believed? And yet, according to Lea, this was a favourite accusation on the part of the Spanish Inquisition.

She was inveigled into the controversy concerning Molinos the quietist, whose insinuating doctrines spread rapidly and had wrought much mischief among the faithful before they were discovered to be heretical, although she wrote a treatise condemning the views of the subtle Aragonian monk, a treatise which was the fruit of a vision during which Jesus expressed to her His horror that "these persons" would do away with His humanity. This vision is interesting on account of its self-evident genesis; it was generated by her own strong preconceptions upon this subject, for if Christ were to lose His humanity, love for Him, as she conceived it, would lose its flavour.

Saint Teresa was also particularly sensitive regarding the humanity of the Saviour.

So long as she remained superior of Saint Teresa convent all went well, but on resigning the post she was often ill-treated by her successors and subjected to every kind of malignity and petty annoyance.

The most painful episode in her life was her imprisonment in her cell, without the consolation of the Eucharist, for two years and a half, by order of the Inquisition—a humiliation that redounded in the end to her glory, for by decree of the holy office she was liberated in 1691 and declared to be "most innocent of the charges laid against her". I do not know what these charges were; the *Life* hints at the matter obscurely, to the effect that the "holy office was desirous of trying her spirit". It is pretty certain that she would not have been treated so well but for the intercession of her friend the powerful Cardinal Orsini; and the true cause of this violent seclusion is doubtless to be sought in the old rivalry between Jesuits and Oratorians—Sister Serafina was largely under the influence of the latter order—that broke out at this period in recrudescence of a peculiarly petulant character. She had been frequently confessed by Jesuits, who helped her at times but, as is seen in this matter, could also become her bitterest enemies.

Even so, Saint Teresa was frequently confessed by Jesuits, who assisted her on some occasions and turned ferociously against her on others.

Excess of piety and impiety alike aroused the hatred of this infamous band of man-demons, whose repeated discomfiture in the kingdom of Naples does eternal honour to its inhabitants. What, after all, can possibly be the explanations of an institution so anti-human in its aims and methods? Is it not a form of Sadism? The movement towards enforcing sacerdotal chastity which began soon after Hildebrand, and the rise of Orders like Dominicans and Franciscans who strove to make the ascetic principle a reality in life, produced a mania intelligible enough to a modern alienist: a mania for the infliction of cruelty. These flesh-subduing tendencies on the part of the religiously earnest crystallized themselves in the person of the mediæval inquisitor, whose office, ostensibly designed for promoting orthodox notions, was in reality a contrivance for the relief of lust by the infliction of torture. *Usque recurret!* The procedure itself, carefully framed so as to afford the judges every opportunity of tormenting the accused who, by the same rules, was deprived of all chances of explaining himself, proves this sufficiently clearly: a form of Sadism. . . .

I linger upon the personality of this energetic single-minded woman, for she is the embodiment of what the Hellenic spirit was *not:* its very antithesis. Earthly existence she held to be an illusion; the world was death; the body a sinful load which must be tortured and vexed in preparation for the real life—the life beyond the grave. To those Greeks, the human frame was a subtle instrument to be kept lovingly in tune with the loud-voiced melodies of earth and sky and sea; these were the realities; as for a life beyond, let the gods see to it—a shadowy, half-hearted business, at best.

Is it not a suggestive coincidence that her convent at Massa should have been built upon the presumable site of that old

Siren temple, perhaps with its very stones? Here, upon this spot, these two ideals confront one another, threatening, irreconcilable. . . .

And now what of this religion of Sister Serafina?

To pronounce upon it, is to pronounce upon the Christianity of which she is an exponent or, at least, a representative. She was a nun, an enemy of normally constituted human society, and in so far to be highly extolled among her fellow-religionists, since "the true monk"—to quote the words of Professor Harnack—"is the true and most perfect Christian". But the monasticism of the seventeenth century, though it still professed the ideals and conformed to the three fundamental rules of earlier days, could not fail to be profoundly modified in form and method by the events of fourteen centuries.

The Christianity of Sister Serafina is that of Saint Teresa. It appeals to primitive, but not always noble, impulses in human nature. Too indolent to scale the heights of doubt or dogmatic speculation, it avoids those fruitful sources of dissension and finds contentment in phlegmatic submission to authority; too selfish to expend its energies in altruistic schemes, it silently disregards, while professing loudly, the perilous and irksome doctrine of neighbourly love; too sensual to desire or conceive an impersonal deity, it throws the impetus of its misguided sexual yearnings into a sub-carnal passion for the Son of God who, by a presumption unique and degrading, is supposed to appreciate and actually to reciprocate such sentiments: the whole edifice, if it deserve that name, being interpenetrated and enlivened by mysticism, the convenient refuge of all who can feel, but not reason. No wonder its adherents declare themselves ready to die for so comfortable a creed; but martyrdom, whatever Dr. Johnson may say to the contrary, is a test neither of truth nor of usefulness.

And yet, as a religion, it lacks not vitality—the vitality of the tortoise, a living fossil, uncouth, rigid of structure, tenacious of life. For unlike most things upon earth, Christianity cannot be improved. The many "modernized" varieties of that cult which invite criticism with inevitable and fatal results—how unfavourably do they compare with that of Saint Teresa, which not only ignores critical methods but actually thrives on ridicule and turns so-called disproof to its own nourishment. This is its strength, and in this sense, and because it fosters the emotions and leaves reason severely alone, it may truly be called a Christianity after the heart of its founder. *Let him become a fool, that he may be wise.*

This is assuredly not the best that can be said of the faith of Sister Serafina, but it is the truth; and when it is added that hers was a somewhat grim and uncompromising personality—she had all the *adamantine hardness* of Saint Teresa—it may well be asked wherein lies the attraction which she exercises even upon those who differ fundamentally from her in their whole conception of life. Simply in this: that she was a sincere, homogeneous entity. What she believed to be true she sought with all her heart, and this alone entitles her to respect in a world that is only too full of composite, disharmonious characters, where sincerity and saintliness do not always blossom on one tree, where each wears a different face according to the occasion, and the few religiously minded are either sunk in drowsy pragmatism* or distracted by frantic endeavours to reconcile ancient folk-lore and modern science.

The twofold aspects of her Christianity are admirably epitomized by herself in a letter to a confessor: "O that I could shed a thousand times my blood for the saving of souls; I weep for the Turks, heretics, and other infidels, and for Christian sinners", but then follow immediately the words: "O that I could steal all the daughters from their mothers and lock them in a monastery."

She lived in an atmosphere of cowardice, intrigue, and hypócrisy;

---

* Pragmatism: the last ditch in the metaphysico-sentimental steeplechase; a bastard Buddhism which the artistic Professor James has conjured up, like an enchantment, out of the rubbish-heaps of Koenigsberg and Athens. And yet, watching the antics of a certain disciple, he must sometimes experience sensations akin to those of a domestic fowl which has hatched a duckling. "The only certain and ultimate test of reality is the absence of internal friction." What is this but Newman's *illative sense*? I like a thing, therefore it is true: pleasure the test of truth! Rather let us ask: what reality has ever been established without internal friction? Or again: "The Beatific Vision as the ideal of knowledge." What is this but the "divine frenzy" of Plato or Saint Teresa? Under such auspices, conscientious intellectual labour may well take a back seat; after pragmatism—the new Messiah. I have not followed recent phases beyond noting that Mr. Hobhouse, in the *Aristotelian Proceedings*, has made short work of these mystic, creative-feminine dreamings, while Mr. Peirce, the inventor of the word pragmatism, has been obliged to coin a new one "pragmaticism", in order to explain what he originally meant: an ominous symptom which reminds one of Goethe's "*wo der Gedanke fehlt, da stellt das Wort sich ein*". What is the whole of pragmatism but a systemization of those disordered flashes of intelligence that animate the savage or child, who create realities to coincide with emotional states? Its votaries yearn for the nonreal, for consolation from the bewildering stress of phenomena: the *horror of a fact* underlies all such conciliatory, "*demi-vierge*" systems of philosophy.

she saw mankind in some of its worst aspects and suffered experiences that might well embitter a saint; but her faith remained childlike and mild. There are, to be sure, occasional spasms in her writings that savour more of the ferocious vindictiveness of the Old Testament than the unwholesome slave-morality of the New; yet, on the general score of tolerance, she may be held up as an example to Christians of all colours. Our intelligence, our humanity, turns with loathing from the unspeakable cult that thirsted for the blood of the noblest, and would gladly furbish anew its rusty engines of horror: had its adherents thought and felt as Serafina did, there would have been no burnings and thumb-screwings, no hagglings as to probabiliorism, *filioque*, or Gadarene pigs—unlovely phenomena, calculated to make the world-reformer despair of uplifting a race that can wallow in such abysses of criminality and absurdity.

We may unhesitatingly condemn the compulsory seclusion in convents of sane and well-behaved individuals, but it is well to suspend judgment on certain other aspects of her life. She cultivated fasting "in order to have the mind more free to think of God". What, in itself, more laudable? And if early training and natural disposition had caused her exalted tendencies to run in one particular direction, are therefore similar mortifications wholly to be eschewed, or is it not rather true that, mischievous if carried to excess, they constitute nevertheless a veritable means of procuring enlightenment? No advancement in learning will come from gross feeders; whoso seeketh knowledge must mortify the flesh; the wisdom of all ages is proof of this. Many who are paid to preach continence to others would be listened to with greater respect if they practised it themselves, and some of Sister Serafina's "spiritual exercises" would assuredly have no harmful influence upon the pampered prelates of our own Church.

But the majority of those who divine this truth fail to grasp it entirely, and thus it has come about that the splendid ideal of self-discipline, which has given to humanity so much of beauty and of use, has likewise created monstrosities of the type of Macarius or Simon Stylites; for the machinery of the mind is artfully balanced and the penances must be precisely such that the nerve-centres respond to the finest impulses—beyond that point lies the dream-region, where the ravings of an ill-nourished brain are mistaken for divine truths.

Self-macerations can be defended only on hedonistic principles.

5*

Arguing on these lines, it may clearly be contended that neither the philosopher nor yet the Christian dare disapprove of the maxim that each may do as he likes with his own body (*If thine eye offend thee, cut it out:* contrary texts, as usual, are at hand), and that pleasure, which entails no harm on others, may be sought where it can be found by every one, according to his varying tastes and temperament, let the manner of it be condemned by the physician, derided by the worldling, and imitated only by the fool. Such practices bring their own reward, for saints who despise the flesh will necessarily leave no children to inherit this idiosyncrasy, which perhaps accounts for the extinction of the saintly species in these later days.

Above all things, she must be judged in relation to her times. Devil-beatings were commoner then than now, but sane thinking is still at a discount; *incubi* have merely been replaced by "Christian Science". . . .

And lastly, it is important to remember that the appearance in these regions of types like Sister Serafina is of an episodic character; they are not an indigenous growth, but a fruit of that graft of Spaniardism which—if we are to believe modern Neapolitans—is the greatest evil that has ever afflicted their province. Spaniardism is responsible for the cloud of monks and confessors that settled like locusts upon the land and of whose deadly works the reader may form some opinion from the pages of Giannone—himself their victim; for the shattering of political life and of wholesome domestic ideals by spy-systems, Jesuit-horrors, and the enforced seclusion of women in inner chambers, of children in convents; Spaniardism brutalized the Neapolitans by beast-shows, dazed them with ultra-Oriental ceremonials, maddened them by outrageous exactions, bad faith, by the gallows, the rack, and the wheel; Spaniardism filled the provinces with the fierce unrest of brigandage, shackled in ruffs and grandiloquent buffooneries the old native freedom of costumes and of speech; it smothered letters, music, arts, and science in the sandy deserts of theology and infected decent Catholic observances by an alien ascetic taint, by gloomy absurdities of the Saint-Teresa type,* and by a hideous and still-persisting realism

---

* The viceroys introduced her cult, and one may speculate to what an extent such a tissue of puerile fictions, forcefully disseminated by confessor and civil magistrate, sapped the well-springs of common sense and of common morality. "It was a curse of the Spanish administration, to make the present unendurable

such as when, on Good Friday, the head of the Crucified is orna-
mented with real human hair, while His body and the snowy
winding sheet are bespattered with fresh cow's blood, in order to
make the effect more "life-like". There have been unceasing protests on the part of Neapolitans of all classes, priests and laymen,
against these abominations which the viceroys imported from their
savage and sombre Spain, the least Christian of all Catholic
countries. Thus, Signor Manfredi Fasulo has discovered at Sorrento
the declaration of two young girls of noble family, aged twelve and
sixteen respectively, who in 1555 went before a notary and publicly
avowed that "they did not wish to become nuns, being, on the
contrary, somewhat in favour of the married state". Great must have
been the abuses ere timid children could be driven to take a step
of this kind. Indeed the history of Siren land during this period is
one long wail of suffering; it will be long ere the Spanish virus is
eliminated.

Her end was full of griefs.

For many years she had suffered ill-health and a variety of
calamities. A rebellious faction sprang up in the convent of Saint
Teresa; the superior lost no opportunity of ill-treating her; the
nuns were at discord among themselves; a slip of paper with a
variety of improper words on it, was found pinned to the door of
her cell. Her own niece drowned herself in the cistern of the convent,
a sad and mysterious affair that "caused much gossip"; some spoke
of incurable melancholy, others, in whispers, of harsh treatment.
Powerless to help, she saw a rapid decline going on under her very
eyes. Meat, which she had contrived to eliminate from the bill of
fare (Saint Teresa had done the same), was plentifully eaten; the
nuns refused to rise at early hours for prayers; the spirit of chastity
abated; a friendship between a priest and a *conversa* gave her much
pain, and the dismissal to Naples of a young doctor to whom many
inmates of the convent had shown themselves more attached than
may have been needful, was attributed to her machinations and
gave the signal for open rebellion.

During her last days all was trouble and confusion. She was
hated and avoided by the whole establishment, and some of the

and to sow no seed for the future . . . a pattern of what a government should not
be"; so says von Reumont, in his *Carafa von Maddaloni*, a carefully documented
study of this period, which deserves to be brought up to date. (An English translation in Bohn's Edition.)

nuns insisted upon leaving it, although they were warned that they would lose one half of their dowries. Simultaneously with these inner convulsions there arose such a mighty tempest at sea that no doctor could come from Naples, and her ordinary confessor, who had been apprised of the approaching end, was unable to console her dying moments. She had to content herself with the ministrations of two Capuchin monks who happened to be on the island, as she seems at this time to have been on bad terms with all the local secular clergy.

Nor was this all. For the devil, driven to desperation by his repeated failures to undermine her saintliness, took violent measures and was heard beating her in her cell. How the nuns were able to distinguish these diabolical flagellations from those which Sister Serafina habitually inflicted upon herself—sometimes a thousand strokes without interruption—we are not told; but we may rest assured that this somewhat brusque method of persuasion, not unknown in the histories of other saints, met with as little success as it deserved.

Sister Serafina viewed all these tribulations as a particular favour of Heaven, for she had always prayed that she might depart this life purified in the crucible of griefs, in torments, and alone.

Even so it fell out.

After lying for some days in an ecstatic condition, and in the attitude of crucifixion, she expired on March 17, 1699, in the seventy-eighth year of her age. And immediately there followed a general reconciliation in the convent; all were united in such love and perfect charity "as had never been her lot, during life, to witness". She passed away in a trance of love and with paralysed tongue. Her corpse, assuming a roseate hue, remained incorruptible and flexible for a long time and exhaled an ineffably sweet perfume; her blood flowed as freely after death as in life. . . .

Thus went to her rest, in the *odour of sanctity*, the venerable Sister Serafina di Dio, and as to her present state no Christian can be in doubt, for if Paradise be reserved for those who practise poverty, chastity, and obedience with all the sincerity of a simple heart, then assuredly she is sitting there now. She performed miracles three years after death and gave advice as ghost; her picture sweats and speaks, the oil that burns before it being medicinally useful; pieces of her clothing are efficacious as talismans, and pilgrimages to her tomb have been known to produce cures for various ailments, though I have been unable to obtain authentic records of any recent cases.

She was buried, amid an incredible concourse of people, in the church of S. Salvatore on Capri; but in 1813 her coffin was taken out and reverently entombed in the parochial church of that island, and, in 1820, once more reverently changed to another part of that church, whence, in 1856, it was again shifted, reverently opened and closed again, and deposited in a different locality, whence, in 1893, her remains were once more removed, examined by the chief medical officer and other notabilities, sealed up again, and laid to rest elsewhere, with a lengthy inscription to record these reverend exhumations and peregrinations.

May she now rest, if possible, in peace!

Before her burial, however, a number of pious experiments had been made with her corporeal parts, in order to justify a claim to saintliness. A death-mask was taken thirty-four hours after her demise, but the plaster of Paris became warm from the heat of her corpse, the cause of which was soon seen to be the heart, which exhibited miraculous signs and, like that of Saint Teresa, maintained heat throughout her body. The lungs, the liver, the kidneys were all taken out and found to bear tokens of a holy life; the bowels were likewise removed and examined, and on the fourth day after death her veins were again opened and blood flowed freely, proclaiming her miraculous state. Five days later her scattered remains were collected in a coffin, and crowds of men and women came to satisfy their *pious curiosity* by gazing upon the decomposing organs of this venerable ascetic. To their hallucinated senses these poor shreds of mortality appeared more lovely and fragrant than ever. Truly an edifying spectacle! The pagans, for superstitious purposes, scrutinized the entrails of beasts: the Christians, those of saints. . . .

The concordance with the Spanish nun, in these latter events, is so amazingly close that, were not similar parallelisms observable in the life-histories of many other saints, a critical reader might almost be tempted to suspect the biographer's *bona fides*. Without dilating upon these extraordinary coincidences, it will suffice to report that Saint Teresa, too, died in a trance of love and with paralysed tongue; that her corpse, assuming a roseate hue, remained incorruptible and flexible for a long time and exhaled an ineffably sweet perfume; that the blood from her dead body flowed as freely as during life; that her coffin was frequently shifted about, while her soul performed miracles and gave advice as ghost.

Nevertheless a medical practitioner, who was called to view the remains of Sister Serafina, refused to depose that they were *in statu miraculoso*, whereas the physician who examined those of Saint Teresa had no hesitation in giving a certificate to that effect.

I cannot say how far this conduct on the Italian doctor's part proved a hindrance to the beatification of Sister Serafina, or to what an extent his Spanish colleague's certificate weighed favourably in the balance when the case of the Spanish nun was considered. Save in this one microscopic detail, the saintly lives and works of these two mystics are so alike that it would seem hardly just to refuse the highest honour to one of them merely by reason of the pronouncement of a worldly professional, who may well have been mistaken, prejudiced, or even bribed to conceal the truth. Nor will I endeavour to solve the enigma of the quasi-miraculous concordance in the lives and deaths of these two women, but my reason for referring so frequently to Saint Teresa will now be clear: namely, that the reader should observe what apparently trifling circumstances can influence the decisions of the Vatican. A carnal doctor's certificate *seems* to dispose of Sister Serafina's claims to the honour of beatification; outweighing a lifetime of saintliness, of miracles and Christian propaganda in which—to judge by the official biographies sanctioned and approved by the Pope—she differed not a jot from the more fortunate Spanish ascetic. In view of the issue at stake, such a respect for the pronouncement of a nameless man of science would be regarded, even in lay circles, as a kind of rationalistic bigotry.

Her contemporaries, at least, judged well of her merits; hardly was she in the grave before the project was set afoot to procure her beatification; among the number of these early promoters I find the name of "Jacobus Tertius Magnæ Britanniæ Rex". The attempt has been repeated up to the days of Leo XIII without success; and thus she, who deserves the title of Beata as well as many another one, must content herself, meanwhile, with that of Venerabile. A Carmelite Pope would doubtless entertain the project if the necessary gold were forthcoming, and Monsignor Canale, the religious historian of Capri, naively but correctly laments the poverty of the island as the cause of its failure. Yet saints have often waited long for their final honours—Saint Elizabeth, for instance, three hundred years; Saint Leopold, three hundred and fifty. These regions have also grown richer of late, while the price of canonization, according to Silvagni, has now been reduced to 200,000 francs.

Thus the hope of many may still be realized, if the stream of wordly prosperity at present flowing into Siren land from Argentina can be diverted into channels of unworldly zeal.

X

OUR LADY OF THE SNOW

How strange is that process of mental association, and how a mood, the most volatile of things upon earth, will often persist and grow into a suggestion and become attached to some locality, twining itself inextricably among houses and fields and pathways! Can anything be more unlike these many-folded radiant coast-lands than the interminable plains of Russia, with their pale skies and weary humanity? Yet the first time I came here I fell in with a Russian gentleman and his daughter, and memories of that ephemeral acquaintance have tinged the country for me. He was not even a true Siren worshipper, such as I have met many since that day; he came here on account of his health, and she, either to be near him or to think out certain problems for herself. Parthenope was Greek to both of them.

Still there are Sirens, too, in the chilly waters of the Baltic, and the name of one of them, Roussalka, was soon to have a mournful sound in many Russian ears.*

Although I never met them after that winter, the septentrional mood is apt to return, like the subtle odour of birch trees clinging to the olives and myrtles of an alien shore. No harm in this, for things are best perceived by contrasts; the Englishman, who never submerges his identity, is a good describer of foreign lands, and the image of the South is not seen so clearly on the spot as when it rises like an exhalation before the mind's eye amid hyperborean gloom. That was a sage remark of him who said "the material furnished by the tropics can only be utilized in a Northern atmosphere".

The good Ivan Nicolaevitch was probably a professor of philosophy or geology at some public institution, but I never had the curiosity to inquire; I like to taste my friends, but not to eat them.

* *Roussalka* (Mermaid) was the name of a training-ship which went down in the Gulf of Finland.

He can hardly be alive at this day. As for the daughter, she may well be sojourning in Siberia, for she was a liberal of the type which Russia needs and therefore banishes. As I remember her now, she seems to have been one of the million good-humoured Northern girls with barbaric splendour of complexion and eyes of intense velvety blue, eyes like twin mountain lakes lying deep down in fringe of fir, calm and mysterious. The father was of another type, pale with a straggling beard—meekness graven into every line of his face; full of perplexing and suggestive theories, one of them—based, he said, on "statistics"—to the effect that the next Messiah would be a Russian pauper, and another, that parents ought to be forbidden by law to argue with their children (he detested Locke). His ideal was state management in everything, a delusion which crops up in the "anticipations" of many modern writers who would complicate life instead of simplifying it.

Forcibly were those times recalled to me when I revisited the Cimentaro, where we had been together. The Cimentaro is a bank of volcanic tufa which lies in a valley above Massa; they hew tunnels into the soft material and extract it as a building stone. You can cut it with a knife. It becomes more valuable—that is less spongy—the deeper you excavate, and the rock is not blasted, but artfully split away from the cliff with wooden wedges and then chopped up into blocks of convenient size. Walls built of such friable stone must necessarily be thick and coated with plaster against the damp, but it is none the less cheaper than limestone in the long run.

My friend was hugely interested in the operation. At last he said:
"We have no stones in our country. Before a house can be built, a road must be laid down to bring the stones for the house. And before the road can be built, a railway must be laid down to bring the stones for the road from God knows where—Finland, perhaps. The railway? It is laid, at first, on wood."

It struck me as an extraordinary statement. But I found it sufficiently true when I visited his country some eight years later.

The tufa of Naples is of yellow tint and harder in texture than this, which changes, in proportion as its moisture evaporates, from a rich purple-brown through mouse colour and hyacinthine shades to a bluish grey. They tell me it costs four centimes a brick at the quarries, but the price is doubled and even trebled by the time it reaches its destination, for it must be transported on the backs of mules who can only carry about seven bricks apiece. These volcanic deposits probably date from the times of the grand Phlegræan eruptions.

Days of the Titans! Like a section of an Emmenthaler cheese is the map of that smoking Cimmerian region west of Naples with its craters, great and small, many of them now submerged beneath the waves but still traceable with the sounding-line, that belched forth in prehistoric ages a fiery deluge; the sea must have turned solid, for its caves and inlets are chocked up with cinders; the air likewise, since deep deposits, like this one, are everywhere. At Villa Nova, on Capri, you can see bombs of pumice over a metre in circumference: conceive the height to which they must have flown in order to reach this spot in their parabolic descent! Vesuvius, whose last column of ashes rose eighteen kilometres into the firmament, is a child's popgun when compared with these engines of primeval wrath. And the sport went on for centuries. No wonder the firm-seated limestone was "dislocated" in these earth-convulsing battles of the giants, and Capri and the Siren rocks shook themselves free from the mainland.

The church of Pastena, higher up the stream which flows past the Cimentaro, reposes on a bed of this material, and here and there along the sides of the valley, at various elevations, can be seen patches of tufa resting upon its limestone ledges. They tell a curious story, namely that the river-bed was already fashioned by water at the time of the catastrophe: the stream was temporarily choked up and obliged to do the work of erosion over again. Whence I conclude that the Cimentaro is an aerial formation—that it fell from the sky to where it now is. And if this be the correct way to account for these upland deposits, it would surely be more logical to extend this explanation to the immense contemporary layer on which Sorrento stands, rather than to postulate an aqueous origin of which we have no proofs.

From here we walked, I remember, through the village of Monticchio up to the summit of Monte Arso, the burnt mountain, which Maldacea described as an extinct volcano—so easily are legends formed from names. It was *burnt* only because unproductive in his day and has now ceased to merit this designation, being crowned with a house and green vineyards. The rock of the Tore is a soft Tertiary sandstone called *macigno*, which overlies the limestone in many places; all the lanes are paved with it, and often have

I thanked Providence for causing Massa to be built in the neighbourhood of its quarries, for it is never slippery in summer and never
wet in winter, whereas the limestone is objectionable at all seasons
unless one goes barefoot or wears the corded shoes called *paragatti*
which were introduced from Spanish South America. The peasant,
with characteristic anthropomorphism, calls this sandstone *pietra
morta*, dead stone; as opposed to the *pietra viva* or limestone.

It is hard work, at first, bringing such recalcitrant stuff into a
fit state for cultivation; the stones must be crushed and mixed with
earth and the trenches for the vines excavated to a depth of six
feet. But the trouble is amply repaid, and green oases, like this one,
are now springing up in various parts of the Tore. I have tried to
obtain data of revenue and expenditure, but in vain, as the cultivators are shy of giving information which might lead, they think,
to an increase of taxes. Certain it is, after the vines have begun to
thrive, that the produce of a single season will often exceed the entire
initial outlay including the cost of the land—not a bad speculation,
therefore, for those who can afford to wait a few years.

This peasant on Monte Arso has also had the luck to strike water,
if luck it can be called which is the inevitable result of digging. The
Tore are saturated with springs which dry up, for the most part, in
summer, but there must be a permanent supply of liquid between
the porous *pietra morta* and the impenetrable limestone. To Ivan
Nicolaevitch it seemed a simple matter to tap this reservoir by
means of artesian wells sunk through a few feet of sandstone, and a
profitable one, seeing that the villages are largely dependent on
rain water collected in cisterns which is apt to fail or to become
tainted, although living eels are kept in them for purposes of
"purification". But I should like to see the faces of the gentlemen
of the *municipio* if his proposal were submitted to them. No doubt
the water of clean cisterns is purer and cooler than this surface-
flow, but they are not always kept as they should be; many hundred
people draw their supply from one not far from here which was
recently found to contain 1440 micro-organisms to the cubic centi-
metre.

Here, beside the "burnt mountain", stands the burial ground of
seven villages; it is called Santa Maria della Neve—Our Lady of
the Snow. A depressing place. Nature is cheerful all around, but
within—an ill-kept square of earth, immense and bare, surrounded
by high walls and overgrown with weeds. Are these people so poor

that they cannot do anything for its appearance? It is hard to
believe; money is pouring in from America.

No Sirens will sing dirges on a spot like this. Yet that was their
charge in olden days; they were divinities of death, symbols of
funeral chant and lamentation, and this one attribute of their many
was reverentially clung to by the Athenians.

Upon the grave of Sophocles was sculptured a Siren, bewailing
the loss of the master whose golden voice was to be heard no more,
"and even now", says Pausanias, "the Athenians are wont to
compare the persuasiveness of his poetry and discourses to a Siren's
song".

Siren-vases, such as that formerly in the Pourtalès collection, have
been discovered at Sorrento, but no Greek tombs with these elaborate ornaments. Those that have been unearthed seem to have
belonged to the lower classes; they are simply inscribed; FAREWELL.
It is touching, this simple word, though our modern conscience
might well be disquieted with such eloquent and candid brevity.
And yet—after the conventional sepulchres of our ancestors, with
their paraphernalia of skulls and cross-bones, their laboured lies in
barbarous Gothic Latinity or worse English, setting forth virtues
which the dead never exercised and hopes of Heaven he may well
have derided—how true is the pathos of this last greeting; how it
speaks of a time when men looked serenely into the eye of death
and found in their hearts, not in their heads, the feelings they would
utter! Some ancient funeral inscriptions are as untrustworthy
as our own, and the Roman *vale* had doubtless grown to be a
mere formality; but the men who first of all carved this salute on
sepulchres meant what they said: farewell!

Hither—to Our Lady of the Snow—they bring the dead for
burial from various villages. The road is a mere track in many
places and the discomfort must be considerable for all who take
part in these scrambling processions, especially during the many
wintry days of rain and storm. I have often asked why these communities do not buy a burial ground nearer home, and have received
a variety of explanations—none convincing. The truth seems to be
that irksomeness is counterbalanced by cheapness, for a plot of land
near a village costs money, while the waste of time counts as nothing.
Orientals! At Tramonti, further inland, the cemetery is at the head
of the valley and on the summit of a truly formidable hill—a funeral

there must mean half a day's loss of time for those who attend it from beginning to end. One would think that the expense of conveying the coffin up these rough tracks would alone swallow up a considerable sum. But this is avoided by the system of confraternities, each member of whom pays a small yearly contribution which entitles him to a free burial when his time comes. No wonder everybody belongs to these societies, for they make interments enticingly cheap.

But will they sleep in peace?

Ay, there's the rub. Soon enough their bodies will be ousted to make room for others, even as in old England men were "knav'd out of their graves" in the same callous fashion. Surely this disrespect for those who have gone before is a sinister feature of catholicism, and a sensitive person, haunted perpetually with the spectre of Unrest after Death before his eyes, may well become predisposed in favour of the fiery resolution. Poor men's bones are cast to the winds, for an avaricious progeny denies them even a few square feet of earth wherein to repose; the skeletons of their betters are periodically resuscitated and examined, put into new coffins, and reverently moved about: lucky the saint or warrior whose anatomy is complete after all these posthumous perambulations. The ancients displayed more piety in this matter. The Romans, it is true, had their Esquilinus, their *ager informis*, but their respectable dead were respectably dealt with and left in peace. Yet even the present system is an improvement upon that which was in vogue up to a short time ago, whereby the poorer dead were simply pitched, uncoffined and head foremost, into a black hole, *fossa carnaria*, which lay below the church. In this pit of abominations they lay undisturbed, until some newcomer, sliding down, jolted them into another position. The *fossa carnaria* at Massa is closed with a marble slab inscribed "The Way of all Flesh"; others bear the familiar but wholly untruthful legend "Return whence Ye came".

Can these bones live? If so, great will be the confusion in such caverns when the last trumpet sounds. The Italian government abolished these horrors under vehement protests on the part of the Vatican; but it will be long ere the priests can bring themselves to countenance cremation, which would cut off one of their chief sources of revenue. Religions should stand on their merits, no doubt. Yet there is something to be said, even for a State-paid clergy. . . .

Not all the cemeteries of Siren land are in this sad case. The two burial-grounds on Capri are decent and harmonious spots, and a picturesque one crowns the summit of Santa Maria above Massa, where the scarlet geraniums grow to gigantic clusters. It is forlorn but still fair, this ancient citadel; they fought furiously here in the fifteenth century—Ferdinand of Aragon besieging it for two years to oust the obstinate Anjou adherents. When at last it yielded, the citizens were emptied out of the contumacious rock and made to settle at its foot. Their devotion to the Anjou cause had been constant and not unrequited. There has lately been printed, from a manuscript in the Paris National Library, a really interesting book —the diary of Jean Le Fèvre, who died in 1390, after being Bishop of Chartres and chancellor to the Anjou kings Louis I and Louis II. Reading this honest old-world journal, one might think that the inhabitants of Siren land were an exceptional order of beings to be favoured out of all proportion to the rest of mankind—honours and benefits of every kind being showered upon them by the Court. A positive infatuation: on one day alone—July 2, 1387—the queen wrote over twenty-five letters to private citizens of Capri. Where are these letters now? *Muribus corrosæ*, no doubt; eaten by the mice, which already fattened on Capri documents in old Le Fèvre's day.

And a charming site is the new cemetery at Capo Corno near Massa, where the ordered cypresses, flame-like children of Zoroaster, overhang the sea and sway to its breezes. Here one can realize how greatly the appearance of the country would be improved if there were more of these queenly growths punctuating the landscape, as in Tuscany. The natives will not have them, on account of their funereal associations: a puerile prejudice, which gives to churchyards the monopoly of a beautiful and useful tree.

Resting, the other day, outside the walls of the desolate cemetery on the Tore, I found at my feet an unusual object—a pebble of flint. How came it here? Soon enough I discovered others; a mine, a vein of it. Is this, then, the place whence the prehistoric cannibals who lived in Siren land drew their supply for their weapons? No; the quality was not good enough for these fastidious creatures who, nor content with flints of the first water, imported obsidian from the distant island of Palmarola, or rather Lipari, and jade, or rather jadeite, from the Alps. The Tore are utterly barren in useful minerals; there is nothing worthy of exploitation to be found on these hills; no salt or iron or petroleum or coal. Perhaps we ought to thank God for this.

Perhaps not. For are these things really the curses which dreamers like Ruskin would have us believe? I thought of pre-commercial Scotland, a land of brigands and bigots. And now? A swarthy mineral, hidden in the bowels of the earth, has woke up latent possibilities in human minds, transforming uncouth savages into thoughtful citizens; giving to England some of her best adminis-trators and to the world a number of glowing writers and of thinkers, deep and daring, who have overturned pernicious maxims of con-duct and set up sound ones in their stead. Many a single county in Scotland has produced more men of original genius than tracts twice as large in the more favoured climates of Europe. Coal! For if you reckon it out, it will be seen that most of the great men of that country have been born within a remarkably small radius of time and an equally restricted one of space; the commercial rise of the central plain, conditioned by the discovery of coal, has led to this unprecedented intellectual rise. True, the pristine beauty of Edinburgh is now shrouded in coal-dust and smoke—but there! you will never satisfy an artist.

Would a similar quickening effect, I wonder, be produced by the discovery of coal on these hills?

At this awkward question my musings were interrupted by the arrival of a funeral procession; a young man had died; he was preparing for some notarial post to enable him to help his large family with occasional contributions and had succumbed to a brain fever from over-work. He seemed to have been a general favourite, yet no one was here to testify affection or esteem on his last journey. Besides the two priests who received three and five francs respectively and who walked about a hundred yards in front of the coffin chatting and laughing, there was only the carpenter, the confraternity in their white frocks, and the youth's two brothers, whom custom compelled to attend; no comrades, no unpaid priests, no teachers, not a single woman, not one of his fifty relatives— every one is related hereabouts—not a soul, in fact, but went under compulsion. They had not even the questionable pretext of bad weather for avoiding the ceremony, as it was a lovely day; but that, perhaps, afforded an even better one. And the service was of barbarous brevity—a Toda would have been ashamed of it. Then the confraternity and priests dashed their vestments into a box and tripped back over the hills in work-a-day clothes, a merry group. Only the carpenter, a serious-looking man of middle age, paced along apart from the others in solitary and sombre abstraction, smoking a black pipe. I inquired why he did not join the rest of them, and received the enigmatical reply: "It is ever thus." He had driven a harder bargain than usual on this occasion—eighty-five francs.

"Walnut?" I queried.

"All imitation! Assassin of the poor! . . ."

"I know a cemetery in my country," Ivan Nicolaevitch once said to me, "which is liquid mud. The dead are lowered into it, but soon enough they rise and float on the surface."

There is no end to these unnecessary horrors.

At Capri they excavated, a good many years ago, an urn of blue cameo glass reposing in a leaden casket. It contained ashes and a coin and was of such fine workmanship that its price quickly rose to £100. These fair and fragile vessels, of which the Portland vase is the best example, were used both for festive and funereal purposes, and so dignified ancient life in two of its aspects—the cinerary purpose, to preserve intact the ashes of the dead, which we allow to rot, in an imperishable envelope; the festive one, inasmuch as their conviviality was a less trivial function than ours, almost a rite, in the performance of which nothing was considered too good, however precious or liable to be broken on such occasions. But these choice urns lead up to the glass sarcophagus of Alexander the Great, to the mummies and exquisite tomfooleries of Egypt, where Death tyrannized over Life. So the treatment of the dead, taken by itself, is hardly an index of a people's intelligence or kindliness; the clever and humane Parsees have a custom which appals us, and the Eskimos, warm-hearted folk, are as callous as beasts in this respect. . . .

After the stragglers of the procession had vanished round the hill, I retraced my steps and conversed awhile with the guardian or grave-digger, who was amiable enough, but rather commonplace for a man of this absorbing occupation. "This," he said, "is the chapel of Monticchio; this, of Sant' Agata; this, of Termini—and life is short, signore, and we must all manage somehow to eat." *Dobbiamo tutti mangiare:* that was the extent of his worldly philosophy.

In the last of these burial chapels I was struck by the frequent recurrence of an historical name upon the tombstones, that of

Amitrano. According to Capecelatro, an abbot of this name was beheaded by Masaniello, and his brother also killed in that tumult. In those days many conspicuous men in Naples came from this peninsula, which was populated more numerously, and by better classes, than it is nowadays. This clan presumably draws its name from the spot called Metrano or Mitrano near Termini, which now consists of only five houses, but seems to have been larger formerly, for Persico reports that sixteen captives were taken from here in the corsair raid of 1558. Perhaps it overflowed into Termini, which is of comparatively modern growth, having only become a parish in 1615, and where the name Amitrano is very common. A-Mitrano —from Mitrano. On the same principle, Amalfi has been derived (wrongly, they say) from A-Melfi, as though originally a colony from the town of Melfi.

Another member of this family wrote a description of that same corsair raid, and yet another one was a celebrated local brigand who died not so long ago and who had hit upon a singular method of impressing the country-folk. He gave it to be understood that he had sewn a consecrated wafer into his body, with the consequence that however much blood he might lose in encounters with the police, his wounds immediately healed again. His pursuers were taken in like the others, for, to corroborate this fraud, he used to carry a skinful of animal blood about with him and spill large quantities of it wherever he had exchanged shots with them, turning up safe and sound a few days later. The theory of his charmed life is still believed by some of the old people.

And the derivation of Mitrano?

From Mithra, I think: the sun-god. He is known to have been worshipped at Naples, Pompeii, and Capri, and votive chapels sprang up in his honour all over Italy. Why not on these hills? The Oriental element was not lacking in the courts of Augustus and Tiberius; at later periods, too, when the cult of Mithra became more widely disseminated, these coastlands must have been the residence of Eastern merchants from their natural attractions or from convenience of situation near the great trade-routes; of freedmen, or retired military officers who had become attached to the cult of the Persian god which accompanied them on their campaigns into the remotest parts of earth.

Thus Siren land has contributed its mite towards unhinging the reason of the Western world. For Eastern religions lose their finest strains when transplanted out of their native soil, and that of Mithra, imported into Italy, efficiently carried on the work of undermining the common sense of Europe. Only the modern Scotchman, the Roman of the Republic, and a few other favoured races whose minds are constructed on the watertight-compartment system, can withstand the toxic effects of certain speculations which in no wise impair the sanity of those among whom they originated. We lack the light touch in spiritual matters. Our climate and racial development has made us strenuous and prone to turn words into deeds; of the many things that we take too seriously, none have wrought greater social havoc than the airy religious dreamings of the East.

Christianity has moulded our destinies; if the sun-god, to whose former worship these engraved tombstones on the Tore remotely testify, had supplanted Christ, what then? The answer is not difficult. They underwent a progressive convergent development; the world-spirit that presided over their birth (to use a now antiquated mode of speech) drew from both what its then bilious appetite craved for, and rejected the rest. It would have ended in a mere difference of name. And not even that: Mithra, like Christ, is the "Light of the World", and Cybele, his whilom associate, is the Madonna or *Gran Madre di Dio*, the Magna Mater of old, who was worshipped both at Capri and Sorrento. The *Monumentum Ancyranum* has shown that Augustus was not unfavourable to her cult—a fact which may have contributed to her popularity in this part of Campania which he visited so frequently.

Tertullian laments that the institutions of Christ and Mithra were alike from the beginning; thus December 25, the feast of Mithra, was the only occasion of the year when the king of the Persians was allowed to get drunk: a custom of this kind still lingers in parts of the Christian world. They grew up together and engaged awhile in fierce competition; like rival trading concerns, each copied what was successful in the other. But the religion of the sun-god was too rational to survive, for it solved the problem of sin and evil without recourse to predestination, and kept the door of hope ajar for the believer who, by personal endeavour, should purge away his guilt. That did not suit the hysterical spirit of an age which required faith and prearranged damnation for its enemies. It succumbed also because it seems to have excluded women from participation in the mysteries—a fatal error, if propaganda was its aim. Yet, before expiring, Mithraism had been permitted—"by an inspiration of the devil", says Saint Jerome—to leave many of its leading characteristics as a legacy to the younger cult.*

In these days, when humanity is infected with observances whose grotesqueness is their only claim to success, it is well to look backwards and to realize that there exists on earth no nearer approximation to verity than the original figure of Mithra the Mediator, the God of Light and Truth. He is the hypostasis of intelligent human effort adjusting itself to a non-moral environment. Ormuzd and Ahriman are dim cloudy shapes; none can tell us what they are about; Mithra, the Redeemer, is made man. In favour of dualistic religions it has been contended that a single god, knowing all things and responsible for all, is a profound immorality. The sun alone, passionless contriver, enemy of lies, is above reproach. He makes and unmakes the atoms in our brains which make and unmake Jehovahs; he is responsible for all things on earth, good and evil; yet his name is unsullied as his face. What divinity shall be compared to him? The wise man of all ages will not hesitate whom to adore when he beholds the Great Fire by whose operation all things derive their first breath of life and the faculty of continued living; when he remembers that the ruby is kindred not in colour only, but in substance, with the arterial life which flows through his veins—a kinship of blood binding the cosmos to himself, whose body contains the common properties of the earth, whose humours, they say, are swayed by her satellite, whose very thoughts are but expressions of solar virtues.

Our vistas on Mithraism and such themes have been widened by the labours of men like Rawlinson, Champollion, and Cumont. The myth of the sungod was a simple matter for our grandfathers. Now that we know a little more, we know a little less; and it is really worth contrasting the diffidence of a modern writer on this subject, like Reville, with the facile *ex cathedra* utterances of the great Dupuis and his school. We are confronted by an agglomeration of facts and ideas, by a complexity of geographical, psychological, and

* Original to Mithraism are: the idea of moral regeneration; draught from the mystic cup; sacramental rites; consecration of bread and water; confession of sins; the sacred flame on the altar; asceticism; veneration of the Sabbath; the last judgment; martyrdom; resurrection; hope of immortality; expiation of sins; baptism; lustration of neophytes; confirmation; penitences.

historical data, that staggers the intelligence. Who will now unravel the mysteries of Zeus, of Heracles? These protean phantoms, that figure forth every aspect of human thought and passion, elude our grasp. True it is that, modified almost beyond recognition, the old gods are still alive within us; antique ideals permeate our spiritual life; the blood of Apollo and Aphrodite flows through the veins of Christ and his Virgin Mother. Yet these venerable shapes, though vital, remain intangible. Their birth-places are beyond our ken. We pursue them, but they flit tantalizingly into wilds of Thrace and Tartary, past Memphis into regions of god-fearing Æthiopians where old Nile collects his waters—from Italy to Greece and over cloud-capped Aryan uplands they lead us on till, looming gigantic through the haze, they vanish in the twilight, in the limbo of Oriental tradition, Promethean workshop of the gods.

So I mused; but the radiance of Mithra did not avail to dispel a spectral image floating before my eyes, the *phantasma* of that funeral with its unseemly haste and callousness, which I finally decided to regard as a perversion of the ancient point of view—of that serenity in the face of death which was praised as distinctively Hellenic by men like Herder, whose enthusiasm for things Greek may sometimes have overshot the mark, based, as it was, upon the contrast between Periclean sunshine and the political and metaphysical fogs of their own country.

It was another of these enlightened Germans, Lessing, who remarked that without the help of revelation no intelligent man could ever have come to regard death as a punishment. He was alluding to Christianity; but the early Christians, to judge by the sepulchral monuments of the catacombs, did not hold this sad and wrong view. And although certain Romans like Seneca already began to dwell with luxurious introspection upon the terrors of the grave—a habit which grew into an obsession during the Middle Ages, when mankind was haunted by the fearfullest shapes of gloom—yet it was reserved for later ages to cast the full blight over reasonable men. We had not thrown aside our mirthfulness with our mail-shirts; our ancestors took themselves less seriously than we take them; the merry England of Chaucer, with its masks and mummeries, has many affinities with South Italy of to-day. For so long as indulgences can be cheaply purchased, the religious conscience cannot be troublesome: that unction *in extremis*—what a glorious salve! But when the ghostly intermediary was taken away and man found himself face to face with a god whose time was occupied in noting down his inmost thoughts, then the reign of haunting terror began; well might he dread the approach of death and tremble for his chances hereafter.

Siren land has been affected by these mediæval fermentations, but chiefly on the material side; on the moral, it seems to me that the identical causes which have co-operated to form our Northern sensibility in certain matters have here produced a clean contrary effect: that spiritual blunting or anæsthesia of which this funeral was an example.

And the Greeks? The idea that we entered into the world tainted from birth, that feeling of duty unfulfilled which is rooted in the doctrine of sin and has hindered millions from enjoying life in a rational and plenary manner—all this was alien to their mode of thought. A healthy man is naturally blithe, and the so-called joy of life of the ancient Greek is simply the appropriate reaction of the body to its surroundings. And if Greek life was heaving with a soft undercurrent of melancholy, it was the melancholy not of psychic constipation but rather of wistfulness; it was what Pater called a "pagan melancholy". They did not brood; a sane mind broods over nothing; it insists upon being distracted. The death of a comrade needs must convulse our organism, but, if sound, it resents the intrusion and seeks to regain its equipoise; it must have certain safety-valves of which our puritan conscience, speaking dimly of something beyond the objective fact of death, does not approve. Or is it not going too far to say of such calamities, as a well-known American writer has done: "Every other wound we seek to heal—every other affliction to forget; but this wound we consider it a duty to keep open—this affliction we cherish and brood over in solitude." We consider it a duty. Why a duty? The masochistic note of modern life. . . .

Those men of old who carved upon sepulchres that single word "farewell" struck the mean between our hyper-sensitiveness and the indifference of the South.

It is easy to see that, in a general way, the inhabitants of the Parthenopean region have deviated less than ourselves from the standard of rightness as regards these tracts of primitive feeling, the reason being that they received Jewish ascetics upon a foundation of classical culture, as men; we, "as a little child" whose organism was susceptible like that of the Pacific islanders when catarrhs were introduced. They were never taught to disrespect the *encumbrance* of Oriental dreamers—the human body, that exquisite engine of delights; the antagonism of flesh and spirit, the most pernicious piece of crooked thinking which has ever oozed out of our poor deluded brain, has always been unintelligible to them. That is why they remained sober when the rest of us went crazy. There were no sour-faced Puritans in Naples, no witch-burnings, no inquisition—the Neapolitans never indulged in these fateful extravagances; they held that the promptings of nature were righteous and reasonable, and their priests, whatever they might profess to the contrary, still share this view and act accordingly; anti-asceticism is the key-note of their lives, and pruriency, offspring of asceticism, conspicuous by its absence in young and old, in literature and society. More than ourselves, they have kept in view the ancient Hellenic ideal of Nemesis, of that true temperance which avoids troubling the equilibrium between man and his environment.

The *ancient* Hellenic ideal: for Greeks themselves overthrew it; soon came Orphic mysteries, and Plato, and the rest of them, stuffed with Eastern lore, and men found it easier to babble charming nonsense about souls and essences than to investigate the facts of life. The old idea of sanity perished; ethics ceased to be a department of physiology; an ego-centric and introspective existence began. Men regulated their behaviour not according to nature, but according to the imaginary exigencies of an imaginary life beyond. From such incorrect premises it was impossible to draw correct conclusions. Would it be wrong, I wonder, to call Pythagoras, albeit he hit upon a few good things, one of the corner-stones of the temple of crooked thinking, or even to say that all mankind, from Socrates to Kant, had lost their bearings in the search after verity? Surely not, if the leaders are to be taken as representative of the rest.

Most of us have learned to distrust apothegms. You may cram a truth into an epigram: the truth, never. Did not the stoics and epicureans, for example, rebuild the old striving under the title of "virtue"; have not sane men lived sane lives from the beginning of the world, despite their teachers? Thus every epigram requires a foot-note.

. . . . .

Assuredly, this sentimental lingering in burial-places is unwholesome. For last night I had a dream, a horrible dream, one of those dreams that endure, that haunt us with their white faces through all the sunshine of the day.

It was evening, and the train had left me at some unknown spot. It might have been a town or village in the English "black country", for coal-dust had crept over houses and roads and trees, and a murky cloud hung in the sky as though some demon, with outstretched wings, were brooding over the land. Troubled in mind, I wandered about the streets. Uncouth buildings, with a thousand chimneys and projections, towered into the sky; everywhere lay, in chaotic confusion, mountains of black mineral wealth, and carts, and iron contrivances of menacing aspect, whose purport I could not fathom. Pallid men and women, straggling home from the pits, scowled at me. It was all, very gloomy and evil; the fearsome exaggeration of dreams got hold upon me. Some catastrophe was about to happen. I began to run.

My steps took me to a squalid cemetery. It contained tombs without end—a wilderness of tombs. And there, suddenly, a tall grave-monument, leaning against the enclosure, beckoned to me as though to invite attention, and I found myself examining it carefully. It was in good taste and had evidently been reared by some person of means, but although scarcely ten years old, it already wore a look of dismal neglect, for the stone was encrusted with unclean lichens and, instead of bright flowers, a generation of rank summer weeds, black with soot, had thrown themselves over it and there decayed.

Ah, the cemetery on the Tore! And yet. . . .

What a spot, I thought, to lie in for all eternity! If this should be my lot! And—how soon are we forgotten! For this tombstone must have been built and tended by some loving heart not so long ago; but that friend had now died in his turn, and there was none left to cherish the loved one's grave. A world of tenderness and affection wiped out, as though it had never been . . . and only ten years: how soon, how soon! Certain events flashed through my consciousness, until an intensity of grief and compassion, such as only dreams can inspire, overwhelmed me at the thought of this unknown fellow-creature.

Then curiosity tempted me to see who lay beneath this stone, but it was too dark to read the inscription and, searching in my pockets,

I discovered that I must have lost or mislaid my matches. After all the direful impressions of that evening, even this pleasure, this harmless little caprice, was to be denied me. I felt like crying with the peevish impotence of a child.

On the wall sat an old man, smoking a black pipe. The guardian! And yet—he was changed somehow; his face wore a curious look. Can he have guessed my very thoughts? With suspicious alacrity, he jumped down and stood at my side. There was a lantern in his hand: a stream of light poured from it.

"Now," I said, "we shall see."

The name on the tomb was plainly legible.

It was my own.

XI

ON LEISURE

COME, let us discourse beneath this knotty carob tree whose boughs have been bent earthward by a thousand gales for the over-shadowing of the Inspired Unemployed, and betwixt whose lustrous leaves the sea, far down below, is shining turquoise-blue in a dream of calm content—let *me* discourse, that is —for if other people are going to talk, as Whistler used to say, there can be no conversation—let me discourse of leisure, the Siren's gift to men. But, first of all, pass nearer those flasks. They contain the closest approximation to that "gold of Sant' Agata"—*oro stravvecchio, oro del padrone*—the formula of whose composition was peevishly thrown away, like any ordinary Great Seal of England, what time the inn became a menagerie. Its label alone may be read on some bottles which need not be uncorked. "Never," said an august personage long ago to me, "never give a man cigars, wine, or food above ten per cent better than what he gets at home. Never." The serpent's wisdom! On this principle these caravanserais are worked, and all we can do is to seek our "gold" elsewhere. Meanwhile: your health! Drink, my friend, and let me see that smile of yours; soon enough, I daresay, neither of us will smile any more, though we may grin for all ages to come, if the soil is dry. . . .

A sorry preamble, this; not exactly a "captation of benevolence" in the Ciceronian style. But what matters the exordium, if the *oro* is to our liking? Let us drown it in four inches, and begin again.

They had no *oro* in those times. Cicero's son, that ineffable drunkard and vagabond, knew this right well; if he had lived a little later, he might have found a substitute in the pages of Athenæus. But he was born before his time, like all great men. For where the *oro* now grows were forests; Pollio built his temple with their beams and the Amalfitans their fleets, and at their feet grew the wine of Sorrento, which Caligula called "a respectable vinegar". A dangerous liquor, by Hercules: did not doctors recommend it to their patients? In those days, the boughs of the grapes at Sorrento waxed so high and mighty that labourers were wont to insure their lives before climbing up to gather them.

Be prepared, under such a mere boughing acquaintance, for indifferent wine; like that inky fluid of the Naples Campagna where the grapes likewise clamber up to heaven out of sight of the peasant, who periodically forgets their existence and plants hemp and maize in their earth. No vine will endure this treatment; personal contact is the first requisite for good results. Where is that "master's eye"? He would need a telescope to see his progeny. And the cultivator must also be a man of feeling, for there is a communion between the vine and him who tends it more subtle than between master and dog or lover and his beloved, and, bless you, more enduring. They end in resembling one another. Think of the priest-ridden Niederoesterreicher and his sour vintage! Then wander through golden Provence, wander to the Mainthal and Deidesheim of old romance, where the farmer loves his vines as children, and tell me if the liquor does not reflect the man? The taste of the wine depends upon the heart of the vintner.

And leisure is the *primum mobile* of the universe.

Without leisure, the sun, moon, and stars would not have been created, for it stands to reason that the Creator could not have carried out this idea if He had been busy at the time. Are not mankind and all the beasts of the field also products of leisure moments?

The wine of Capri used to be famed throughout Italy. It has now become a noisome sulphur-and-vinegar compound that will etch the bottom out of a copper cauldron; and though the natives still drink it by the gallon—what older· travellers tell us of the sobriety of the Capriotes is hard to believe—yet, in the interests of public health, it would be better if the manufacturers of *vero vino di Capri* were confined to the distillers of the relatively harmless Neapolitan preparation which goes by that name. Montesquieu lodged with the Carthusians on Capri and praises their wine in his journal. This shows that the exigencies of French politeness are not necessarily at variance with truthfulness: no man of the world will sniff at monks' liquor. But the amiable monarch Ferdinand, whom the Capriote Arcucci used to entertain for weeks at his house with "Tears of Tiberius", a self-coined and self-manufactured native wine of noble pedigree, hit upon a more original way of showing gratitude, for he hanged his good host in 1799—hanged him, that is, after the Christian Bourbon fashion, when white-haired patriots and delicately nurtured women and mere lads of sixteen were attached by the neck to tall gibbets, and while one fiend in human shape, called *tira-piedi*, clung to their feet, the executioner climbed up from behind and seated himself firmly, like the Old man of the Sea, upon their shoulders, where he was swayed to and fro by the victim's convulsions till at last the vertebræ were broken—all this, amid the shrieks of ten thousand ruffians, applauding the wit and wisdom of their lazzarone-king. It is well to bear these things in mind when one hears so much, even at Naples, of the good old times. Murat, the royal *tartarin*, had a finer conception of humanity; instead of murdering his benefactors, he planted French champagne grapes upon the heights beyond Naples, out of which they still extract a drinkable stuff called Asprigno. Try it, when you have the chance.

Another bottle?

So be it.

Now, leisure should be spelt with a capital "L", otherwise it runs the risk of becoming materialized, like many similar things which have ceased to be abstractions. This is what they call "treating a concept as if it were an entity". *The Unknown*, for instance. I have passed that stage: the *Hibbert Journal* stage. We create a word for our convenience and forthwith, unless we are on the look out, there comes over it a horrid change. The word was made man. It puts on flesh and blood and begins to give itself airs. Soon enough, it stares us in the face, as though we were total strangers. "Know you?" it jeers. "Know you for a fool!" Many respectable men have been eaten alive by the words of their own creation, for their appetite exceeds that of Frankenstein's healthful monster, and I have reasons for suspecting that, like the ferocious Scythians of old, they only drink milk.

Milk! That explains everything.

Try, also that of Ischia. As a *vino da pasto*, it is surpassed by none south of Rome; indeed, it is drunk all the world over (under other names), and a pretty sight it is to see the many-shaped craft from foreign ports jostling each other in the little circular harbour, one of the few pleasing mementoes of Bourbonism. Try it, therefore, through every degree of latitude on the island, from the golden torrents of thousand-vatted Forio up to the pale primrose-hued ichor, a drink for the gods, that oozes in unwilling drops out of the dwarfed mountain grapes.

Large heart in small grape.

Try also the red kinds.

Try them all, over and over again. Such, at least, was the advice of a Flemish gentleman whom I met, in bygone years, at Casamicciola. Like most of his countrymen, mynheer had little *chiaroscuro* in his composition; he was prone to call a spade, a spade; but his "rational view of life", as he preferred to define it, was transfigured and irradiated by a child-like love of nature. "Where there is no landscape," he used to say, "there I sit (i.e. drink) without pleasure. Only beasts sit indoors." Every morning he went in search of new farm-houses in which to *sit* during the afternoon and evening. And every night, with tremendous din, he was carried to bed. He never apologized for this disturbance; it was his yearly holiday, he explained. He must have possessed an enviable digestion, for he was up with the lark and I used to hear him at his toilette, singing strange ditties of Meuse or Scheldt. Breakfast over, he would sally forth on his daily quest, thirsty and sentimental as ever. One day, I remember, he discovered a cottage more seductive than all the rest—"with a view over Vesuvius and the coastline—a view, I assure you, of entrancing loveliness!" That evening he never came home at all.

Everything which distinguishes man from animals is the result of leisure.

There must have been moments, for instance, when reclining at the entrance of his cave, with his head in the shade and his feet in the sun, the progenitor of our race amused himself with scratching cabalistic signs upon his grandmother's skull or wondering how to propitiate the rain-demon that spoilt yesterday's dinner. Here we have the *prima stamina* of art and religion accounted for—by leisure. Or, to take a corporeal illustration: we still have muscles for flapping our ears, but leisure has made them useless. A fly settling on our ear, we soliloquize thus: "Ha! A teasing insect, as I conjecture. Let me see if I can kill, capture, or at least disable it"; and, instead of an automatic and beast-like ear-twitching, we execute a careful movement of hand and arm. Our godlike physiognomy is due to leisure which has permitted of meditation, brain-changes, and consequent skull-modification. How could we have become the cosmopolitans we are without leisure, which has allowed of observation, deduction of conclusions, mathematics, astronomy, and navigation?

Unlike the beast, we walk upright because leisure has induced curiosity, tools, hand-specialization, and back-bone alteration. Our teeth and digestive system are different from those of the apes— leisure, forethought, seeds, settled habits, regular meals, changes in stomach and teeth.

Leisure first made man formidable on earth. And our virtue, so far as it differs from that of animals, is purely the result of leisure. What is virtue? The conduct which conduces to the actor's welfare; the line of least resistance along which the sage walks and the fool is driven or kicked. In this sense, a flea is exactly as virtuous as a man. But a difference arises, when man begins to argue on the subject. Can anyone argue without leisure?

No—not altogether; the taste of the wine does not wholly depend upon the heart of the cultivator; it also depends upon the heart of him who drinks it. Wine is like friendship: we must meet it half-way. But often this is impracticable; one cannot try all brands; two faces peering at one another through the windows of lighted railway carriages. . . . The world is full of untasted liquor, of inchoate friendships swallowed up in the murk of night. And even when possible, what would it profit if a man carved out his heart and laid it at your feet? The postman would return it next morning with an extra fee for overweight. So the wise man, like our great English philosopher, will slobber out his gruel if too hot; but not his heart, however ardent. We be solitaries, despite our leisure.

Who is this exquisitely arrayed shadow that shakes its hyacinthine locks in disapproval? Ah, I recognize you now, you precious creature, though your hair has grown longer than ever since the angels took you—quite absurdly long, in fact. No, you were never a solitary, I grant; you were sociable enough; you found your friends very useful. So young and so wise, you used to remind me of that grey-haired babe, the Etruscan god—with a difference. He never would drink wine, would this quintessential, Cinque-Cento Symbol; it disturbed his delicate thinking faculties and likewise, I doubt not, his complexion; he never would listen to good Monsieur Janet, who has proved, to every one's satisfaction, that "intolerance of alcohol is one of the stigmata of degeneration".

Another bottle?

. . . . . .

For this class of persons are built the hotels in the larger towns of
South Italy, where, even when the food will pass, no wine can be
procured at any price. Whoever wishes to taste good native vintages
at Rome or Naples must gird his loins and crawl into the bowels of
the earth, into dank tartarean caverns such as Rembrandt loved to
paint, where a greasy oil-lamp, sputtering overhead, casts flickering
lights upon a double row of Gargantuan vats receding into the
gloom and strikes warm tints from the red noses of a group of
coachmen, wood-porters, and birds of that feather who are perched
on rickety chairs in the black gulf between, helping down their
liquor with an occasional plateful of some dubious vermilion stew
that simmers in a corner of the wine-soaked floor. These are the
customers who get their money's worth; theirs the wine that never
enters the big hotels, whose proprietor buys up falsified "Margaux"
for the élite and, for the simple tourist, poisonous local mixtures by
the shipload, which he sells at two francs fifty a bottle as *vin du pays*,
making a profit of 350 per cent.

A Neapolitan costermonger would throw this stuff in his face:
if we all did the same, we would soon be better served. But we come
to this country armed with too much patience; the real "signore"
pays gladly; he never complains, even when at death's door from
the effects of our treatment; he would drink our ditch-water, if it
did not cost us more than the wine we give him. No wonder that
word *signore* has become synonymous, in the vernacular, with
simpleton, for nothing amazes these people more than to see a man,
apparently sane, meekly submitting to outrageous extortion. For
the rest, there is little connoisseurship in the matter of Bacchus
surviving in this country; centuries of misrule and starvation have
blighted the delicate flower. The ancients, whatever may have been
the real state of the case, at least talked as if they had judiciously
filled cellars; they bragged in good style and in good cause. Their
descendants have inherited echoing subterranean vaults, dim and
cathedral-like, full of possibilities; but nothing more. And yet I
have sometimes heard them saying that the Germans are—relatively
to themselves—savages. Body of Bacchus! When D'Annunzio shall
compose an ode equal in ethical significance to *Im tiefen Keller sitze
ich*, I may be prepared to consider that proposition.

A nation without a cellar-lore can hardly be said to exist, save
on the map.

Yet the lower classes occasionally display a pathetic reverence for good wine. I once intercepted a familiar acquaintance returning to Siren land from Gragnano, where he had been transacting some macaroni business. He informed me with a proud smile that he was bringing back a present to his family. What was it, I asked? A scarf for his wife—toys for the children? Nothing of the kind. It was a six-year-old bottle of that sparkling dry wine of Gragnano for which the devil, unless I am much mistaken, will sell his soul at any hour of the day or night; the poor fellow beamed all over in anticipation of the family treat. I was quite touched by his kindliness.

"Will they really like it?" I queried.

"Won't they!"

But they never got it, for I loved him so dearly that I drank it myself, then and there.

And those early Italian builder-monks, clearly, were connoisseurs of the right kind. That was an ultra-modern yearning which led them to dwell on lonely hill-tops and there to plant and ponder; depend upon it, they felt impulses which the common herd never feels: the poet's craving for solitude and rocks and clouds; the gourmet's stimulation of a wilderness without and good cheer within; the creative joy of the artist who covers the naked canvas with teeming life, of the god who bids waters flow in dry places. Such retirement necessarily took on the religious complexion of its age, but the cowl does not make the monk: they were Strindbergs and Huysmans who dwelt at La Cava. At Cassino the Benedictines built nobly and meditated, but here amid careering cloud-wisps and moist forest-gloom these cowled academicians junketed and entertained princes, caring nothing for external parade. Those thick, plain walls tell their story; they are not the faltering language of men who doubt; they have analogies, none too remote, with the solid luxury of a London club. And if you would taste the fruits of this mediæval epicureanism, go to the archives. Hither came, tottering with age and cares, the Wizard of the North, and knocked at the gate; then sadly turned to go. No magic key was found to open for him the world of glittering romance that slumbers within those parchments; his age of miracles was over. Walter Scott at the portals of La Cava—a fine subject for a picture. . . .

And another also came in later years in whom Italy lost a perfect lover. A Siren worshipper was Gissing, though his Sirens were not always of the right kind. That is surely a strange criticism which deplores the personal note in his *Ionian Sea;* as if the moods of such a

man were not as vital and veracious as the reasonings of others!
I am inclined to think that he died of congestion, for there was that
within him—some macrocosmic utterance—which vainly endeavoured to pierce the gathering mists of introspection; the Rycroft
litany, beloved of the weaker brethren, marks the parabola into the
enfolding gloom. The old, old story: inefficient equipment, not of
intellectuality but of outlook and attitude, and likewise of *bête
humaine;* of that tough, cheerful egotism which, sanely regarded, is
but sanity itself. When they asked the Leontine philosopher how he
managed to attain a hundred years with such glowing health and
jollity, the sage was wont to shake his hoary locks and roar out:
"BECAUSE I NEVER WENT A STEP OUT OF MY WAY TO PLEASE ANYBODY
BUT MYSELF!" With a spark of that spirit, Gissing might be alive to
this day. To allow one's body to be torn to pieces by harpies is a
freak of chivalry beyond the dreams of Amadis.

These convent-builders loved old wine and, on this account
alone, cannot be accused of wholly misusing their leisure. But what
chapters could be written on that subject! Diseases due to misuse
of leisure: toothache, baldness. Customs due to misused leisure:
tall hats, picnics. Thought-products due to misused leisure: envy,
fraud, the *evil eye.* Institutions due to misused leisure: codes of
honour among schoolboys, army officers, and other imperfectly
civilized associations; the *vendetta.* Modern examples of misused
leisure: German feudal barons (Sudermann's *Frau Sorge*), or those
Spaniards who can sustain life for a week on a glass of sugar-water,
while, if their conversation be stopped, they pine away and die.
The subject-matter of this endless debate? *Pesetas.*

Leisure is the curse of the poor in spirit.

What a mistake to say that complexity argues culture! Nobody
but savages, wasters of good leisure, could invent solemn, sense-
defying buffooneries like totemism, or the vendetta, as still practised hereabouts. It is in the blood—the whole *Iliad* is nothing but a
vendetta; it is the soul of the people, their all-in-all; not a man you
meet but has half a dozen on hand, of one kind and another, to
amuse his idle moments, and if you suggested expeditious English
methods of settling accounts he would laugh at you; he does not
want his accounts settled; the *brooding* is exactly what he likes. There
are vendettas of a thousand kinds, each with its regulations and
mode of procedure firm-fixed as the Polar star; the simplest are
those of the young men and boys who, when they have differences

to adjust, retire to the nearest wine-shop and dig knives into each other; a kind of game, they will tell you; if five or six are wounded on such occasions they call it *mezza-quistione*—half-a-dispute.

Which reminds me of a fine old-fashioned game they play in the Caucasus. The Caucasian swells, like the Scotch, take great pride in keeping up their time-honoured sports, and one of them is this: In order to break the monotony of their interminable banquets and drinking-bouts, the host, at a given moment, causes all the lights in the room to be extinguished. This is the signal for the ancestral game to begin. Forthwith each guest unbuckles his revolver and fires six shots at random across or under the table. It is done in perfect good humour, as the rules require. After that, the lamps are re-lighted, the corpses counted and carried away, and the bowl passes round once more. They call it "odd man out" —in the Georgian tongue.

Or the Evil Eye, which we all learn to believe in, sooner or later. At Capri there dwells a tottering hag known as Serafina who, sixty or seventy years ago, was useful for carrying postal telegrams to their destination. She can barely crawl now, but, in spite of protests as to her inefficiency on the part of ignorant visitors, she retains her official place undisputed. So the authorities have ordained; and for the best of reasons.

She has the Evil Eye.

"What would you, signore? Supposing we turned her out, and something afterwards happened to our wives and children? We should have only ourselves to blame."

Whence it follows that the *fascino*, the evil eye, is something of a commercial asset, if you know how to use it; it is as good as a fixed income, as was demonstrated to me by a soft-voiced, lamb-like individual with whom I happened to be conversing the other day, and who told me the following, absolutely truthful.

Tale of the Evil Eye

"There is a restaurant in Sorrento, the 'Ace of Spades'—you have heard of it, signore?—which was successfully managed, long ago, by the masterful Don Peppino until his wife died and old age and infirmities began to creep upon him. Having no sons and only one daughter, a great beauty, who was going to inherit all his money—every one was after her, but the old fellow never joked on that subject: quite the reverse, in fact—he looked about for some one to help him with serving the customers, and finally hit upon a penniless youngster nicknamed *cagnapezzo* (Autolycus, trash-collector)—a miserable person, whose real name was Pasquale.

"Imagine, signore, Don Peppino's amazement when, the first day after they had come to terms, this individual quietly observed—

"'I've been expecting this job for some time. And now, dear Peppino (the impudence!), I must ask you not to call me *cagnapezzo* any more, but Pasquale, *Don* Pasquale, see? Because, in a month or so, I think I'll marry your daughter.'

"'Out you go!' said Don Peppino, seizing him by the scruff of his neck.

"'Wait a bit, old man. A pretty girl, your daughter; re-markably pretty.'

"That same evening she was run over by a carriage and killed.

"In short, Don Pasquale, as he insisted upon being called, had the evil eye; he was a *iettatore;* there was no denying the fact. And there was no getting him out of the house again. That affair of the daughter had established his reputation; the whole town began to fawn upon him, and soon enough old Don Peppino died and the other appropriated all his worldly goods and presently married a rich wife and had a family of his own.

"The years went by, signore; and the lamented Don Peppino's business flourished so well under the control of the evil-eyed Pasquale and his three children that, his own wife having died, he too was obliged to find an outsider to help in the concern. This was a smart youth called Antonio; yes, signore, a very smart youth.

"'And mind,' said the landlord, after explaining to him his duties, 'mind I don't see any goings-on with my daughter Concetta. Because if I do, you know—well, *you know* . . .' hinting, signore, at his notorious capacities as *iettatore.*

"'No, I don't,' said the new waiter, quite calmly. 'Good-looking young fellows, those sons of yours.'

"'Say *benedico!*' shrieked Don Pasquale, threateningly.

"'Say it yourself. Uncommonly fine boys; both of them, I mean.'

"Within a week they caught smallpox and died.

"A pure accident, signore."

Don Pasquale had unwittingly engaged another *iettatore* as

waiter: at least, so he thought. Here was a mess; two evil eyes under one roof! People thought that the business would go to pieces, but, like sensible men, they arranged affairs between themselves in a kind of armed truce, exercising their peculiar *fascino*-functions on alternate days—so the priests said. But Antonio knew what he was after.

As soon as due mourning for the sons was accomplished, he observed, casual-like—

"'Pity they died. But Concetta would make a good manageress.'

"Don Pasquale pretended not to hear.

"'I was saying that Concetta would make a good manageress. *That was rather awkward about the boys, eh?*'

"'Take her and be damned,' growled Don Pasquale.

"This marriage, signore, was the beginning of an unbroken friendship in the family. The establishment is now thriving under their triangular supervision to an extent which would have made the lamented and masterful Don Peppino green with envy, green! Come and see for yourself, signore! Old Pasquale, I am sure, would be delighted to welcome you, and so would Concetta."

. . . Rather a queer story, I thought. Who ever heard of two Evil-Eyed Ones living together?

"How do you know all this?" I asked my lamb-like informant.

"How do I know it?" he echoed. "Because I am Antonio, Concetta's husband—at your service."

"Oh. Have a cigar, my friend! Here, take two of them. . . ."

Then there was the wine of ——. I recall the times when as much of this nectar as was good for any Christian could be drunk for a franc; nowadays, the widow only sells it as a favour to old clients, "in memory of her dear departed husband"—at four francs a bottle! It was insidious stuff, most insidious. Your head remained serene like the snowy peak of Olympus which reflects, above its misty girdle, the crimson rays of sunset; the tongue wagged with eloquence and discrimination: the rest was turned to marble. Even as that Indian plant whose bended twigs incline to the soil and presently sprout up around the parent stem, a goodly family of daughters—often the brown herdsman, faint with the noonday heat, seeks refuge in that pillared shade: even so your feet, hitherto free to move at your bidding, had noiselessly descended into the floor and there taken root. You rose to bid farewell—that is, tried to rise—and found yourself anchored to earth firmer than rocky Olympus. Then, indeed, that frank departing gesture crystallized into a strange phantasm of a grin; you smiled, like the suitors of Penelope, "with alien lips". In this petrifying, gorgonizing action it resembled the wine of the Glotterthal, the wine that Sybel loved. Not that he disparaged other vintages; he liked them all; he was "no monopole", as the kindly hostess often had occasion to observe.

A propos, are there any cases of women being held captive by the Sirens? I know of very few. Have they been too preoccupied with their own charms to take notice of any others? The Sirens themselves were women, you know; and probably dressed rather oddly. Also, they were idle fowls who kept men from their duty, whereas our wives and sisters used to be stern champions of male drudgery—for man must work and woman must dress—and this has led to a little bickering in the past. But woman is changing once more; she is becoming free as after Pericles or the Renaissance, and can therefore laugh herself out of that time-honoured privilege of saying foolish things in the grand manner which seems to have bewitched our gallant forefathers. She is beginning to realize what songs the Sirens sang.

Let me explain, my young friend—I am in the mood for indiscretions—how it happened. Man, the infatuated idealist, always on the look-out for something to adore, created, in one of his moments of mediæval vapours, the Madonna-woman. It was a benignantly grinning idol, inanely oracular, to be approached on bended knees. In those days, women had to acquiesce in all his unhealthy whimsies, and many of them began to take the thing seriously and to play his game. Now, they mean to have no more of it; they are sick, utterly sick, of the Madonna business. They mean to laugh again and to enjoy life like other beasts of the earth: like men, in fact. Whenever, therefore, you catch yourself thinking that women are saints and angels, be sure you take a blue pill. The whole epidemic would have been avoided if our ancestors had thought of that.

By the way, it was rather an unflattering definition of a "real lady" which I read not long ago, to the effect that *she alone knows how to wear diamonds*. However that may be, the real gentleman, I conceive, is he who knows how to employ rationally any amount of leisure that may fall to his lot. Every other of the ten thousand definitions of that word is lame beside this one, which Aristotle already formulated, or at least divined, when he bound up gentlemanliness with elegant leisure and contra-distinguished between ἡδονή and εὐδαιμονία. And well may we pause before condemning such Hellenic ideals, if we call to mind what Galton says of the average intellectual standard of the Athenian as compared with ours. These men wrought not only in marble; they were the master-critics of the art of life. What constitutes, I wonder, the real test of a refined state of society? The existence of a preponderating class of intelligent and good citizens, not actively engaged in self-defence or the pursuit of wealth. This is honourable leisure, the flower of human development. It may be said that such a condition resembles that of the mariners who have dropped their oars, spell-bound by Siren voices. Likely enough. But while it lasts, it represents civilization. Everything else, at its best, is only progress. If the flower wither not, how shall the seed prosper?

We called him Sybel, because he seemed to have stepped straight out of Auerbach's cellar. He liked it old and sweet and plentiful, no matter where it came from. He used to take a nap halfway through and then, waking refreshed, laugh at us youngsters for being already so far gone, which of course made us more uproarious than ever. But one evening he sobered us effectually. He had lain down with a beaming countenance as usual, and we were beginning to wonder when he would wake up again, for it was considered right never to disturb him, the sleep being good for his heart, as he explained (he was far too fat ever to mean what he said). Beside myself, only the theologian and an Æsculapius had remained articulate at that hour; the latter, I remember, was setting forth the symptoms of hydrophobia to the hostess, who listened with an air of abstraction, having heard the story before. A shred of conversation still lingers in my mind.

"I tell you, madam, the dog was a mad as could be. He was as mad—as mad—as mad——"

"Then how did you escape?"

"Why (confidentially), you know, of course. By pretending to be a mosquito."

But Sybel still slumbered and we began to discover that his behaviour was disrespectful to the company at large. It was resolved that energetic measures be taken. The theologian's eye wandered round the room and finally reposed upon a stick of sealing-wax;

but a hot liquid drop, falling upon Sybel's outstretched arm, produced no effect. He only beamed.

"Which goes to prove," said Æsculapius, gravely, "according to the precepts of Hippocrates and Peter of Bokhara, that life is extinct."

And so it was. Poor Sybel must have been dead for two hours at least. Yes, he sobered us effectually that evening.

Fear not, long-suffering friend; I am not yet in my anecdotage; I will speedily make an end on't, so far, at least, as you are concerned. As for me, I am only just beginning to enjoy myself, and I will not be put out of my humour—no, not for the treasures of Mogul or Montezuma. Say me, shall I explain how it came about that the Mexican nobles, while quaffing *chocolatl* at sunrise upon the summit of their vapour-belted *teocallis* to the martial chant of *itzli-putzli-popocodl*—how it came about that these warrior-chieftains were in so far not forgetful of their rank and pedigree as to wish that some other kind of beverage could at last be invented? *Chocolatl*, indeed! No wonder they were bloodthirsty ruffians, for all their feathers.

There shall be no *chocolatl* in the land, when I am king. A song, ho!

> My mother bids me bind my hair
> With Cinque-Cento ribbons rare,
> But oh my daddy, won't he swear—

—What, another bottle?

We be creatures of habit, and it matters little what a man's habits are, so long as they are regular. Besides, what says this letter, just received? *All strains to be avoided.* To resist is ever a strain. I have been subject to temptations from earliest childhood, and always know beforehand whether I shall yield or not. I always yield—the line of least resistance. But it is time, methinks, to recapitulate the most salient points of the discourse. Let me see. . . .

A flea hath virtue.

Excellent fooling, i'faith! Why, what a flea has cannot be worth much. I'll have none of it.

Here is something better. Your health, my patient friend, and—as they say hereabouts—*cento figli maschi!*

One of the most noteworthy features of that ancient Mexican civilization was the prevalence of the snuff-taking habit. Regarded as an isolated phenomenon, there is not over-much to be said on

the subject; but when viewed, as the historian should view it, in
conjunction with the wonderful astronomical knowledge and other
accomplishments of this tenebrous and sombre race, it assumes
another import—quite another import. His Grace the Archbishop
Lorenzana, in his account of New Spain. . . .

XII

CAVES OF SIREN LAND

WHAT shall we think of that immense homogeneous civilization which is said to have covered the shores of the Mediterranean basin from neolithic to Homeric times? Did it receive, in the course of ages, affluents from wiser East or sterner North, or was some spark enkindled in its midst—some skin-clad Gutenberg or Flavio Gioia or Roger Bacon—that lighted the way over the dim gulf of years? For if it laboriously worked itself upwards step by step, the mind grows dizzy at contemplating the abysm of time between the most cultured of these men and the still rude society of prehistoric Troy or Cnossos. But why a "homogeneous" civilization? Because their weapons and dwelling-places are similar? So are those of the Papuan and Swiss lake-dwellers. Necessity produces these things by analogous variation—even as certain snakes, nowise related, have in different parts of the world hit upon the identical method of defending themselves by poison. Their cranial capacity or configuration? Skull-measurements are laudable studies, but when a wise man begins to discuss their bearings upon race-problems, it is time, as the Persians say, to put one's trust in God. And if "homogeneous" implies contemporaneity, what is there to show that there may not be a lapse of a thousand years between a flint knife from Tunis and a similar one from Apulia? Sooner or later, I suspect, this homogeneous civilization will go the way of the Aryans, who probably never existed; being a kind of nebular hypothesis which, in our present state of ignorance, explains a small bundle of disconnected facts—not always correctly.

They tell me that prehistoric spear-heads have been found buried under the soil of what afterwards became Pæstum and Cumæ. If this is true, it shows that the Greeks were probably in contact with these people; or, at all events, that they were satisfied with the localities once chosen by them as settlements.

Previously to that they lived in wigwams or skin-shelters, for the supply of caverns, though considerable, cannot possibly have been equal to the demand. This is the first step in the direction of social habits; God created the cave: man the wigwam. To this period must be assigned the numberless fragments of hand-made pottery, red without and black within, that litter the slopes of Anacapri. Some of these pieces have a horizontal line of corded ornament in relief at the rim; it seems to have been done by affixing a raised band of clay to the vessel while unbaked and then modelling it with a turn of the thumb. Into what wonderful phantasies has not the art of ceramics blossomed since those days! And yet this prehistoric embellishment is identical with that on the modern earthenware washing-tubs that stand outside every cottage in Siren land. So pottery, universally distributed, slow-moving and serving easily ascertained purposes throughout the globe, is to the ethnologist what shells, despite their infinite variety, are to the geologist—Ariadne's thread.

Wherever caves have been explored in this region, as the Grotta Nicolucci at Sorrento or the Grotta delle Felci on Capri, interesting results have been obtained; stone celts, terra-cotta vases, remains of domestic animals, and knives of obsidian. Some seeds, too, seem to have grown, for hand-mills are among the relics. But the people were cannibals for all that; cracked human bones, mixed with those of pigs and sheep, suggest marrow-sucking propensities. Likely enough, these were the *Sirens* of early navigators—the women being sent out by their men-folk to lure sailormen ashore with their songs. And they actually had cosmetics, the minxes; a shell containing a mixture of red ochre and fat testifies to neolithic vanity. The skeleton of a rachitic child has also been found. Ointment boxes and scrofulous infants—here are some of the delights of modern life in embryo, to say nothing of "a little music", not the least of them.

I can name various caves in this region which might well contain relics of these anthropophagous Sirens. But such excavations, to be of value, must be carried out cautiously and systematically, in order to obtain some idea of the age of the embedded remains and of their age in relation to one another, which can only be done by means of sections and photographs showing their juxtaposition with the cave deposit. And this deposit is a study in itself, for it varies greatly; in some caves it is of extremely slow growth; in others, which are more accessible to wind-drifts, vegetable matter, or materials falling from above, it is relatively rapid. To excavate a cave on these scientific lines requires a greater outlay than may be thought, without which the remains are best left to repose where they are, in expectation of some future enlightened amateur.

Excavating accidentally some years ago I came across the charred remains of a fire, beside which lay a celt of jadeite, another of limestone, and two or three round pebbles to be used for slinging. The green celt is a rolled river-pebble, carefully worked up (it must be a rare pleasure when a scientist like A. B. Meyer, who has fought a lifetime for his pet theory of the European origin of these jade implements, once hopelessly discredited, at last sees it universally acknowledged). A certain pathos attaches to these objects, all lying close together as they had been left thousands of years ago, for they cannot have been lost, in the ordinary sense of that word, seeing that their owner would have remembered where he lit his fire and returned to seek them there, and they were far too precious to have been thrown away. No; the owner never returned because, for some reason, he could not—he was hindered by death or capture.

The introduction of a fine material like jade must have created something of a revolution in the social habits of these people, for its blades are as superior to the ordinary ones of siliceous limestone as a steel razor to one of obsidian.

What songs these Sirens sang, though a puzzling question, is not beyond all conjecture. We may be sure that these fierce wenches were not capable of modulating subtle strains. Their melodies may well have been the original of those primeval chants, the Linus-song, the *wailing in the vineyards* of Isaiah—autochthonous, sphinx-like, fraught with the hopes and fears of a forgotten race—that are still wafted upon the summer breezes of Siren land and defy the musician's art to record them, though Tosti has made the attempt in one of his Neapolitan songs. They call this mournful and veritably prehistoric wail the "peasant's song", *canzone di personale* (=parzionale = a metayer): it can be heard at the time of harvest, vintage, or olive-gathering (some suppose that it was imported by the Moors). Or perhaps they resembled the yodler of the *homo alpinus* or of the London milkman—the most bestial of human cries. Life was simple in those days, and with a little imagination it is not difficult to construct a domestic scene of the period, after this fashion :—

WOMAN (*approaching*). I sang Hoio. Another sea-fool comes.
MAN. Who spoke to you? (*Enter a Greek sailor*). The new green one for *you*—white-faced, seal-eyed man-pig.

WOMAN. Hoiotoho-swar!

SAILOR. That song again! To what land of marvels have these good folks led me?

MAN. See this green stone. It cuts sharp: eia-weia! *You* know.

SAILOR. Opopoi! I do begin to fear mightily. How he rolls his eye under those cavernous brows; and she, with wolfish clashings of teeth—Ai, Ai! Papaiax—they seize me—attatai, papai, pai, io, moi, moi, omoi, ototototoi—

WOMAN. They sing wrong.

MAN. They eat right.

(Interval)

WOMAN. Righter than the last, wallawa-hupla!

MAN. Who spoke to you? See this stone.

WOMAN. I sing right. Ja, ja.

MAN. Atcha! You eat wrong. Fetch another man-pig.

This little scene thows a light not only on the importance of jade in the prehistoric household, but also on the theory of these savages regarding the inverse ratio of musical talents and edibility which alone explains how it came about that the Siren family did not end after the fashion of the Kilkenny cats—namely, because, like the modern inhabitants of Siren land, they devoured not each other but only strangers from over the sea. Note, likewise, certain resemblances between the neolithic, Teutonic, and Hindustani tongues, which may help to elucidate the Aryan question.

It must have been these decoying arts which induced Servius to think that "according to the truth" the Sirens were ladies of questionable reputation. This is going too far. You ungentlemanly old fellow, what maggot has got into your grammarian's brain? Those Sirens who strewed the shore with whitening bones were respectable mothers of families finding food for their husbands and little ones; but yours—what occupation would they have on lone Tyrrhenian rocks? Seek them, rather, in Memphis or Babylon.

This same Grotto delle Felci at Capri was afterwards transformed by the ancients into a sylvan sanctuary of Pan or Priapus—to judge, at least, by the remains of an altar and by three huge stalagmitic growths now broken off which may formerly have been of ceremonial significance. The influence of these caverns upon the religious life of olden days is easily underestimated. When one remembers with what reverence these mysterious openings into the fertilizing mother earth were regarded, it might have been expected that many of them would have been devoted to the worship of generative forces, even without the written testimony of Suetonius, who connects these very *antra et rupes* with sexual orgies. Apposite popular names, which will not be found on maps, have been given to some of those grottos and towering rock-needles. "*Le culte de la génération,*" says Lefèvre, "*a exercé une influence, vraiment énorme, sur la pensée humaine, sur la conception de l'univers, sur les institutions sociales*", and among a population with an historical record like that of this province, relics of ancient sex-worship can be found by whoever looks for them. Strange, for instance, in a land where every beast, however harmless, is doomed to death, is the serpent-worship which the Mosaic curse and Christianity alike have not succeeded in extirpating; it brings misfortune to kill those that establish themselves in the neighbourhood of houses, and a drug prepared by chemists out of others purposely caught on the hills imparts virility and long life—another instance showing how frequently the attributes of this animal as a priapic emblem and as one of eternity coincide (I presume the conception of health, Æsculapius, is to be regarded, philosophically at least, as intermediate between the two).

And not long ago I came across a striking relic of these unholy observances at Torco: the larger intestine of an ox inflated with air and affixed upright over the lintel of a private house, with a streamer of red cloth attached to it—*for good luck*, the proprietor told me (coalescence with horn-emblems against the evil eye). The fish is another of these phallic symbols that go back into hoariest antiquity; its Italian name has a very different colloquial signification—in this province only—from that which the piety of early Christians drew out of those mystic characters. And in the now removed flooring of the church at Positano was a large marble phallus—women knelt on it and maintained that prayers thus offered up were of peculiar efficacity. I might mention also the shape of amulets and, in certain localities, that of bread as baked at Easter-time, the procreative festival of spring; the "sexes" attributed to domestic objects like hinges, screws, bolts, mortars, hooks and eyes, etc.—indeed a volume could be written, though perhaps not published, on the subject.

The introduction of Attis, Cybele, Flora, Liber, and so forth must have helped to sustain these deeply rooted primitive cults which began in fetichism and, after a thousand elaborations, are once more relapsing into it. The church, meanwhile, unable to expel these lewd shapes from their cloven rock of ages, has changed their names, and Our Lady of Lourdes now occupies a cave on

Capri: some weeks ago was celebrated the tenth anniversary of her installation amid incredible pomp and circumstance. Simultaneously, it was thought well to purge the Blue Grotto of its Tiberian associations by the erection of a plaster-cast Madonna over the entrance, the passage of this image across the water being attended by certain childlike religious buffooneries which scandalized the more godly among the foreign spectators.

Numberless are the caves in Siren land. They vary from minute fissures to vast oval amphitheatres capable of sheltering a population, like that one at Capri wherein the natives took refuge during Saracen raids; some are dry, others distil water from invisible rifts or pendent beards; they were all moister in the days when there was timber overhead, as can be seen by the many distorted, discoloured, and perennially dry stalactites which hang from their roofs. Some of these caves, like that above Sant' Elia, are beautifully tinted in a pattern of orange stripes converging towards the centre; nearly all of them are decked out with fantastic pinnacles and niches, suggesting a fairy-scene on the stage. The maidenhair fern droops in clusters from the ledges; tufts of *campanula fragilis* dangle their porcelain bells of pale amethyst from the fretted vault overhead; here and there a leafy fig, emblem of fecundity, thrusts formidable roots into the crevices or writhes like an octopus over the stones. The flora of these caverns would be worth studying, since even common flowers that find their way into these rainless and dewless recesses begin to look a little different from their companions outside. In some of them, like that which lies opposite the islet of Isca—a spacious grot, divided into two chambers by a natural arch, with a fine southerly prospect, a right royal abode in prehistoric times—can be found the *mesembryanthemum nodiflorum* and other rarer plants. At their entrance, on the sun-scorched rock, grow the eglantine, the rosemary, thyme, and caper plant.

The materialistic peasant cuts down this fair vegetation and stores it within against the winter; other caves he converts into goat-shelters by a rude enclosure. Of the lore attached to these hollows, he remembers chiefly the plutonic legends of buried wealth with its guardian spirits.

In the narrower fissures, which often run into the bowels of the earth, foxes establish themselves, to his great annoyance. They and the wolves are the only wild beasts of the country. The latter descend during the cold months in all directions from the clefts and beech-woods of Faito on Mount Sant' Angelo; they seldom attack "Christians". Yet only two years ago a boy of fifteen was devoured near Cava by one of these furies—nothing was found save his feet encased in their thick boots; and a woman was lacerated by another while cooking macaroni in her kitchen. The ravening she-wolves are blamed for these desperate deeds. It was calculated that during last winter over one hundred dogs had been eaten by them in the district of Preazzano and Ticciano, which lies just outside the gates of Siren land—these gates being the openings which lead from the Sorrentine plain between walls of rock into higher regions, the flying buttresses of the mighty Sant' Angelo.

The village of Sant' Agata, they say, owes its foundation to a wolf, which carried off the daughter of a certain knight of Massa. The father, having vowed to the virgin that if he rescued the child alive he would then and there erect a church in her honour, found the little one uninjured, and on that very spot built the church round which the village of Sant' Agata subsequently grew up. If we laugh at wolf-stories now, it is because we have forgotten what that grey horror, with eyes aflame, meant to our ancestors—how for untold ages it terrorized mankind, leaving a deep scar on lore and literature.

Few superstitions are more firmly rooted hereabouts—all over the world, nearly—than that of the werewolf. The word *lupomanaro* can be heard every day as a vituperative, and any child will tell you that there are two kinds of wolves—dog-wolves and man-wolves (*lupo-cane* and *lupo-cristiano*). Certain mortals and certain animals are dowered with the gift of distinguishing the *versipellis* even in daytime, when he appears in human garb; a sure test is this—if a shrine or crucifix happen to be on the path along which he is going, he cannot proceed, but must turn back. There lives a *lupomanaro*, a poor peasant called *il lungo*, in a solitary cottage near Sant' Agata. When the moon is full, he runs about exactly like a wolf, with his hands resting on his knees; when he comes to a cross-way, he howls fearfully.

"Does he change his skin?" I enquired.

"No."

"What do you call his disease?"

"*Male grande—male di luna.*"

Thus lycanthropy, with advancing civilization, is merged into epilepsy. Other werewolves are men who work in hot bakeries at night and suffer from *male piccolo* or convulsive asthma; they crawl about the streets in the early hours of the morning, panting and groaning. Then is the time to cure them. If you can creep up from behind and stab them in the back with a piece of steel—a knife, for instance—they will exhale all their wolfishness in one wild howl.

Even to the very tail of the peninsula these marauders penetrate; not a year passes without some dogs or goats being killed at Termini, and last winter they forced an entrance into the so-called *grotte delle capre* or goats' caves on San Costanzo, and did a fearful massacre among its inmates.

The summer is fast drawing to its close. But it will not do to say farewell to Siren land without visiting this line of caves which lie on the southern flank of the mountain, one above the other, under a projecting wall of rock. Every morning some two hundred far-tinkling quadrupeds issue from these caverns to graze the coarse herbage on the slopes. A rough path leads past them up the steep incline, and I never walk that way without a feeling of reverential awe for these immemorial shelters whose stones are polished by the footsteps of bygone ages. They lie high up, in the solitude, among stones. The glittering Tyrrhenian rises into the firmament and its many-tongued laughter floats up to their threshold which, in olden days, may well have been shaded by holm-oaks and laurels and pines. There is a fine flavour in the wild landscape all around; but within, the atmosphere is rank and murky with the odours of a thousand generations of goats. For these grottos, remote as they are from human habitations, must have been useful from earliest times as a refuge for flocks. On the hill-side near at hand you may find fragments of the familiar black and red prehistoric pottery. These men, already, took shelter here.

Whether the goats have greatly changed since those primeval days, I cannot tell.

And the shepherds? The skin mantle was cast aside for a shapely tunic, and the tunic replaced by the blue cotton shirt of yesterday; popes and emperors have come and gone; the woodlands are swept away and the very mountains have put on new faces, but these goat-boys are the same dreamy, shy, sunburnt children as in the days when Phœnicians sailed in their black ships past yonder head-land. They "think of nothing". Simpler than fisher folk or tillers of the soil who must ever revolve contingencies of weather and market, gentler towards their charges than keepers of horses and other beasts, they glide through youth watching the combats and loves of their flocks, rescuing the little ones from craggy ledges and tending the lame and weary, while day by day an intense feeling of endearment towards these warm and frolicsome comrades grows up in their breasts. This is their world—a goat-world; their very countenances reflect it.

Stumbling upon such primitive conditions, we seem suddenly to step outside and beyond the decent Hellenic civilization, with its ordered household, its sceptred kings, well-greaved warriors, and grave dames; its cornfields and broad-browed oxen. We seem to enter that outer world of hollow rocks where men neither sow nor reap; the monster-engendering cycle of Polyphemus and his goats.

To what pipings have these caverns listened, when Troy was yet unsung? To what mad, hot whisperings? The moon alone can tell, for she has looked straight into them time out of mind. But the moon is discreetly silent, having seen many things upon earth; she knows the ways of man and beast, and is not easily made to blush. Maybe some Daphnis, when the world was young, drove his flocks into them night after night and year after year, thinking of nothing. And one day there emerged, casting a wild glance about him, the progenitor of that troop of faun-like creatures, whose poignant truthfulness first appalled, then enslaved, our reluctant imagination.

Dreams?

Perhaps not altogether. I, too, have dwelt with shepherds in Arcadia. And saints of God, wandering in the stony wilderness, have encountered the fauns, face to face, ay, conversed with them; while Monsieur Hedelin, advocate, priest, and preacher, has demonstrated their existence beyond all possibility of doubt, if the facts in this book are true. The fauns *are*: they have been ever since Hellenic days. But the Greeks did not invent them—they only found them. Pathetic animalesque shapes, nymphs and fauns, titans and chimæras, the offspring of human intercourse with nature in her seductive and sterner moods, crept into Greek art and were made man. Sometimes, by an intuition of genius—how difficult the feat is, can be seen by those who would imitate it—a compound imaginary being was artistically fixed; the human element emprisoned in beast body (sphinx), or remorselessly welded upon it (centaurs). But not all these sub-human forms beloved of children and heralds express single-hearted strivings like Pegasus—strength wedded to heaven-soaring flight—or the winged Psyche.

The griffin is merely picturesque.

Yes; it was a feat of genius to arrest those composite phantoms in that precise moment when, trooping past the mind's eye, their grace outweighed their grotesqueness. An ingredient of strangeness, says the English sage, is requisite to full beauty, and doubtless there is no lack of strangeness in these conceptions. But what distinguishes Greek man-beasts from those of other nations is that this ingredient, though inevitably present, is forcefully subordinated to a human note of pathos or graciousness. If, as I think, Greek artists held that the grotesque, the horrible, may be a means, but rarely or never to an end, it is easy to understand why certain things were beyond their power or desire of expression. The man-wolf, for example, is recalcitrant to the chisel under such conditions. Not that there is any lack of foundation in fact; he is as well authenticated as the fauns and has been circumstantially described by eye-witnesses from early times; but short of falsifying the truth immeasurably—a sin— nothing could be done towards investing the beast with that ele- ment of graciousness which they deemed indispensable and which even their direst imaginings, the medusæ or furies, display. Also: he does not allow of the requisite vagueness of interpretation. Enviable fauns! In their happiest moments they were espied and eternalized by loving friends: how many of us mortals will share their fate?

In the Sirens too, in the old Sirens, the Greeks had a hard task before them. Gradually they moult; the feathers drop off their limbs and bosom; it is a downward process of purification, the nobler parts being the first to glow with the new light. Whatever Baudelaire may have thought to the contrary, there is nothing so incontestably anti-bestial as the naked human body, and this per- haps explains the startling fact that Greek gods and goddesses, in proportion as they become civilized, tend to discard garments and covering devices of all kinds. The brute may still lurk within fine clothing or feathers. But only the Etruscans despoiled the Sirens of all bird-like attributes.

Did the Greeks sometimes go too far in their rejuvenations? It was well that those bearded Sirens were done away with, but what are we to say of the old and new Bacchus, or that absurd Eros-baby, which had supplanted the fair and pensive youth, fraught with a burden beyond his years? Venus Urania, methinks, ought to have a beard.

One point strikes me as noteworthy. From whichever country

these creations entered Greece, and whatever may have been their original guise and import, they were quickly remodelled and stamped with the hall-mark. It may be a trifling matter, that of these mixed symbolic art-productions, but it serves to illustrate the whole trend of Hellenic thought. Nothing overmuch. . . . Two attributes, such as the Minotaur possesses, are sufficient for the mind to assimilate at a glance.

In Assyria they wrought man-headed winged bulls. A people nursed in Chaldæan modes of thought may have found no difficulty in rapidly grasping the inner coherence of so much allegory, but a simple, unprepared spectator is taken aback by this plethora of attributes and ponders as to their meaning; these Assyrian bulls, like Irish ones, seem to become valuable in proportion as they are pregnant.

The Greek sculptor thought otherwise; he demanded an instantaneous flash of comprehension, and therefore rejected them and their fellows. For Greek art remained objective long after philosophy had gone the way of Plato, as we know from late masterpieces like the Nike of Samothrace and the Venus of Milo, which speak, in clearest language, to the beholder. The artist feels: the philosopher reasons, and reasoning, the latest and most delicately etched pencilling on the mind's surface, is the first to become blurred. Clear feeling will outlast clear argument, because it is older: the drunkard, who strips off the various layers in the order in which he has put them on, is an admirable illustration of this. Gorgias might grow grey in discussing problems of immortality; he might interpret them this way and that and never solve the knot; but if the Greek citizen remained for a moment in doubt as to the significance of a work of art, its purport was missed.

And nowadays?

Nowadays we are become somewhat metaphysical and subjective to these matters. The meaning of a picture or statue may not thrust itself upon us in this crude, straightforward fashion; the morsel must be chewed before swallowed and relished only of the elect; prayer and fasting are requisite to initiate us into the mysteries which the master sought to express. It is all for the best, no doubt. Times are changed. The Greeks liked garlic.

As for the fauns and their fellows—these dream-creatures wander over flowery meads in the dim borderland between the monstrous and the sublime, and whoever seeks them will not seek in vain, for their existence is coeval with man and Hellenic art only discovered them in the sense that Vasco de Gama discovered the Indies or Volta electricity. Critics, meanwhile, shake their heads in sagest fashion; but whether they approve or not, who shall say? These conscientious gentlemen are puzzled and disquieted, having no clear preceding exemplar to guide them. They wish such things had never been invented. There are *pros* and *cons;* besides, there are fauns and fauns. . . .

"Not guilty, but don't do it again," they mumble at last; a reasonable verdict, when one comes to think of it, and one which might well be extended to certain faun-makers of later days.

POSTSCRIPT

Nobel says that the Slav religion was largely fashioned by forests. Even so, it seems to me that the *prima stamina* of what was afterwards known as Hellenism were originally hewn out, so to speak, under threats of a discordant and destructive environment.

Pelasgian immigrants, the stock of old Greece, the builders of bridges and canals, the sowers of seeds, were leagued against a common enemy—nature. Old Mother Earth was false and ferocious to them; she thwarted them at every turn; the land was peopled by things hostile to man and his ordered ways; there were torrents and gloomy forests and yawning clefts and swamps; the sea, unconquered, grim, or smiling only to destroy; shaggy men, acorn-devouring, who skulked in caves. So those early settlers learned to feel acutely on the subject of humanity, of man the regulator and restrainer of savagery; they held in horror the crude shapes and forces of the outer world, and the keynote of their spiritual strivings became an intense anti-bestiality—far intenser than it is easy for us to conceive nowadays. For times have changed, and we regard ourselves as a portion of nature, rather than her foe.

Long afterwards, when earth and ocean had put on a friendly or at least familiar demeanour, and when the infusion of fresh blood had given to these people their plasticity and versatility, we find persisting this venerable ideal, this humanizing tendency, product of forgotten struggles with the brute and sombre forest. It tinges to latest periods their conception of art and literature and conduct, cropping up in the most unexpected places.

I spoke of the Eros-baby, a late apparition, and one of their relatively few representations of the infant-type. And the odd thing is, that these infants in Greek art are not only few, but also of rather indifferent execution. The Plutus-infant, the baby Hercules, even the Dionysus-child in the arms of Hermes—they have all come in for a share of adverse comment, and Mr. John M. Robertson, who is not given to talking at random, merely voices the general opinion of critics when he says that "the Greek sculptors never learnt to model a tolerable infant".

Can it be that from ignorance of its true genesis this particular aspect of their creative genius has been misread? That the Greeks, rather, never *deigned* to model a tolerable infant?

I think they were quicker than ourselves to detect in the infant-type with its convulsive movements, eyes far apart, flattened nose, crooked legs, and prevailing animalesque characteristics of structure and locomotion, something abortive, incomplete; a caricature of that human body which was for them the full expression of what I have called anti-bestiality; particularly offensive, because it accentuated the features which we possess in common with the brute. This made their artists so niggardly and uncharitable towards babyhood that they never cared to figure it, unless conventional reasons obliged them to do so. Even we, who have outgrown such sensitiveness and become more robust than the Greeks in such matters, still discover in infants a resemblance to the ape, and in the ape the most odious distortion of ourselves.

As soon as—without violating that approximation to truth which canons of good art demand—the infantile traits could be made a subject for idealization; as soon as the child unveiled its heart and ambiguous simian lines dissolved into the soft-stirring smile of boyhood, giving promise of new beauties about to emerge triumphantly and drive the bestial strains back into the dusky caverns of the past, no one has treated the human form with more loving appreciation. But it is as if they hesitated to give their artistic imprimatur to what was not convincingly human, and in this one may be tempted to recognize an echo of those old struggles with the brute.

The change in family life and the new position of women have fostered greater intimacy between the father and his helpless offspring, and from this relation has grown an infant-type, and a mother-type, unknown to the Greeks. The Madonna, myrionymous like her prototype Isis, and the infant Jesus—Horus in the arms of Isis—have also contributed to the establishment of this new ideal.

If Greek art was stepmotherly towards babies, ours went too far in the other direction, for the Christian conception of this divine infant, which may justifiably be idealized in virtue of its unique character, disturbed our artistic treatment of ordinary ones. We over-idealized them, expunging the simian traits before they had shown any indication of fading away. Thus arose, by judicious modelling, a new infant, a composite being with the features and limbs of man, woman, or child à discrétion, and in whom the naturally vacant stare of dawning life was metamorphosed into a gaze of concentrated piety of world-wisdom, reflecting sentiments such as no infant ever possessed; sentiments such as those recorded of Saint Nicolas of Tolentino who, as a suckling babe, was already so convinced of the propriety of ascetism that he voluntarily abstained from partaking of his mother's milk on two fixed days of each week.

Whoever looks for such babies in Hellas will look in vain, for this is the anti-bestiality of an age which regards man himself as the brute, to be contrasted with a diaphanous angel-type hitherto unrevealed. The Renaissance, too, was not over-conscientious in its plastic representations of the infant-type: witness the "Cupid" of Donatello, whose *torso* might be mistaken for that of a Zeus or Neptune. Altogether, this delirious blossoming is to be appreciated for what it wrought upon the minds of men rather than for its artistic achievements, which are flawed with introspection and not for ever young. These men painted nature as they saw it, with seraphic simplicity; but their renderings of the human form lack the universal application of antiquity; they revived the form, without assimilating the spirit, of their masters.

A scholar might amuse himself by tracing back the whole Nemesis-conception of the Greeks to those old Pelasgian nightmares —to the violence of nature, the immoderation of the beast, teaching them their lesson of measure. He might speculate, too, upon the various shapes that floated through early Greece without being artistically adopted—upon the many creatures of earth and air and phantasy which were thrust aside as abhorrent to this rather narrow sense of what was good or fair. The primitive Sirens, I suspect, escaped this fate by a miracle, the miracle of Homer's adoption and transmutation of them; poets and writers of a more refined age would have been merely puzzled or repelled by such fearsome forms. These demons of putrefaction, but for the *Odyssey*, must have waited long centuries to be appreciated.

They must have waited till our day.

For, unlike those old farmers on jungle-clearings, we live on terms of sympathy with our natural environment. We can afford to do so, even as the Romans could afford to cherish conciliatory relations with their conquered enemies. Thus, nature becoming our hand-maid, new fountains of enjoyment have sprung up for us, such as the picturesqueness of the desert, of poverty and squalor, of decay; the weird and droll and uncouth, the sumptuous and exotic, have all found a place in our catholic estimation; we admire the extravagances of Egyptian carvings or Gothic skeletons, and gloat over grotesque *chinoiseries* which a Greek would have dismissed as abuses of man's higher faculties.

Humanity alone, as a subject for treatment, has expanded into a many-voiced organ when compared with that clear but thin reed of theirs. What did Hellenic art know of the humour of old age—of those kindly wrinkles? Of the haunting charm of youthful etiolation? Of barbarian strength and virtue? In the *Iliad*, again, we hear only of captains and kings—the common herd does not exist. But nowadays even vulgar persons, with vulgar hopes and fears, may be made interesting. We relish it at least on a level surface, in homely scenes, Delft-ware style; for when a tragic passion with heights and depths is to be sounded, none save a cunning master, who cheats us into giving them the feelings of their betters, can make the thing endurable; they *will* wallow, these good folk, having, as Schopenhauer observed, "no height from which to fall"; their griefs and toys are alike lowly, and oftentimes past comprehension.

All this, even without the intervention of the Jesus-Horus ideal, would have paved the way for a conception of beauty so extended as to include the simian features of the infant.

The outlook is widened—forest-gloom dispersed.

But those keen human notes, the wild cry of Hellas, are no longer heard: a choral symphony has drunk them up.

XIII

THE HEADLAND OF MINERVA

THERE is a project afoot to continue the driving-road from Sorrento, which now ends at Termini, as far as the point of Campanella. Italy is full of such designs of local patriotism. Often enough, after some thoughtful mayor has collected money during his term of office for an undertaking of this kind—roads, drainage, or water-supply—his successor will spend the whole sum in pyrotechnics in honour of the village saint: thousands of francs carefully hoarded up being thus thrown away in a wild orgy of a single night. Shoulders are shrugged; a new collection begun: *Italia farà da sè*—that charming mixture of enthusiasm and inefficiency! It will ever be thus under a communal system as established here; no public spirit can exist where the good intentions of a few are absorbed by the vices to which the institution lends itself; where each reacts upon the other by ties of relationship or business and by preordained obligations of love and hatred; where the caprice or envy of a single man will suffice to frustrate a project secretly approved by all. What they require, these villages, is an independent and benevolent tyrant after the pattern of the old *podestà:* the municipal system marks a theory of government which ill accords with their habits of life.

Not that the building of this road is a pressing need. There are too many roads in the country already and, were nothing else to be amended, I could wish that the inhabitants might long continue to waste their superfluous wealth in making noises and bad smells to the glory of God—for such are the local fireworks.

The time to take this walk is the early morning, before the sun has begun to beat down upon the western slope of Mount San Costanzo, along which the path runs. The road leads gradually downwards, at first through olives and then along the bare hill-side, fragments of Roman masonry and paving-stones proving that it follows the ancient track, till we reach the platform on which stand the lighthouse and the tower of Campanella—so called from a gong which used to be sounded there at the approach of pirates. Here are abundant old remains, but no trace of Minerva's temple. Holstenius, who wrote his annotations to Cluver in 1666, and who seems to have visited the place, says that the temple (of the Sirens, he calls it) stood upon the site of the present Campanella tower, which was built with its materials; adding, however, "so the inhabitants say"—which makes his testimony almost worthless.

And, favourable as the site is for a public building of this kind, yet the Roman poet's description of the "Sorrentine peak" from which the goddess looked down is somewhat inappropriate, seeing that Campanella is only about thirty yards above sea-level; unless, indeed, the whole mountain was identified by a figure of speech with the deity herself, whose shrine lay at its foot. The cosmographer of Ravenna has "Syrrentum, Minerva", and Guido, about whose age there is some uncertainty, speaks of "Minervum, in which is the temple of Minerva, where Anchises the father of Æneas first saw a man feeding horses, as Virgil reports". No horses could pasture here nowadays. He was alluding to the *castrum Minervæ* near Otranto.

I do not know when the promontory ceased to bear the name of the goddess: in the Golden Book of King Roger (1154) it is called *ras M.ntirah*, which its latest editors consider a mistake for *ras Manirbah* (Minerva); the tower was erected *in loco ubi dicitur Minerva* in 1334, and is similar in shape to that on the Galli, which was built at the same time, though in better repair. Many antiquities have been found at this spot, but the traveller Borch, who landed here in the eighteenth century to collect coins, was sadly disappointed, for the natives whom he calls "*aussi fourbes que bêtes et méchans*" brought him "*un petit écu de France usé et une pièce d'argent aragonaise, disant que c'étaient deux antiques de grand prix*"—which annoyed him considerably.

In the fourteenth century, too, the corals between *Capram et Minervinum* were a royal monopoly: so says a document which has been excavated by Monsieur Georges Yver in that vast post-tertiary deposit known as the Archivio at Naples.

Among the stones to be picked up at the site are certain lumps of red volcanic scoriæ. I regard them with interest, as proving that some, if not all, of the buildings at Campanella date from the early imperial epoch. For I have found this material, which was used by the Romans for the modelling of vaults, and where lightness was to be combined with strength, nowhere save in those ruins of Capri which cannot have been built before Augustus. Now if this scoriæ, as I strongly suspect, was brought from Vesuvius—like the "tufa of Herculanum" concerning which there have been learned discussions—before that mountain was covered with ashes in 79, the age of these buildings is determined pretty accurately within two close-lying limits. Mason-bees now construct their houses in its almond-shaped cavities, selecting it for the same reasons which commended it to the architects of Roman palaces: because it is dry, porous, and adhesive to plaster.

In winter the waves dash fiercely against this hoary promontory, and even in the bluest days of midsummer there is an unquiet heaving of the waters near the point. No wonder the Sirens chose it for their seat, for once ships began to pass between here and Capri, there can have been no lack of wrecks and victims. A part of the fleet of Augustus was shattered against these very rocks in the year 34. Gold and silver galore must be lying under the waves in those narrow three miles; anchors and chains, too, and rusty implements such as were used on one memorable occasion when the great medical school of Salerno was flourishing; flourishing and yet envious; envious of the fame of the mineral waters of Pozzuoli which attracted travellers away from their own town—for the waters, you perceive, cured patients gratis, while the Salerno doctors used to send in heavy bills—so envious, that certain rich and well-reputed physicians of that school, to wit, Sir Antoninus Sulimella, Sir Philippus Capograssus, and Sir Hector de Prochyta, after taking counsel how to remedy this vexatious state of affairs, decided that it was no time for half-measures.

They therefore embarked in Salerno upon a small vessel carrying certain iron instruments wherewith to deface the marble inscriptions and figures at Pozzuoli which set forth the blessings of those healing waters. That, they thought, would ruin the reputation of the sister-town. But alas! on the return journey after this impious expedition the boat was "miraculously submerged between Capri and Minerva" and the iconoclastic physicians engulfed together with their crow-bars, hammers, and chisels. The defiant letterings were doubtless engraved anew, there being no lack of Roman marble tablets at Pozzuoli; as for the waters, they flow on health-giving as in times of yore, for have not their virtues been contrived, ere the beginning of the world, by Virgil, the archimage?

It was a frankly mediæval expedient of revenge, inconceivable nowadays; and yet—hearts do not change so quickly; we only weave new garments in which to clothe hopes and fears that are for ever old. And a relative or descendant of this same Hector de Prochyta was the most un-mediæval of Italy's sons—John of Procida. Often enough he sailed through these straits. If we could but read his diary! What perils by sea and wanderings in lonely places, momentous battle-councils, beggarly rags exchanged for the splendours of Byzantine court or Vatican, and as easily resumed again; what shifts and intrigues! How comes it, I wonder, that none of our scholars has written a monograph on him and the great Hohenstaufen, their aims and aspirations? Why does our reading public, so greedy of things Italian, know of him nothing save schoolboy recollections of Sicilian Vespers? If they would turn aside from their Cinque-Cento infatuation and forget, for a while, the squabbles of microscopic Tuscan princelings and the hallucinations of neurotic monks and carvers of saints, they would behold, in John of Procida, a MAN. They could watch how this man's character is drawn out by adversity, *educed*, till he towers like an Ifrit above his fellows and his age. More than this: they would be confronted by a phenomenon rare indeed in mediæval history—by a striving, an ideal, that would do honour to themselves in this twentieth century.

Vengeance is mine, said the Jewish god who liked to keep all the good things for himself; such was not the notion of *Dominus Iohannes*. He tumbled into a dishonoured grave the proudest prince in Christendom, and the tremors of his splendid, sanctified hatred were felt from London to Constantinople. His ambition was the unity of Italy—a portent, a dream undreamed in that night of barbarism, a cry that none save the prophetic voice of Dante echoed down the centuries to come. This doctor of Salerno was endowed with an astuteness and a tenacity that verge on the preternatural; he was no party conspirator, but an independent statesman of singularly modern cast, who drove popes and kings and emperors, with the precision of an automaton, the way he meant them to go. That transient gleam is the "wolf's tail" of our present political status; it prefigures the triumph of reason over its hereditary enemies, monkery and militarism. With a keen eye to the advantages of trade in an age of feudal putrefaction, he built the harbour of

Salerno and instituted an annual fair, which is still held in that town. And amid a life of breathless State activity, he calmly continued to practise medicine; he was *facile princeps* in the land; great men travelled hundreds of miles to consult him, and some of his recipes are printed in pharmacopœias of to-day. At his advice, no doubt, the Emperor Frederick actually permitted the dissection of dead bodies for anatomical purposes, a concession to common sense not rare, but unique, in mediæval times. It was John of Procida, too, who thought fit to adorn, at his own expense, the last resting-place of Hildebrand, Prince of Popes. This act alone would suffice to stamp the man: there was, without a doubt, an element of grandeur in him.

It is easy to be modern nowadays, though not all of us have discovered the secret; it was easy, maybe, at Rome or Cuzco or Nineveh; but to be modern under the sterilizing, paralysing blight of European mediævalism was reserved for a few prodigies—martyrs, rather, since most of them paid for this distinction with their blood. And even in the matter of dying, John of Procida was phenomenal. At a patriarchal age, he expired in his bed; almost forgotten, as one historian remarks. Likely enough he was "almost forgotten". Mont Blanc does not show to full advantage from the Grands Mulets, and it takes a far distance of time to see John of Procida in his true perspective.

In these waters, too, his friend Roger de Lauria, with a resourcefulness and audacity unparalleled up to that day, crushed the fleet of the Anjou king and captured his son. . . .

One is apt to forget that Athene was a *parvenue* in these lands of the Sirens; travelling westwards, she ousted them from their headland whose oldest name, Sirenusson, was then changed, in her honour, to Athenaion. In early days, before the temple of the Sirens was actually built at Massa, their residence was probably imagined to lie on the south side of the promontory and about its storm-tossed capes and islands; they gradually crept away from their homesteads, Athene following in their wake. It is quite intelligible, that these old but deathless maidens of the sea, in whose nature were elements incongruous and hard to expound, should yield before a wholly beneficent goddess with clearly marked sexual and mental attributes. For, previous to setting out on this voyage, she had passed through the crucible of Hellenic purification—it is as far a step from the astute companion of Odysseus or the Egyptian

Tritogeneia to her whom we know, as from the wooden xoanon of Athene Polias to the idealizations of Periclean art. Man first appeases, then worships, his devils. There was nothing left to appease or disentangle in bright-eyed Athene; she is cast in one mould and her ægis gleams with fine humanity, flashing the message onward into furthest ages. The older Sirens were enigmatical, if not hostile. They retreated before her and never turned to look back, and when the sanctuary of Parthenope at Naples became celebrated, that in Massa decayed—the familiar movement from East to West, to which the township of Massa itself and of Sorrento, of Naples and Paris and London, all bear witness.

This was explained somewhat differently in the Middle Ages. Says the old Cronaca di Parthenope: "A virgin girl, unmarried and called Parthenope, of surpassing beauty, daughter of the King of Sicily, came with great number of ships to Chiaia (Naples). By a chance she sickened there and died of that same distemper and was buried. And here, on her grave, was the temple erected."

If you are in the mood for a scramble, you can be rowed from Campanella a mile in the Massa direction as far as the Cala di Mitigliano, and thence climb up the ravine to the summit of Mount San Costanzo. It is rough walking till the farm of Mitigliano, about half-way, is reached. In the vineyards here may be seen a few Roman remains and four huge amphoræ, one of them still intact and in its original position. This, then, is the ancient Metellianum (there is another place of this name near Cava). And not far from this site were unearthed, some six years ago, a "shepherd" of gold and a metal helmet which were sold for fifty francs to a Sorrento jeweller, though "who knows how many millions they were really worth". It is impossible to obtain clear details of such discoveries; not only are the natives incapable of describing what they see with their eyes, but also, like the Irish, they hesitate to reply until they know what one would be glad to hear; if one persists in merely asking for the truth, they suspect hidden motives and become evasive. The Oriental influence, I suppose—the same which always prompts them to answer one question with another.

"Why do you invariably answer my questions with another question?" I once enquired.

"Why shouldn't I?"

Above this farm stands the venerable chapel of Mitigliano with a "miraculous" picture, and the ruins of a small convent whose inmates, they say, were enslaved by the Turks. A furious nocturnal treasure-hunt took place here not long ago in which cellars, walls, and cisterns were demolished. "They found nothing," the farmer told me; "at least (with a wink) so they said."

Mount San Costanzo has two summits divided by a saddle-shaped depression—La Croce and the chapel itself. The mists of Byzantium still cling to those grey rocks, for Saint Costanzo was patriarch of Constantinople, whose body, carefully packed in a barrel, floated from the Euxine into the Bay of Naples; it arrived fresh and uninjured, nor is there anything profane in the conjecture that the occupant of the barrel had been treated with bitumen, large quantities of which must then have been stored at Byzance for the manufacture of *Greek Fire*. His relics, what is left of them, are now lying at Monte Vergine, that vast repository of bones which were imported in ship-loads from the saintly East to the confiding West; nearly every calendar saint is represented in the official catalogue by a tooth or a knuckle, and among the items I observe, to my astonishment, "the skeletons of Shadrac, Meshac, and Abednego", which Frederick II, who could never resist a joke, is supposed to have sent over from Jerusalem.

Now: how did this come about? For, if I remember rightly, the patriarch Theophilus was also anxious to possess these anatomies and despatched the monk Colobi on a boat of clouds to Babylon for the purpose of fetching them, but the three saints stoutly refused to quit their tombs, though promising to oblige the patriarch in other matters. How did they come to reach Jerusalem, and to change their minds on the subject of exportation?

It is all rather incredible nowadays; men like Trajan, Pericles, or Sardanapalus are of yesterday, in comparison. Yet the bone trade revived quite recently; not with the East, but with His Holiness the Pope, who forwarded saints' skeletons from the Vatican to Naples in exchange for castrated boys to warble the praises of God in the Sistine Chapel. San Domingo and other travellers have collected details of this interchange of commodities.

The Oriental notes lingered long in these regions: San Costanzo, Santa Maria di Costantinopoli, Sant' Elia, Santa Sofia, and others all date from the times when the shadowy exarch still reigned at Ravenna. And mediæval Greek was spoken here up to remarkably late days; the Suabian laws were promulgated in Greek and Latin;

Greek was in familiar and official usage up to 1450, and six Greek churches, says the learned Mazzocchi, survived in Naples up to the thirteenth century. But the Normans whose piety, or shrewdness, generally placed them on the side of the Roman pontiff, had meanwhile dealt an unexpected death-blow to the power of Byzantium in the West, by introducing the silk-worm into Sicily.

We are apt to be unfair to Byzantium. It must not be judged, I think, by what it created or wrought into fresh forms, but by what it preserved. As a period of repose and conservation—as a mere wedge of time and dominion interposed while the savage North was ripening for its legacy of antiquity—its services to mankind are past all reckoning.

In those centuries, when the inhabitants of this district may often have wondered to whom they owed allegiance, were laid the seeds of that opportunism and lack of living conviction in public affairs which now, after another thousand years of misgovernment, have borne such baleful fruits. It is good to read, now and then, in the old chronicles, of the deeds of those improbable creatures, of Sikard and Grimoald, Radelchis, Gaidelgrime and Sigelgaita, whose very names sound like a roll-call from the Niebelungen-lied; of the Greek dukes of Sorrento and other lordly phantoms that conjure up visions of Shakespeare's mellow geography.

A seething witches' cauldron was South Italy; dark and passionate shapes emerge from the brew, clash their weapons or mutter a prayer, and again sink down.

In those ages, too, when men really believed the unbelievable, they built sanctuaries upon the hill-tops—proximity to heaven being esteemed favourable for the exaudition of prayers; nowadays, mankind refusing to climb, the churches have descended into the valleys to suit the convenience of a lukewarm generation. An attractive site like San Costanzo hill must have been occupied from earliest times: Christianity in Siren land under Marcus Aurelius is no impossibility, if we are to trust Tertullian and Origen. Yet the arch-pagan Symmachus praises for its (heathen) religious zeal the town of Naples where they used to say, "it was easier to meet with a god than with a man". Hill-worship in the provinces gradually declined: the saint-bishop Antoninus of Sorrento was charged before the Pope, in the ninth century, with "celebrating mass on mountain summits against Christian usage, and thus propagating a new and most pernicious heresy". Why *new*—why this exacerbation? There is more than meets the eye in this indictment. The good man's heresy would be no heresy in these days when every Catholic bishop, according to a convenient fiction, is accompanied by a "portable altar" wherever he goes.

And the crucifix on the sister-summit also goes back, I suspect, to the days of Constantine the Great, being a repetition of one of those legendary crosses on which the archangel Michael, the Apollo and Lucifer of Christianity, who then winged his way westwards and settled upon cloudy peaks all over Europe, was wont to alight; the material emblem surviving while the Oriental tradition faded away before the western one of Calvary. Yet not all the crosses hereabouts can claim this venerable origin. That on the rock Vervece was erected only a few years ago in commemoration of some sailors who were shipwrecked there; two others, which do not improve the landscape, were placed on peaks behind Sorrento, in order that storm-tossed mariners "might have something to look at", by certain mighty landlords to whom much may be forgiven, for they have planted much.

There runs a legend at Termini to the effect that the chapel on San Costanzo hill was built by the saint himself, under protest. The elders of the village having determined to construct his shrine lower down, the saint sent several messages to say that he preferred the hill-top; and all in vain. The site of the new church, they told him, was already mapped out, and the sooner he acquiesced the better.

"You won't?" he said. "Well, then, I must build it myself."

So saying, he collected stones and mortar, and in a night the whole edifice was completed. That settled it. This, of course, took place hundreds of years ago, or even more; but what he did to the men of Nerano who refused to send their *figlie di Maria* to his feast at Termini, even under promises of payment, is a matter of yesterday. He simply "shook his chains"—is this a reminiscence of some Typhœus-legend?—and an avalanche of rocks poured down upon their village* from the heights overhead. Since that time, the *figlie di Maria* of Nerano are the first to put in an appearance at Termini on the festive 14th day of May, and the last to depart homewards— and gratis.

---

* The rock-strewn relics of this place can be seen about half-way up on the left side of the direct footpath connecting Nerano with Termini, and immediately under the hill. Or this may have been one of the villages destroyed by the Corsairs in 1558.

Then, two years ago, there was that affair of the grasshoppers. . . .
Sometimes, too, he fashions a boat out of a walnut with a tiny
sail to it, and steps on board. In this cockle-shell he paddles out
from among the rocks with the merest phantom of an oar; but the
barque swells to a goodly size as he recedes from land, and lucky
fishermen have sometimes met the saint cruising about in broad
daylight: he likes to take his pleasure on the water, like any other
cristiano.

A very mysterious transaction took place in the Middle Ages.
The present patron of Massa is no longer San Costanzo but San
Cataldo, an Irishman who terminated his mild mission in the
seventh century at Taranto, where there used to be a wonderful
wooden statue of him (now replaced by the usual metal abomina-
tion), and where his epitaph, which has a familiar sound, may still
be read—

> *Me tulit Hibernae, Solimae traxere, Tarentum*
> *Nunc tenet: huic ritus, dogmata, iura dedi.*

In Capri, however, there is a deserted shrine of San Cataldo, and
we are told that long ago the men of Capri "piously robbed the
bones of San Costanzo from Massa, where he used to be protector,
and made *him* their patron, which he still is". In short, it seems as
if the two communities, with some little violence, had "swopped
saints".

In those troubled days, San Costanzo was useful at Capri for
scaring away the Saracens with his torch, and this is the attitude
in which he used to be conventionally depicted. Now, inasmuch as
it stands to reason that an ordinary torch would have been in-
effectual for this purpose, we must assume that he was granted the
power to brandish some more conspicuously effulgent meteor,
probably a *fax ardens*; or perhaps a *capra saltans*, a *lancea*, a *trabs
verticalis*, a *draco volans*, a *clypeus*, *stipula*, *pyramis*, *jaculum*, or
some other of those fiery coruscations which Cardan*—or is it

---

* Correct as this particular proposition of Cardan's may be, it would be wrong
to esteem him unassailable at all points, as has been done. He errs, to my thinking,
in respect of the salamander. Your salamander is a cold lizard, hairless and
poisonous by nature, and while all of this family have four legs and a head, yet
none save the true salamander can withstand the action of fire. Though generated
in the flames, as Aristotle in one passage affirms (he contradicts it in another), his
cold is nevertheless held to be such as to extinguish them. Pliny, Galen, Aelian,
Dioscorides and others of the ancients hold this view. Olympiodorus and Saint
Augustine, with other Christian Fathers, likewise. Even so Nierembergius, who

Paracelsus?—conjectures to be the excrements of the stellar firmament.

Yes, I can well believe that THE INFINITE was the one original product of mediæval cogitations and their chief intellectual legacy to posterity; that word epitomizes the intellectual inertia and moral dyspepsia of those times.

Lucky the mortal who arrives on the summit of San Costanzo during one of those bewitching moments when the atmosphere is permeated with a glittering haze of floating particles, like powdered gold-dust. The view over the Gulf of Naples, at such times, with its contours framed in a luminous aureole rather than limned, is not easily forgotten. They are rare, and their glory of brief duration. On other occasions this fairy-like effect is atoned for by the clarity; not only Siren land, but half Campania, lies at our feet. Far away, the sinuous outlines of Tyrrhenian shores with the headland of Circe and the Ponza islets that call up grim memories of Roman banishments; the complex and serrated Apennines whose peaks are visible into the far Abruzzi country; nearer at hand, Elysian Fields, Tartarus and Cimmerian gloom, and the smoking head of Vesuvius decked with a coral necklace of towns and villages. Not an inch of all this landscape but has its associations. Capua and Hannibal; the Caudine Forks; Misenum and Virgil; Nisida, the retreat of a true Siren-worshipper, Lucullus; the venerable acropolis of Cumæ; Pompeii; yonder Puteoli, where the apostle of the gentiles touched land; here the Amalfitan coast, Pæstum, and the Calabrian hills.

And everywhere the unharvested sea. The sea, with its intense restfulness, is the dominant note of Siren land. There is no escaping from it. Incessant gleams of light flash from that mirror-like expanse; even when unperceived by the senses, among squalid tenements or leafy uplands, they will find you out and follow, like some

elucidates certain of the opinions of his predecessors touching the matter. And likewise, to my amazement, the illustrious Cardan. For is it not improbable, I ask, that so exiguous a creature should quench a fire however great, or even permanently live in it? Wherefore I submit as follows: That the salamander, by reason of his chilly humour, may well extinguish a small fire, but never a great one; and that, if placed in a combustion similar to the one which flickered about the above-mentioned Shadrac, Meshac and Abednego, he may, and does, survive for some days or even years, but not—like the pyrausta, Charistian Birds and other fire-loving creatures—for ever. *Profiteor me haud alio sensu hanc sententiam proferre, aut accipi ab omnibus velle quam quo ea solent, quae humana tantummodo auctoritate, etc. etc.*

all-pervading, inevitable melody. How the *Odyssey* throbs with those luminous vibrations! Forest voices are the music of Bach; we seem to wander in cool wooded glades with sunlight pouring through leaves overhead, to breathe the fragrance of dew-spangled moss and fern, to hear the caress of light winds playing among the crowns and the rustling of branches and streamlets and all those elfish woodland notes which the master himself, in his solitary wanderings, had heard and thenceforth emprisoned everlastingly—coaxing their echoes into those numbers whose enchantment none but chosen spirits, little less than angels, can unseal. Some are of multiple voice, like that god-gifted Tschaikovsky, whose melancholy is flecked by exotic passions such as Mozart or Beethoven never sang—for how shall that come out of a man which was never in him?—lilting, super-sensuous measures from old Samarkand where they loved with the love of dæmons; muffled pulsations, oft-repeated, doom-enforcing; or an ominous metallic quaver—the wail of the myriad Tartars who fell by the blood-stained waters of Tengis, or, it may be, some premonitory cry of his own tormented soul that fled from earth, all too soon.

Others may reflect the camp or court. But Homer voices the sea. . . .

There are many spots on earth as fair as the Parthenopean bay—equally fair at least to us moderns, whose appreciation of art and of nature has become less exclusively human. The steaming Amazonian forests and the ice-crags of Jan Mayen appeal since yesterday to our catholic taste; but whoever takes the antique point of view will still accord the palm to the Mediterranean. Here, true beauty resides with its harmony of form and hue—here the works of man stand out in just relation to those of nature, each supplementing the other. Elsewhere, she is apt to grow menacing—gloomy or monstrous. In the North, the sun refuses her aid and man struggles with the elements; he vegetates, an animated lump of blubber and dirt, or rushes frantically in starving hordes to overrun the bright places of earth; in the tropics his works shrink into insignificance, he is lost in a fierce tangle of greenery, sucked dry by the sun, whom he execrates as a demon—he dwindles into a stoic, a slave. Here, too, an ancient world, our ancient world, lies spread out in rare charm of colour and outline, and every footstep is fraught with memories. The lovely islands of the Pacific have a past, but their past is not our past, and men who strike deep notes in such alien soil are like those who forsake their families and traditions to live among gipsies. Niagara will astound the senses, but the ruins of Campania wake up sublimer and more enduring emotions.

No person of culture, however prosaic, will easily detach himself from such scenes and thoughts—is it not the prerogative of civilized man to pause and ponder before the relics of his own past?

It is time to depart. The swallows have flown overhead on their long journey, and the redbreast's plaintive whistle announces that the summer is ended.

And how much there is still to see—the remains of Pollio's temple with the baths of Queen Joan, and crumbling towers and sites innumerable! Yonder is Erche, for instance—a commanding plateau opposite Santa Maria surrounded by ravines on three sides and within a few hundred yards of which the old Roman road to Minerva's temple must have passed: how came the name of Hercules to wander so far inland? And only the other day I found my way to a solitary group of houses called Scuola, a singular appellation which reminds me of that *school* of poets and philosophers which was imagined to lie near the promontory of Athenæum; the Sirens' songs, according to Pontanus, being nothing but the irresistible seduction of eloquence and literary pursuits. "What has been said of the sweet voices and songs of the Sirens is a fable illustrating the attractions of eloquence, and the cult of knowledge of letters." Was it not good of the old humanist to associate the Sirens with lettered ease? At Scuola, too, there stands a decayed chapel with a pavement of hand-painted tiles that depict the expulsion of our first parents from Paradise. They shine with the lustre of eternal youth and, to judge by the date, the work may well have been executed by the hand of the celebrated Lionardo Chiaiese who, together with his two brothers, was a pioneer of majolica in Naples, and whose two other pavements, at Anacapri and in the Neapolitan nunnery of Suor Orsola Benincasa, are considered masterpieces impossible to reproduce with modern methods. The scene is drawn with great freedom and taste, and I have endeavoured, twice, to interest certain folks at Naples to safeguard it ere the crazy roof,* through which green plants are vigorously sprouting, shall crash

* It has since fallen in. See my *Looking Back*, p. 225.

down upon the stern young archangel and all the wondrous beasts of the garden.

It is the same everywhere. Go where you will, new discoveries and suggestions are lying in wait; impossible to avoid stumbling upon relics of Roman rule, of old Hellas, or mediæval romance that are crowded into these few miles. The memories start up at our feet, like the fabled dragon-brood of Cadmus. These are the delights of Siren land.

But the summer is ended, though there may well be another kind of Siren land where we can take our joy at all seasons, if so disposed. Not in the stars, however: nobody but Plato would have thought of making the Sirens live in those remote spheres. What you cannot find on earth is not worth seeking.

Yet there will still come days of sunlit splendour—Saint Martin's summer, they call them—when the sea uplifts an unruffled countenance to the crystalline dome overhead, which then looks so securely built as though it could never be broken up—days when it might be well to sail over to Capri once more or to examine the site of the old Siren temple at Fontanella near Massa (if such it was), whose marbles were hammered to pieces and scattered broadcast in the year of grace 1896. "It is best not to speak of these things," said my informant, who witnessed the desecration. Montorio, though he knew nothing of the temple buried beneath the soil, relates that a religious procession used to wend to this spot in former days and to salute it with cannon-shots, as if a spectral Siren-cult had persisted far into Christian times—— Enough! The half is better than the whole, and whoso hurries unduly will never catch the *genius loci* of these regions. Fontanella and the rest of them must wait for another season, since the scanty olives are gathered and vine leaves changing to yellow.

Cicadas no longer sing.

Green patches have sprung up on the burnt Tore yonder.

The summer is ended.